The Law and Practice of the International Court of Justice (1945-1996):

A critique of the Contentious and Advisory Jurisdictions.

First Published 1999 by
FOURTH DIMENSION PUBLISHING CO., LTD.
16 Fifth Ave, City Layout
P.M.B. 01164
Enugu, Nigeria

ISBN 978-156-448-2

Produced in Nigeria by
Fourth Dimension Publishers, Enugu

CONTENTS

Page

Dedication vii

Acknowledgements viii

Foreword ix

List of Tables xii

Abbreviations xiii

List of Cases xiv

List of Statutes xvi

Chapter

1. JUSTICIABILITY OF INTERNATIONAL DISPUTES 1
   - Introduction 1
   - Definition of International Disputes 5
   - Antecedents in International Arbitration and Adjudication 12
   - The Hague Conferences and the Permanent Court of Arbitration 14
   - The Permanent Court of International Justice 16
   - The UN and the Court (ICJ) 17
   - Forms of Pacific Settlement 20
   - Negotiation 20
   - Inquiry 22
   - Arbitration 24
   - Conciliation 26
   - Good Offices 28
   - Mediation 29
   - Administrative Tribunals 30

2. ROLE AND FUNCTIONS OF THE INTERNATIONAL COURT OF JUSTICE 33
   - International Conflict Resolution 34
   - Cooling off Function 35
   - Diplomatic Function 38
   - Arbiter Among Nations/Guardian of International

Morality and Legality 40
Advancing Jurisprudence and Elaboration of the Law 41

3. CONTENTIOUS JURISDICTION OF THE ICJ 45
Jurisdiction and Seising 45
Jurisdiction of the Court in Contentious Cases 46
Consent Ad Hoc 49
Jurisdiction Post Hoc (Forum Prorogatum) 50
Jurisdiction Ante Hoc (Compulsory Jurisdiction) 53
Treaties in Force 56
Transferred Jurisdiction 58
Incidental Jurisdiction of the Court 58
Matters Specially Provided for in the Charter 59
Multiple Jurisdiction 60
Jurisdiction to decide *Ex Aequo Et Bono* 61
The *Non Ultra Petita* Rule 62
Interim Measures 63
Chambers of the Court 66
Chamber of Summary Procedure 66
Chamber Provided for in Article 26 Paragraph 1 of the Statute 67
Chambers Formed under Article 26, Paragraph 2, of the Statute 67

4. THE PROBLEM OF RESERVATIONS TO THE COURT'S JURISDICTION UNDER THE OPTIONAL CLAUSE 69
The Special Problem of Self-Judging or Automatic Reservations 74
Reservations Properly So Called and Improperly So Called 79

5. PROCEEDINGS IN CONTENTIOUS CASES 85
Preliminary Steps 86
Written Proceedings 87
Closure of Written Proceedings 90
The Oral Proceedings 91
Submissions and Closure of Oral Proceedings 94

Deliberation of the Court 95
Effectiveness of the Judgments of the World Court ... 97

6. ADVISORY JURISDICTION OF THE WORLD COURT 103
Definition of Advisory Opinions 103
The Development of the Advisory Procedure 104
The Jurisdiction of the Court in Advisory Cases 106
The Legal Basis of the Court's Advisory Jurisdiction .. 113
Seising the Court (Advisory Opinions) 115
Legal Questions 116
Authorised Bodies to Request Advisory Opinions 118
Requests must be Written 119
Other Conditions to Fulfil 120
The Advisory Procedure 120
Composition of the Court for Advisory Proceedings .. 124
The Reception of the Opinion 125
The Effect of Advisory Opinions 128
Binding Effects of the Opinion 132

7 STATISTICAL EVALUATION OF THE COURT'S WORK IN ITS FIRST 50 YEARS 135

8 OVERVIEW OF THE COURT'S JURISPRUDENCE .. 171
Questions Involving Territorial Rights 171
Disputes involving Questions on the Law of the Sea .. 174
Disputes Involving Questions of Treaty Interpretation and International Economic Law 176
Cases involving the Interests of Natural Persons 180
Cases Bordering on International Criminal Law and Extra-Territorial Rights 180
Cases Bordering on Environmental Issues 188
Nigeria Before the Court 193

9. PROBLEMS OF THE COURT 202
Reluctance of Developing States to Submit Disputes to the Court 202
Need to Accept Judicial Settlement 205

Structure/Composition of the Court and the Law Applicable as Factors Militating Against the Acceptance of the Court 216
Procedure of the Court and the Problem of Time and Costs 227
Rationalising the Procedure of the ICJ 228
Cost of litigation in the ICJ 229

10. ALTERNATIVE FUTURES 235
Opening the Floodgates 236
Increasing Access by Individuals 237
Non-governmental Organisations (NGOs) and the World Court 240
A Chamber of International Criminal Justice ....
Developing Regional Chambers 244
An ICJ Bar Association 247

Bibliography 252
Index 256

Dedication

To those who genuinely believe in and pursue Justice and Equity at all times, for all mankind.

Acknowledgements

It is always difficult to acknowledge the contribution of all those people who have given support in various ways, material and intellectual to the writing of a book which has had a fairly long period of gestation. The present work has its inception in a masters thesis started in 1989 (at the University of Jos). It thus has the rare opportunity of being incubated with the fatherly but uncompromising aid of some of Nigeria's most brilliant minds on the subject of international law. My debt goes to Associate Professor I. Gabriel of the University of Jos who supervised the M. A. Thesis and to Professor U. O. Umezurike of the University of Calabar who externally assessed and chairmaned the viva session. I owe sincere gratitude to the duo of Professor I.O. Agbede (who remains in the position of "Doctorvater" to me) and Professor A. O. Obilade both of the University of Lagos who took time to go through the script at various times.

No serious writer on the International Court can refuse to recognise his obligation to his predecessors in that area. I refer particularly to renowned scholars like Rosenne, Elias, Prataap, Gross, Schwarzenberger, Lauterpacht and Jennings. I plead guilty of diffidence and hesitation in differing from their learned positions on most matters. Many thanks as well to those services of the ICJ and the UN in general which have made the Court one of the best documented of international organisations.

It remains a pleasant duty to make public acknowledgement of the assistance received from family and friends. I remain specially grateful to my wife Anke Weiler-Oduntan, little Jimi, (my son), my parents Mr. and Mrs. E.K. Oduntan, Ilse, and Günther Klinge (my parents-in-law), Ololade Oduntan, Kayode Oduntan, Mr. and Mrs. Femi Taiwo among others.

I am grateful to Mr. L.E. Oni, Abieyuwa Lawal and Late Joan Alabi who basically for friendship's sake performed the task of typesetting and proof reading various drafts of the work. I wish also to pay my tribute to the courtesy and kind collaboration of the Printers and Publishers.

Needless to say that I am responsible for all errors, flaws and inadequacies that are bound to exist in this work. For "we all make mistakes and if anyone makes no mistakes in what he says he is a perfect man" (James 3:2).

FOREWORD

International Law is a living organism and like all other living organisms, has grown tremendously since the Middle Ages, but more especially since .1945 when the United Nations Charter was signed and the International Court of Justice (ICJ) as one of its most important Organs was brought to life. In spite of imponderable problems which have confronted the Court, it has nevertheless developed both in terms of its substantive jurisdiction as well as in the procedure and practice of the court. There were many who had predicted that the court did not have long to live; and until quite recently some cynics still thought that the court had better be given a decent burial. This has been largely as results of problems which must obviously confront such a body set up to adjudicate disputes between States claiming to be equal, one with every other, and guarding their sovereignty jealously with an understanding that each will accord to the other its claim to almost unlimited sovereignty. In spite of all these, the court has weathered through about half-a-century of what many may regard as useful life.

Soon after the end of World War II, that is, at the early years of the existence of the Court, World War III appeared imminent but for certain reasons chief among which is the existence of the UN which has together with its agencies especially the ICJ been tottering along. This of course has led to the devotion of greater time and attention to the study of the ICJ by scholars all over the World. However, Nigerian scholars have not contributed much to that study, the outstanding contribution of late Professor Taslim Elias, later a Judge of the Court, being a notable exception. It is this reason among others which has excited me to read the manuscript of this book by an on-coming Nigerian scholar, Mr. Gbenga Oduntan, and to write this Foreword at his request.

What the author has done in ten chapters is to examine with the greatest possible care not only the Statutes of the ICJ, but also the practical application of the Statutes as well as the Rules. All these he has done as an academic jurist, placing reliance not only on the bare provisions of the applicable Statutes and Rules but by reference to the actual practice of the Court as exemplified by judgments and orders given or made by the Court. In Chapter one, the author gives a very brief history of the Court and its antecedent, the Permanent Court of International Justice (PCIJ), and discusses very briefly those other 'Forms of Pacific Settlement' known to International Law as he calls them. These are Negotiation, Enquiry, Arbitration, Conciliation, Good Office, Mediation; and of course the UN's domestic Administrative Tribunals. This chapter serves as a good introduction to the subject matter of the book, thus enabling a fresher to have a grasp of it and to understand more easily what is to follow.

The author is not shy in taking definite stands on a number of issues known to be controversial. He aligns himself with Sir G. Fitzmaurice who asserts that International Courts have recognised the development of law as an essential part of the function of the ICJ, and that multiple judgments of the Courts are to be encouraged, not discouraged. The author then touches and discussed the vexed question of the jurisdiction of the Court. He discusses this question in all its ramifications with care and in a lucid manner by copious references to actual decisions of the Court. It is the parties to disputes before the Court that have the right to accede or not to accede to its jurisdiction either generally or as well as in specific cases, and it is sometimes thought that a party could withdraw from its approval at any stage of a proceeding. The author asserts from decided cases "that the court would render null and void unreasonable reservations to its jurisdiction. One such case is the withdrawal by the United States of its consent in the case concerning Military and Paramilitary Activities in and against Nicaragua."

The Author discusses in some detail the proceedings in contentious cases before the Court, from the commencement by written memorials counter-memorials and replies similar to pleadings in our procedure in domestic trials, up to the presentation of oral arguments. He even gives a graphic description of the Court when in session and how the Judges deliberate on the issues in controversy and come to decisions on them, and how those decisions are brought to the attention of the parties. He then says that "ultimately the effectiveness of the Court's orders, interim measures, decisions, or judgments, lies in the overall political will of states to give effectiveness to the Court."

Under our domestic law, the Courts have no obligation to give what is generally regarded as 'Advisory Opinion', but under the League of Nations regime, the Permanent Court of Justice was conferred with the right to give Advisory Opinions to the League. It was not surprising therefore that the Charter of the United Nations in Article 96 provides that "The General Assembly or Security Council may request the International Court of Justice to give an advisory opinion on any legal question." The Author of this book discusses in some detail the scope, practice, and application of this procedure. He informs us by reference to copious statistics that "the General Assembly in particular has made use of the Court's Advisory jurisdiction" and that "a radical and new development is the employment of the advisory procedure as part of the machinery for judicial review of the judgement of a tribunal between an individual staff member and the organisation in a contentious case." Apart from these he informs that between its first sitting in 1946 and 1996, the Court has dealt with 75 contentious cases, delivered 22 advisory opinions, and made 295 Orders. The Author then highlights some of the major judgments and opinions given by the Court. He does not forget to look at the cost of litigation before the Court and to make some suggestions for reform.

The Author requested me to write this Foreword, and I am proud to be associated with this Work in this way. Gbenga Oduntan writes with a background not only of Law but also of other disciplines, all of which have enriched the content and presentation of the contents of this book. I have no doubt that in due course the book will become a worthy contribution of a Nigerian to the enlarging world literature in International Law.

Akinola Aguda OFR;NNOM;LL.M;Ph.D;LL.D
104, Babs Animshaun Road,
Surulere, Lagos, Nigeria.

October 1, 1998.

List of Tables

Table		Page
0	Patterns of Reservations to the Optional Clause in Current and Past Declarations	82
I	Member States of the UN as at July 1996	136
II	Chronological List of Contentious Cases	142
III	Actual use by States of the Court's Contentious Jurisdiction	146
IV	Geographical Distribution of Countries which have appeared before the International Court of Justice	152
V	Cases Between Nations of Europe, Australia and North America	154
VI	Cases Instituted by Developed Nations Against Third World Countries	155
VII	Cases Instituted by Developing States Against Developed Nations	156
VIII	Cases Between Developing States of Africa, Asia and South America	157
IX	Cases Involving Preliminary Objections	159
X	Cases Involving Other Questions of Jurisdiction or Admissibility	160
XI	Cases Where Respondent Successfully Denied Jurisdiction	161
XII	Cases Submitted by Special Agreements	162
XIII	Cases Submitted Based on Compulsory Jurisdiction Clause	163
XIV	Contentious Cases Related to the Cold War	165
XV	Chronological List of Advisory Cases	166
XVI	Pattern of Requests for Advisory Cases	168
XVII	Advisory Cases Instigated by Developing Nations Against the Superpowers	170
XVIII	Judges from Africa who have Served on the Court's Bench	218
XIX	Judges from Europe who have Served on the Court's Bench	219
XX	Academic Qualifications and Place of Legal Training of ICJ Judges from Developing Countries as at 1994	221

ABBREVIATIONS

AJIL	American Journal of International Law
BYIL	British Yearbook of International Law
Diss. Op.	Dissenting Opinion
FRG	Federal Republic of Germany
GAOR	General Assembly Official Records
Hudson cases	Cases and other materials on International Law 3rd ed 1951
ICJ	International Court of Justice
ICJ Pleadings	International Court of Justice: Pleadings, Oral Arguments Documents
ICJ Reports	Reports of Judgments, Advisory Opinions and Orders of the International Court
ICLQ	International and Comparative Law Quarterly
InJIL	Indian Journal of International Law
Intl. Conciliation	International Conciliation
PCA	Permanent Court of Arbitration
PCIJ	Permanent Court of International Justice
Recuil	Recuil des Cours, Academic de Droit World Court Reports Hudson World Court Reports, 4 Vol. (1934-43)
RIA	United Nations, Reports of International Awards
Sp. Sup.	Special Supplement
Supp.	Supplement
UK	United Kingdom
UN or UNO	United Nations Organisation
UNCIO	United Nations Conference on International Organisation
UNESCO	United Nations Education Scientific and Cultural Organisation.
UNGA	United Nations General Assembly
US or USA	United States of America
USSR	Union of Soviet Socialist Republics
WHO	World Health Organisation

List of Cases

Australia v. France
(1973 -1974)

Belgium v. Netherlands
(1957-1959)
Belgium v. Spain
(1958 - 1961)
Belgium v. Spain
(1962 -1970)
Bosina and Herzegovina v. Yugoslovia (1993 -)
Botswana v. Namibia
(1996 -)
Burkina Faso v. Repulic of Mali
(1983 -86)

Cambodia v. Thailand
(1959 -1962)
Cameroon v. Nigeria
(1994 -)
Cameroon v. United Kingdom
(1961 -1963)
Canada v. United State
(1981 - 1984)
Chorzow Factory Case
(1928)
Colombia v. Peru
(1949 -1950)
Compentence of the General Assembly Case.

Danube Commission Case
Denmark v. Norway (1988 - 1993)

Eastern Carelia Case
El Salvador v. Honduras
(1988 - 1992)
Ethiopia v. South Africa.
(1960 - 1966)

Federal Republic of Germany v. Denmark
(1967 - 1969)
Finland v. Denmark
(1991 -1992)
Federal Republic of German v. Iceland
(1972 - 1974)
Federal Republic of Germany v. Netherlands
(1967 -1969).
France v. Egypt
(1949 -1950)
France v. Lebanon (1953 -1954)
France v. Lebanon (1959 -1960)
France v. Norway
(1955 - 1957)
France v. United Kingdom
(1951 -1953)
France v. United States
(1950 - 1952)
Free Zones Case

Greece v. Turkey
(1976 - 1978)
Greece v. United Kingdom
(1951 - 1953)
Guinea Bissau v. Senegal
(1989 - 1991)
Guinea Bissau v. Sengal
(1991 - 1995)

Honduras v. Nicaragua
(1958 -1960)
Hungary v. Slovakia
(1993 -1997)

India v. Pakistan
(1971 -1972)
Interhandel Case
Iran v. United States
(1989 -1996)

Iran v. United States of America (1992 -)
Isreal v. Bulgaria (1957 -1960)
Italy v. France, United Kingdom and United States (1953 - 1954)
Liberia v. South Africa (1960 -1966)
Libyan Arab Jamahiriya v. Chad (1990 - 1994)
Libyan Arab Jamahiriya v. Malta (1982 -1985)
Libyan Arab Jamahiriya v. United Kingdom (1992 -)
Libyan Arab Jamahiriya v. United States (1992 -)
Liechterstein v. Guatemala (1951-1955)

Minority schools in Upper Silesia Case.

Nauru v. Australia (1989 -1993)
Netherlands v. Sweden (1957 - 1958)
New Zealand v. France (1973 -1974)
New Zealand v. France (1995 -)
Nicaragua v. Costa Rica (1986 -1987)
Nicaragua v. Honduras (1986 -1992)
Nicaragua v. United State of America (1984 -1991)
Norwegian Loans Case

Pakistan v. India (1973)
Peace Treaties case
Portugal v. Australia (1991 -1995)
Portugal v. India (1955 -1960)

Qatar v. Bahrain (1991-)

Reparations case
Right of Minorities case
Spain v. Canada (1995-)

Switzerland v. United States (1957 -1959)

Tunisia v. Libyan Arab Jamahiriya (1978 -1982)
Tunisia v. Libyan Arab Jamahiriya (1984 - 1985)

United Kingdom v. Albania (1947 -1949)
United Kingdom v. Argentina (1955 -1956)
United Kingdom v. Bulgeria (1957 -1959)
United Kingdom v. Chile (1955 -1956)
United Kingdom v. Iceland. (1972 -1974)
United Kingdom v. Iran (1951 -1952)
United States v. Iran (1979 -1981)
United Kingdom v. Norway (1949 -1951)
UN Administrative Tribunal Case
United States v. Czecheslovakia (1955 -1956)
United States v. Hungary (1954)
United States of America v. Italy (1987 - 1989)
United States of America v, USSR (1954)
United States of America v. USSR (1955 -1956)
United States of America v. USSR (1958)
United States of America v. USSR (1959)

List of Statutes

Act of Algeciros of 1906
Act of Lima
Aerial Navigation Convention 1919
art. 34
Anglo Greek Commerical Treaty

Charter of the International Trade Organisation
art. 9 (2) and (5)
Convenant of the League of Nations
art. 7
art. 14
art. 22

Enemy Act
European Convention for the peaceful Settlement of Disputes
art.15

General Treaty of Friendship, Commerce and Navigation
Genocide Convention

Hague Convention
art. ix
art. xiv

I.C.J.
Rules of Court
art, 15-18
art .21
art. 31
art. 32
art. 41
art. 42
art. 43 (4)
art. 44
art. 45 (2)
art. 45-46

art. 49
art. 50 (1)
art. 52 (1)
art. 54
art. 56
art. 56 (3)
art. 57
art. 61
art. 69 (4)
art. 72
art. 73
art. 74 (3)
art. 90 - 93
art. 101
I.C.J. Staff Rules II
- part I
art . 3 `(5)
art. 15
art. 81
International Court of Justice Statute.
art. 4
arts 4 &5
arts 14 &15
arts. 16 & 17
art. 18
art. 25
arts. 26, 27 & 29
art. 30
art. 34
art. 34 (2)
art. 35
art. 36 (2)
art. 36(5)
art. 37
art 38 (4) and (5)
art 39
art. 39 (1)
art. 39 (1) and (5)
art 40
art 41
art 42
art. 48
art. 50
art. 54 (1)
art. 59
art. 65
art 66 (2)
arts. 66- 69
International Labour Organisation Constitution
Art. 37 (1)

Jay Treaties

Law of the Sea Convention 1983
League of Nations Convenant

Mandate for South West Africa
art.7
Montevideo Convention of 1911
art. 12
Montevideo Conventions of 1933
and 1937
Montreal Convention

Nuclear Proliferation Treaty
art. 6

Polish-German Convention 1922

Treaty of Amity, Economic
Relations and Consular Rights
Art. x (1)
Treaty of Conciliation, Arbitration
and Judicial Settlement
Treaty of Friendship and Good
Neighbourliness 1955
Treaty of Versailles, Nationals of the
Allied and Associated Powers
1919.
art. 304 (b)
Trusteeship Agreement for Nauru
1947

United Nations Charter-
art. 1
art. 2 (4)
art. 2(6)
art. 2 (7)
art. 4
arts 7(2) and 22
art. 11(3)
art.14
art. 17
art. 18
art.18 (2)
art.18(3)
art. 27 (2)
art. 33 (1)
art. 34
art. 36
art. 37 (2)
art. 33
art. 38
art.41
art.51
art. 59
art. 65
art. 65 (2)
arts. 66, 67 and 68
art. 68
art. 71
art. 73 (e)
art. 76
art. 92
art. 93
art. 93 (1)
art. 93 (2)
art. 94
art. 94 (1)
art. 94 (2)
art. 95
art. 96
art. 96 (1)
art. 96 (2)
art. 102
art. 103
United Nations General Assembly
Resolution 47/1 of 1992
United Nations General Assembly
Resolution 49/75k of 1994
United Nations General Assembly
Resolution
res. 44/22
res. 186/5/11
res 351 A (iv)
res. 731
res. 748
res. 782 B (viii)
res. 957 (x)
res. 3232 (xxix)
United Nations Security Council
Resolution 276 of 1970
United Nations Security Council
Resolution 284 of 1970

Vienna Convention of 1969 on the
Law of Treaties

World Health Assembly Resolution
WHA46.40 of 1993
art. 2

Chapter 1

Justiciability of International Disputes

Introduction

It is a truism that peace under law has been the desire of man since the Stone Age. In fact it was the need for peace and security that led to mankind's first attempts at social groupings. It is equally a truism that this peace has always eluded mankind. The history of existing international society is that of conflicts and wars among Nation States culminating in the two devastating world wars which occurred in the 20th century. The First World War briefly halted but did not break this trend. This war made the world realise the need to form a League of Nations. A Permanent Court of International Justice[1] was designed for the League and this marked one of greatest events in the development of international adjudication. However, mankind made the same mistakes all over again. After the catastrophic occurrence of the Second World War there was a call for an organisation which would "...save succeeding generations from the scourge of war..."[2] This organisation to be known as the United Nations would, it was hoped, be able to rule by virtue of the power given to it by the Nations which established it. It was also realised following the experience of the League era that the United Nations Organisation[3] needed an International Court of Justice[4] from which the "parties to any dispute, the continuance of which is likely to endanger the maintenance of international peace and security shall first of all seek a solution..."[5] by judicial settlement. In establishing the ICJ expectations in San Francisco in 1945 were very high. The UN held

---

[1] Also to be referred to as the PCIJ.

[2] Preamble to the United Nations Organisation Charter.

[3] Also to be referred to as the UN

[4] Also to be referred to as the ICJ, the International Court, or simply the Court.

[5] Article 33 of the United Nations Charter.

before a war ravaged international community the beacons of international rule of law based on Law and Justice. The Court was to offer the possibility of substituting orderly processes for the vicissitudes of war and the reign of brutal force.[6] It represented the hopes of the smaller and developing States to avoid being invariably drawn into other bloody international conflicts led by superpower rivalries. The sobering concequences of the Second World War lent sincerity even if only momentarily to the efforts of the developed States to construct a truly international Court of Justice. But today over fifty years after the creation of this International Court of Justice[7], there are divergent views among scholars and States alike as to the effectiveness of this Court.

For some especially the much older States and the scholars therefrom, the Court has been more or less a complete success. But to others especially the new generation of States and some of their legal scholars, the Court is a farce, a fiction and a failure, and the basis for its continuance difficult to fathom. Indeed the very efficacy of judicial settlement of international disputes is questioned. Thus the problem this study faces is that of an appraisal of the efficacy of judicial settlement of international disputes and particularly an examination of the role of the International Court of Justice in judicial settlement.

Presently, Nigeria is before the International Court in a case concerning Land and Maritime Boundaries instituted against it by Cameroon. What kind of justice can Nigeria expect? Is it of any significance that Nigeria is anglophone whilst its opponent is francophone? Would it matter if Nigeria were in Court with a European power? Libya, an African country, has for instance, dragged two leading Western Nations--the United States of America and the United Kingdom--before the Court over a contentious dispute arising from the bombing of an American airline flying over

---

[6] Documents of the UN Conference on International Organisation (UNCIO) San Francisco .1945, 13 UNCIO 395 (1945) (Dec. 913 IV /1/ 74 (1), June 12, 1945.

[7] The Court marked its 50th judicial year in 1996, the inaugural public sitting having taken place on April 18 1946. In 1995 the Court celebrated the 50th anniversary of its creation as the principal judicial arm of the UN with the entry into force of the Charter and the ICJ Statute annexed to it on October 24, 1945.

Lockerbie, Scotland. What are the chances of victory or defeat in such cases? How exactly does the Court function or work? How is a dispute referred to the Court's adjudicatory process? What happens between the institution of proceedings and the final disposition of the matter by the Court? These are some of the major questions this work tries to answer.

We are strategically placed in point of time to review the Court's performance. The close of the first half-century of the Court coincides approximately with that of the UN. Thus a review of the problems and prospects of the Court cannot but reflect on the scorecard of the UN itself. We are also fast approaching the close of the United Nations Decade of International Law, which also coincides with the turn of the 20th century. Hence, it falls quite naturally on scholars of this period, particularly those from the developing world (largely silent hitherto) to embark on an assessment of the efficacy of the machinery of the ICJ to apply the ever changing field of International Law to the resolution of conflicts and tensions which seem forever bound to exist if not increase among groups of States and/or International Organisations.

Prima facie, there are many possible methods of attempting a critique or assessing the overall utility of the Court in its over fifty years of existence. One method is to examine the laws, rules and regulations governing the operation of the Court. This brings into consideration aspects of the Charter of the UN, the Statute and the Rules of the Court.[8] Another is to examine the jurisprudence of the Court in decided cases and its effects on general international law. Yet another is to determine the degree of acceptance or non-acceptance of the Court's judgements, orders and opinions--in short the effectiveness of the Court's decisions. Furthermore an attempt may be made to ascertain the real use made by authorised States and international organisations of the jurisdiction and facilities of the Court. The jurisdiction of the International Court is divided into two distinct parts: its capacity to decide disputes between States, or the

[8] The three basic documents are also to be referred to simply as the Charter, the Statute and the Rules. While the Charter (Chapter XIV) contains the legal basis for the establishment of the ICJ, the Statute contains provisions for its organisation and the Rules regulate the procedures.

contentious jurisdiction, and it's capacity to give advisory opinions when requested to do so by particular qualified entities. The object of our enquiry into the law governing these two jurisdictions is to examine its effectiveness as well as the interplay of political and legal factors having a bearing on the Court's work. This interplay has always existed and through time it has exercised a marked influence upon the processes of international adjudication, as was also the case with the Permanent Court of Arbitration, the Court of Arbitral Justice, etc. Whereas it is in the true interest of the entire international community that the ICJ should dispense totally impartial justice based on equal access and standing before the Court, war has been accepted by social scientists as a continuation of politics by other means. The thesis to be tested is whether or not international adjudication before the ICJ is also a continuation of politics by other means.

An interesting development in recent times is the steady increase in the number of cases referred to the Court. Adjudication before the Court is thus beginning to be seen as a normal rather than an extraordinary part of international relations. This fact is somewhat reflected in a slow but steady rise in the number of declarations accepting the Court's compulsory jurisdiction under Article 36, paragraph 2 of the Statute of the Court (i.e., the optional clause). However, it must be realised that the number of States parties to the Statute has more than tripled since the inception of the Court. This may partly explain the increase in submission of disputes to the Court. In fact there really ought to be more cases. Furthermore, the problem of wide and ambiguous reservations to the Court's jurisdiction under the optional clause on the one hand and the numerous objections to the Court's jurisdiction on the other hand leaves much to be desired. It is not possible to assume that real progress is being made without further enquiry. Thus, the main aim of this work lies in the identification of necessary changes in the law and practice of the contentious and advisory jurisdictions of the Court. This must be done in order to popularise the use of the Court by all States, particularly the developing States, based on equal confidence and to enhance the means of peaceful settlement of disputes including the legal means to that end.

In sum, the problems this work addresses include the following: (a) an exposition of the role actual and potential of the Court as the principal judicial organ of the UN; (b) an examination of the rules governing access to the Court's jurisdiction in contentious and advisory cases, as well as the rights of the States to appear or refuse to appear before the Court; (c) the law and practice of the advisory jurisdiction of the Court; (d) evaluation and analysis of both the contentious and advisory jurisdictions, in a manner to discover whether or not the World Court is biased in any way towards the interests of any groups of States; (e) problems affecting the Court's work in particular and judicial settlement of international disputes in general; (f) the development of a better regime for international adjudication within the framework of the ICJ and the UN.

Definition of International Disputes

We should proceed by identifying and delineating what is meant by the term "international disputes" at least in relation to the justiciable issues that could be submitted to the contentious jurisdiction of the Court. This is necessary because the term is central to the paper's topic. It hardly needs to be stated that without international disputes there would be no need for the contentious jurisdiction of the Court. Yet we must state from the very beginning that there is no generally accepted definition of "international disputes." Thus Levi was right when he noted that: "International disputes are nowhere defined in conventions or treaties. Yet legal consequences for States arise from the existence of such disputes."[9] However, the PCIJ attempted a definition in the *Marvrommatis Palestine Concession Case*. Here it was defined as "a disagreement on a point of law or fact, a conflict of legal views or of interests between two persons."[10] The ICJ accepted this as a definition of an international dispute and based on this definition held that there was a dispute in the South West Africa

---

[9] Werner Levi, *Contemporary International Law: A Concise Introduction* (Boulder, Colorado: Westview Press, 1979) p. 286.

[10] **Mavrommatis Concession Palestine Case, 1924 PCIJ Series A, No. 2 - Series C** No. 5-1. See also Kryŝtyna Marak, *A Digest of the Decisions of the International Court.: Permanent Court of International Justice* (The Hague: Martinus Nijhoff, 1974) pp. 78-98.

case and in the Cameroons case.[11] Thus Fitzmaurice said in the Cameroons case, "A dispute must involve more than a mere difference in opinion."[12] The term dispute thus has a technical connotation in international law. This is more so in the determination as to what can and cannot be submitted to the contentious jurisdiction of the International Court. The ICJ has on occasion noted that whether an international dispute exists or not is a matter for objective determination, and that an international dispute will be held to be in existence when two sides "hold clearly opposite views concerning the question," the essential element of a dispute being "a divergence of views between the parties on definite points."[13]

If it is agreed that international law is a complete legal system in itself then it cannot possibly be argued that a dispute could not be settled in accordance with it. However, international lawyers stress that there is such a thing as the justiciability of disputes, with reference to the accepted distinction between legal and political questions.[14] Thus it could happen that a demand to settle a particular dispute made by a State would be rejected by the ICJ. For instance, if a developing State demanded preferential treatment from a developed State such a claim based as it would be on moral and supposedly non-legal grounds could be rejected by the ICJ. As a result of such legalistic distinctions many disputes which could have been well handled by the Court not have been sent to the Court. A political question in the true sense may translate into a demand for the development of international law beyond existing law. Many disputes submitted to the Court involved such demands. There is nothing inherently wrong in this particularly in the sphere of advisory opinions. The UN Secretary General's *Report to the General Assembly* in 1991 wisely counsels that questions which seem entirely political, but which "have a clearly legal component"

---

[11] *Ibid.*

[12] See Judge Morrelli dissenting opinion ICJ *Reports* 1953, p. 15 at p.20 (U.K. Preliminary Objections) 1963 *ICJ Reports*, pp. 105, 109.

[13] *Peace Treaties Case* (1950) at p. 74 and *Asylum Case* (Interpretation) *Ibid* at p. 403. These two judgements have been said to neatly summarise a long line of cases defining the nature of a dispute.

[14] *Ibid.*

could be usefully referred to the Court for an advisory opinion, if for any reason the parties fail to refer the matter to the Court.[15]

The German Government's claims for delineation of non-defined borders in the Continental Shelf Case for instance pushed to extreme limits the justiciability of that case. But the compromise achieved between the parties kept it within legal limits so that the Court was able to decide the issue.[16] Professor Scheuner insists that there is yet another type of political question, namely that which could be legally decided, but which a State might not wish to have legally decided by the Court. This refers to the age old problem of "vital issues," questions of honour or domestic jurisdiction. These are questions which if they really are of international concern, the Court could settle but on which a State may be unwilling to accept the Court's judgement.

It is therefore not possible to isolate any single principle of justiciability and an attempt to do so would only produce unsound legal reasoning. There are certainly cases of functional non-justiciability, for example where the parties have not properly presented the issues to the ICJ. Yet even in such cases it is within the competence of the Court to deal with the relevant issues whether or not the parties plead or argue the cases accordingly. As Brownlie warns, justiciability is a matter of policy and this may be measured, but is definitely not necessarily limited by the standard assumptions of the legal persons most closely affected.

It is, however, clear that the Court would steer clear of such narrowly local questions as the applications of municipal law. Schwarzenberger has expressed the view that the distinction which is frequently drawn between justiciable and non-justiciable disputes lacks any objective criterion. According to him if States are willing to have a dispute decided on the basis of international law this can be done and is the proper function of an international Court. If however,

---

[15] See the address of Sir Robert Jennings (President of the Court) to the forty-seventh session of the General Assembly held on 21 October 1992 reprinted in *ICJ Yearbook* 1993 (Appendix), p.249.

[16] Ian Brownlie, *Principles of Public International Law*. 3rd ed, (Oxford: Clarendon Press), p. 142.

they raise points that involve the necessity of a change in the law, the problem becomes intrinsically a legislative issue.[17]

The distinction between legal and political disputes is particularly crucial with respect to Article 36 (2) of the Statute. That is, in respect of compulsory jurisdiction. The jurisdiction over "legal disputes" enumerated in paragraphs (a) to (d) of that article is not easy to identify. Ehrlich argues that in the strict sense of the term a dispute means only a dispute as to the existence on the basis of Law, of an obligation of one State in relation to another State.[18] In short, only legal disputes are in fact true disputes. A broader view in this respect is taken by Szafara who maintains that the existence of the political dimension is not a bar to classifying a dispute as a legal dispute.[19] It may be concluded then that although not all disputes are legal, all legal disputes are political to some extent. Moreover, Ende was correct in noting that in actual practice, States regard international disputes as fundamentally political in nature. As we will later come to see, States invariably treat all disputes in a political sense and this accounts partly for the phobia of a majority of States against submitting themselves fully to the compulsory jurisdiction of the ICJ or even availing themselves sufficiently of the services of the Court. In practice, however, the Court hardly if ever concludes that it lacks jurisdiction ostensibly because the dispute was not legal in nature.

There is no dispute which inherently is not susceptible to legal treatment once the parties are agreed to depoliticize it and provide the Court with the means to act. The distinction between justiciable and non-justiciable disputes seems to be born more out of practicability and politics than particular theoretical necessities. The important thing to look for is whether or not the pronouncement of the Court is likely to form the basis for the ultimate settlement of the problem and relax rising tensions.

---

[17] George Schewarzenberger, *International Law as Applied by International Courts and Tribunals* Vol. III (London: Stevens, and Sons, 1976) p. 192.

[18] L. Ehrlich *Prawo Mie Dzynaur Odowe* (Warsaw, 1958), p.360.

[19] Renata Szafára, *The Compulsory Jurisdiction of the International Court of Justice.* (Dordrecht: Martinus Nijhoff Publishers.1993) p.11.

The question may still be posed; do "dispute" and "difference of opinion" or "divergence of views" mean the same thing as has been assumed by some writers or is the concept of "difference of opinion" used to indicate a milder form of disagreement? Some writers believe that it would help ease the tension among States and improve the prospects of settling the dispute if the divergent assessment of a point of law were to be brought as soon as possible before a neutral body -- without even waiting for an actual case to arise and before the difference had a chance to became "... unnecessarily entrenched in the course of protracted diplomatic negotiations."[20] Hasty referral to an international court may on the other hand thicken the plot so to speak and bury the chances of negotiated peace and genuine reconciliation.

It appears, however, to have been established that a purely theoretical difference of opinion as to a question of law or fact is not enough to constitute a "dispute" in the legal sense.[21] In the view of Shabtai Rosenne, an international dispute has therefore:

> ... a conception narrower than 'case' or 'matter' which may relate not to a dispute, but to what the parties may choose to call a 'difference' to use the expression appearing in the special agreement in the Minquiers and Ecrehos Case, that is to say, to something broader and perhaps less than a dispute.[22]

A reflection of the extent of conflict in the conceptualisation of international law between the new States and the older States is the way they often differ as to what should be regarded as an international dispute. When they cannot even agree on this, it is no wonder that there are grave differences between these two groups of States on matters of international relations. In the last fifteen years or so the international implications of insurgency and even more the pressure of liberating and separatist movements blur even further the dividing line between international and internal disputes.

---

[20] Hans Von Mangoldt, "Arbitration and Conciliation" in Max Planck Institute for Comparative Public Law and International Law," *Judicial Settlement of International Disputes*. (Berlin and New York: Springer Verlag, 1974) p. 520.

[21] *Ibid.*

[22] Shabtai Rosenne, *The International Court of Justice: An Essay in Political and Legal Theory* (Leiden, A. W. Sijthoff; Dobbs Ferry; NY: Oceana, 1957) p. 307.

However, we are of the opinion that since the whole purpose of defining an international dispute is the maintenance of peace, the terms should neither be too narrowly construed nor made too elastic For instance, upon the outbreak of hostilities within a single State, various factions--liberation movements, freedom fighters, insurgents, defenders of the *status quo, etc.*-- will present a cacophony of discordant voices. Some will affirm the international character of the dispute while others will expressly deny it. In such a situation, it is not uncommon for each side to argue from its own position of understanding based on subjective interests. It is common knowledge that in recent times the international community has been invariably drawn into internal dispute situations (witness the on-going situation in Algeria). It is however true that in many cases disputes start as internal disputes, only to develop into international disputes which disrupt world social order or threaten to seriously violate accepted international legal rules which are *erga omnes*. With the end of the cold war and its super power rivalries and alignments the newer States have a tendency to generate such serious intra-state conflicts and these are presently reshaping the definition of international disputes. The recent events in Liberia, the breakaway Republics of the former USSR, Yugoslavia, Somalia, Angola, Mozambique, Rwanda, Burundi, Yemen, etc., typify this development. To effectively cope with such situations it is necessary to give a broad interpretation to the concept of international dispute. It can be said (employing the words of Article 33 of the Charter) that an international dispute is "any dispute the continuance of which is likely to endanger the maintenance of international peace and security."

We therefore agree with Schwarzenberger that the distinction drawn in the United Nations Charter between "situation" and "dispute" is more important in relation to some articles than others.[23] For instance, the duty of arbitration imposed on the Security Council under Article 37(2) of the Charter applies only to disputes. In other Articles such as Articles 11(3) and 14 of the UN Charter the term "situation" does not form a contrast to disputes but is the wider term

---

[23] George Schwarzenberger, *op.cit.*

intended to include disputes. It is true that in interpreting the meaning of the term "dispute" in jurisdictional clauses both the ICJ and the preceeding PCIJ had always given a liberal construction to the term and defined it in its widest sense as any disagreement between parties.[24]

Civil wars, however, have not traditionally been considered international disputes. What makes a civil war develop into an international conflict is differing decisions reached by different States as to which is the legitimate government and which group should be regarded merely as insurgents, "for if the outsider intervenes on the side of the legitimate government the conflict would remain internal whereas assistance to the insurgents would internationalise the dispute."[25]

Perhaps it could be said at this juncture that an international dispute is a contentious disenchantment between two or more States over points of law and/or fact, the continuance of which can endanger international peace and security. Once an international dispute has been established it is a fixed matter under the general principles of International Law as restated in numerous conventions, treaties and documents including the UN Charter, Articles 1, 33, 36, 94, 95 etc. that the dispute be settled by peaceful means. There is a plethora of such peaceful means at the disposal of States and Article 33 of the Charter provides a fairly exhaustive list of methods to be employed including: "... negotiations, enquiry, mediation, conciliation, arbitration, judicial settlement, resort to agencies and arrangement..." or even to "other peacefùl means of their choice."

It is thus clear that as regards international disputes States under the regime of the UN Charter are not conscribed by a straight-jacketed approach to settlement. This probably was deemed necessary by the drafters of the Charter in order to ensure that solutions and settlement reached are borne out of genuine consideration by the parties involved in a dispute. Also the principle that no State should be forced to accept settlement by a particular means must have been considered by the drafters.

---

[24] *Ibid*, p. 194.

[25] Levi, *op.cit.*, p. 287.

Antecedents in International arbitration and Adjudication

> And it shall come to pass... they shall beat their swords into plowshares and their spears into pruninghooks.[26] Nation shall not lift up sword against nation neither shall they learn war any more... and he shall judge between the nations and shall decide for many peoples.[27]

> ... Kings and States are bound to employ this method (arbitration) of avoiding war... And for this and many other purposes it would be helpful as a matter of fact necessary for the powers to hold conferences, where those whose interests were not involved might settle the disputes of the rest and even take measures to compel the parties to accept peace on fair terms.[28]

There have been many such strong notions on the desirability of settlement of international disputes. Harmonious principles having religious foundations testify to the etymological foundations of the idea of international arbitration. The idea of resolving international disputes by subjecting disputants to arbitration by disinterested third parties, a rule based on the principles of law and justice, developed as an alternative to settlement by the rule of force. This concept was definitely widespread in acceptance, but its application was strictly restricted, because it had a regional flavour. The concept existed in the early periods of Middle Eastern history in the sacred codes of the East.[29] Islamic scholars testify that it is engendered in the teachings of Islam.[30] Moslem scholars in fact are of the view that the concept was intensively borrowed from Islamic principles practised among Islamic States by the Europeans following their contact with Islam through Spain, the Crusades and earlier Ottomans.

---

[26] "Isaiah," Chapter 2:4, *Good News Bible* Today's English Version (London: The Bible Society & Collins, 1979).

[27] *Ibid*

[28] English translation from Hugo Grotius, *The Law of War and Peace*, trans. Louise R. Loomis (New York: 1949), p. 251.

[29] Shabtai Rosenne, *The World Court: What It Is and How It works* (New York: A.W. Sijthoff - Oceana, 1973) p. 11.

[30] M. Khadduri, *War and Peace in the Law of Islam* (Baltimore: 1955), p. 23. For insightful views on the doctrine of Al-Siyar see also Abdur Rahman Doi, *Shariah The Islamic Law* (Ibadan: Iksan Islamic Publishers 1990) pp.420-425.

However, it is claimed by most European scholars that it is in Europe that the concept took root. Rosenne thinks that there was an attraction in the European mind which sought to transfer the absolute values of discipline and the need for respect of the law in the nation-state to the international community.[31] Third party adjudication was common among the small Greek and Italian city-states. In the former it was constructed within the framework of their Hellenic Culture (and especially through the instrumentality of the Delphic Amphictyonies) and in the latter the practice of arbitration was performed by ecclesiastical and secular authorities.[32] In the ancient Roman Empire there was a built-in mechanism for resolving disputes between their many vassal states. This practice was continued by the Popes and Emperors, the major premise being that the judgement in settling a case between parties must begin by judging not by conciliation.[33] It was in this ancient/medieval period that the theologian jurists developed the theory of the just and unjust war.

In more modern times, that is, from the 18th century, the first cases arose under the General Treaty of Friendship, Commerce and Navigation (the Jay Treaty which is so named after an American Secretary of State, John Jay) of 1794. This treaty dealt with all the outstanding disputes between the United States and Great Britain accumulated since 1776, excepting three which were remitted to arbitration by mixed commissions.[34] Simpson and Fox described this development as "a new starting point for the development of international arbitration, often the process in the preceeding period of a century or more, had come to be regarded as virtually in desuetude."[35]

In the nineteenth century, treaties existing between the US and the UK made it possible to submit various issues to arbitral tribunals of commissions.[36]

---

[31] Rosenne, *op. cit.*, p. 11.

[32] *Ibid.*, see also I.G. Tenekides, "International Law and Federal Communities in the Cities of Greece", RADI, 90 (California: 1956) p. 469.

[33] Rosenne, *op. cit.*, p. 12.

[34] *Satow's Guide to Diplomatic Practice*, 5th ed., (London: 1959) p. 84.

[35] J. L. Simpson and Hazel Fox, *International Arbitration* (London: 1959) p. 84.

[36] *Ibid.*

The Hague Conferences and the Permanent Court of Arbitration

A further stage in the development of the judicial settlement of international disputes was reached with the First Hague Conference held in 1899. The powers which took part in this conference signed the Hague Convention for the Pacific Settlement of International Disputes, in which they undertook to use their best efforts to ensure the pacific settlement of international differences with a view to obviating, as far as possible, recourse to force in the relations between States.[37] There was at this time the conviction that the permanent institution of a tribunal of arbitration, accessible to all, in the midst of independent powers, would contribute effectively to the Empire of Law and the strengthening of the appreciation of international justice. Arbitration was considered the fairest and most trustworthy way to settle disputes among nations. Efforts were thus concluded to establish such an institution in the guise of a Permanent Court of Arbitration.[38] Although the latter was a permanent institution; it was not a permanent tribunal in the true sense of the word but a panel of about 150 to 200 persons (four from each contracting power) from among whom States could select one or more arbitrators to form a tribunal for the settlement of a particular dispute.[39] For this reason Cecil Hurst says that:

> The Permanent Court of Arbitration was a court only in name; it was nothing more than a panel of arbitrators, a list of men qualified and willing to sit as members of a tribunal when one was called into being by the parties; agreement on the individuals to be chosen as arbitrators and on the terms of reference had still to be undertaken by the states concerned.[40]

---

[37] UN. Office of Public Information, *The International Court of Justice*, Sixth ed. (New York: United Nations Publications, 1967) p. 2.

[38] David J. Bederman, "The Hague Peace Conferences of 1899 and 1907" *in* Mark Janis (ed.), *International Courts for The Twenty-first Century* (Leiden: Kluwer Academic Publishers) p.9.

[39] *Ibid.*

[40] *See* Cecil Hurst, Legal Adviser to the Foreign Office *in* Wheeler - Bennet and Maurice Fanshawe *Information on the World Court,* 1918-1928 (London: George Allen and Unwin Ltd., 1929) p. 6.

The second Peace Conference in the Hague in 1907 essayed a further step, but it broke down nonetheless. It framed a scheme for a new Court, a "Court of Arbitral Justice," which has been described as the "international prize court." Again this attempt had inherent problems. In many respects this initiative was far ahead of its time. The notion of Compulsory Jurisdiction emerged in the form of calls in certain instances for mandatory arbitration. This drew the objection of Germany and Austria-Hungary, and the idea was dropped.[41] Considerations of sovereignty were still of absolute if not obsessive importance to States and most could not fathom any other system for the planned Court outside that which accords a judge for every State. It is difficult to differ with the opinion of Hurst that this situation arose as "the old bugbear of the equality of States." He further wrote that:

> Judges are the one thing which cannot be dispensed with if cases are to be submitted to a Court and decisions are to be given. Cases cannot be decided by a row of empty chairs, and the conference could not agree as to how the men were to sit in the chairs... all States are equal and there were forty five judges in a Court. To pick and choose between the states meant that some would be left unrepresented, and some of the big states said they were very sorry, but they could not afford to be left out; and the others said they were very sorry too, but they could not afford to be placed in a different category from the remainder and be left out themselves if the others were not to be left out; so that scheme must wait.[42]

Although for various reasons the two attempts discussed above did not succeed, they are today regarded as developments of "... interest since they show that it was in the field of judicial institution that the powers sought to make a first step in the direction of international organisation."[43] We agree totally with this view. The Permanent Court of Arbitration (1899) which was maintained by the Second Hague Conference held in 1907 even existed well into the era of the UN deciding on over 20 cases some of which have been of considerable importance.[44]

---

[41] Bederman, *op.cit.* p. 11.

[42] Hurst, *op. cit..*, p. 687.

[43] UN. Office of Public Information, *op. cit.*, p. 3.

[44] *Ibid.*

A member of the United States' delegation to the Second Hague Conference expressed himself in prophetic words which history has borne out in a striking manner when he declared that: "A court of that kind will deliver its judgements by virtue of the authority of the United Nations."[45] Today as we approach the centenary of the first Peace Conference we still face daunting challenges as regards peaceful resolution of international disputes. Thus we can understand better the problems the founding fathers must have faced.

The Permanent Court of International Justice

The creation in 1920 of the PCIJ, for which provision had been made in the Covenant of the League of Nations, marked the greatest advance to that time in the field of judicial settlement of international disputes. The Permanent Court was in fact "... a court in the real sense of the term"[46] and was ready to function at any time. It is true that, as in the case of the Permanent Court of Arbitration, its jurisdiction depended solely upon the consent given by the parties to a dispute. On the other hand, the fact that the Court was open to States at any time made it possible for States to refer not only particular disputes that had arisen but all disputes which might arise in the future -- that is at a time when we can say all was at ease. This undoubtedly constituted the first international tribunal having what can be described as a "corporate character" before which a State could bring a dispute by means of a unilateral application calling upon another State to appear before it, without any existing prior agreement to the composition of the tribunal or to the questions to be submitted to it.[47] The PCIJ's first sitting was in 1922. Its activities were naturally interrupted by the events of World War II and in 1946 it finally met its demise as a consequence of the dissolution of the League of Nations. In the period of its active existence, i.e. between 1922 and 1939, it dealt with a total of 79 cases (59 of which were contentious) referred to it either by special agreement or unilateral application. The Court's compulsory jurisdiction under Article 36,

---

45 *Ibid.*
46 *Ibid.*
47 *Ibid.*

paragraph 2 of its Statute was recognised by a sizeable number of the League's member States.[48]

The UN and the Court (ICJ)

> There is only one thought I wish to leave with the members of the General Assembly... there can only be one 'principal judicial organ of the United Nations' as there is normally only one supreme court of any legally ordered community; and that position of the International Court of Justice ought to be remembered and strenuously protected.[49]

In 1945 a new judicial organ, the International Court of Justice, was brought into being by the Charter of the UN. The Statute of the Court is annexed to the Charter of which it forms an integral part. Except for a few changes, most of which are purely formal, it is similar to the Statute of the PCIJ. Furthermore, when the new Court met, it adopted the Rules of the Court of its predecessor without any substantial change. Thus, it is recognised today that: "The work of the PCIJ which began in 1922 is today entrusted to the ICJ and therefore continues uninterrupted."[50] However, it needs be mentioned that some authors follow this continuity principle with less enthusiasm. Gore-Booth, for instance, believes, and we agree with him, that, "... although its Statute is based upon the Statute of the Permanent Court of International Justice there is no doubt that the International Court of Justice was created as a new court."[51]

These assertions are credible in their own right in that there are a great number of treaties, conventions and undertakings which provided for the jurisdiction of the PCIJ and which were (and some still are) in force under the ICJ. Here attention has to be directed to the provisions of the Statute of the ICJ, Article 37 which states:

> Whenever a treaty or convention in force provides for reference of a matter to a tribunal to have been instituted by the League of Nations, or to the Permanent Court of International Justice, the matter shall, as between the parties to the present Statute, be referred to the International Court of Justice.

---

[48] *Ibid.*, p. 4.

[49] R. Jennings, President of the Court's address to the General Assembly in *ICJ Yearbook*, 1993-94, *op. cit*, pp.222-223.

[50] *Op. cit.*

[51] Satow, *op. cit.*, p. 356.

The ICJ by virtue of the provisions of Article 7(1) is one of the bodies "... established as the principal organs of the United Nations." Though located at the Hague the ICJ remains just as much an organ of the UN as the General Assembly or the Security Council.

Article 92 of the Charter provides that:

> The International Court of Justice shall be the principal judicial organ of the United Nations. It shall function in accordance with the annexed Statute ... and forms an integral part of the present Charter.

Article 93(1) of the Charter provides *inter alia*: "All Members of the United Nations are *ipso facto*, parties to the Statute of the International Court of Justice."

Thus, it is not possible for a State to be a member of the UN without also being a party to the Statute of the International Court of Justice. Whereas the converse is possible in that, according to the provisions of Article 93(2):

> A state which is not a Member of the United Nations may become a party to the Statute of the International Court of Justice on conditions to be determined in each case by the General Assembly upon the recommendation of the Security Council.

Making use of this provision (and other relevant resolutions of the General Assembly), Switzerland, Liechtenstein, San Marino and Nauru were at various times permitted to become parties to the Statute.

Once a State has acceded to the Statute and/or the Charter it undertakes to accept as final the decisions of the Court and give effect to them. Article 94 therefore states:

> 1. Each Member of the United Nations undertakes to comply with the decision of the International Court of Justice in any case to which it is a party.
>
> 2. If any party to a case fails to perform the obligations incumbent upon it under a judgement rendered by the Court, the other party may have recourse to the Security Council, which may, if it deems necessary, make recommendations or decide upon measures to be taken to give effect to the judgement.

Satow (5th ed by Gore-Booth) found it necessary to comment on the right accorded by this Article to States (including non-Members of the UN) to have recourse to the Security Council. He wrote:

> According to the normal rule of International Law treaties cannot confer any rights upon states not parties to them (*pacta tertiis nec nocent nec prosunt*), and if this rule were not applied literally, it is difficult to see how a State not a member of the United Nations could acquire any right of recourse to the Security Council.[52]

However, it is our view that non-members of the UN have access to the Security Council and can be rebuked for non-compliance with judicial decisions by the Security Council for two reasons. The first reason flows from a correct reading to be given to Article 2(6) of the Charter which states:

> The Organisation shall ensure that states which are not Members of the United Nations *act in accordance with these Principles* so far as may be necessary for the maintenance of international peace and security.

Here it should be accepted that "these principles" include the principles of judicial settlement (including recourse to the Security Council) as allowed in Article 94(2). Secondly, having in mind the general intention of both the Charter and Statute to grant access to the Court to non-members of the UN on substantially similar terms as members, it would seem that this case is one of such egalitarian principles on which access is to be governed.

A State not a party to the Statute may also under certain circumstances have access to the Court. Such a State shall previously have deposited with the Registrar of the Court a declaration by which it accepts the jurisdiction of the Court, in accordance with the Charter of the UN, the Statute and the Rules of the Court. It will in the same manner undertake to comply with the decision or decisions of the Court and to accept all obligations of a member of the UN under Article 94 of the Charter.[53]

A last note on the relationship between the UN and the Court: it needs be mentioned that according to Article 95 of the Charter nothing in the Charter shall prevent Members of the United Nations

---

[52] *Satow, op. cit.*, p. 357.

[53] See Security Council Resolution 9 (1946) made pursuant to the provisions of Article 35, paragraph 2, of the Statute (Rules, Art. 26, para. 1 (c) and Art. 41).

from entrusting the solution of their differences to other tribunals by virtue of agreements already in existence or which may be concluded in future.

Forms of Pacific Settlement

Just as disputes vary in type and intensity so also has civilisation fashioned over the years suitable means and methods to resolve them. Modern international law gives recognition to the utility of maintaining many windows for the resolution of international disputes. The UN Charter therefore dictates that:

> The Parties to any dispute the continuance of which is likely to endanger the maintenance of international peace and security, shall first of all seek a solution by negotiation, enquiry, mediation, conciliation, judicial settlement, resort to regional agencies or arrangements, or other peaceful means of their own choice.[54]

States are thus bound under International Law to settle their squabbles by peaceful means but not by any particular peaceful method. It would appear that the obligation to seek a solution by any of the approved procedures only arises in the case of disputes the continuation of which will be likely to endanger the maintenance of international peace and security.

It might be pertinent to mention here that the determination of this likelihood is entrusted under Article 37(2) of the Charter to the Security Council which is more or less the executive body of the UN. Nothing, however, stops States from coming to this conclusion on their own. In fact the more readily States discern and admit the existence of disputes, especially in their formative stages, the easier it is to resolve them through appropriate means. Below are brief discussions of various forms of pacific settlement.

Negotiation

Negotiation has remained a particularly viable means of settlement of international disputes. There is a convergence of opinions among scholars as regards the potency of the use of negotiation in the settlement of international disputes. From a diplomatic point of view

---

[54] Article 33(1) of the Charter.

negotiation means the conduct of direct talks between the parties to a dispute aimed at settling the dispute. H.G. Darwin thinks that negotiations are the simplest method of peaceful settlement of disputes, in the sense that in negotiations the parties to the dispute alone are involved in the procedure. To Levi, "[d]irect negotiation between the parties to a dispute is the most frequent method for the pacific settlement of international disputes."[55] A distinctive feature and an advantage of adopting negotiation as a means of pacific settlement is that negotiations involve only parties to the dispute whereas the other methods enumerated in Article 33(1) involve other States or people.

The ICJ in the *North Sea Continental Shelf Cases* (1969) declared it an obligation for the parties to negotiate, and the PCIJ, in its *Railway Traffic between Lithuania and Poland* (advisory opinion) stated that the parties must "not only enter into negotiations but also pursue them as far as possible with a view to concluding agreements."[56] Though there is in fact no obligation to submit disputes to negotiation procedures first before attempting other methods, the idea of negotiation is more closely linked with the notion of diplomacy, for every diplomatic action ends in negotiation. Negotiation means, at least in part, compromise.[57] Public opinion to a large extent influences the kind of compromises and concessions made by a government which is one obvious shortcoming of negotiations. Moreover, it is quite possible for the government to misjudge public opinion in which case negotiations will fail.[58]

International disputes which require negotiations for settlement may arise out of the diplomatic protection abroad of citizens and body corporates by (or of) one country in another. This is especially so in such shareholding disputes as occurred in the *Barcelona Traction Case*. For such cases the United States Supreme Court made a strong case in favour of diplomatic negotiations over (national) court procedures. The thinking here was that:

---

[55] Levi, *op. cit.*, p. 286.

[56] *PCIJ Reports*, 1931, p. 116.

[57] Nascimento E. Da Silva, *Diplomacy in International Law* (Leiden: A.W. Sitjthoff International Publishing Company, 1977), p. 61.

[58] *Ibid.*, p. 292.

> A decision by the national court that the state's acts were invalid might offend that state and make agreement difficult... If per chance the court should find the foreign state's acts legal the findings could undermine negotiations between the two states aiming at redress regardless of the legal situation for the damaged nationals.[59]

Here it is further posited that: "... national interest might be settled reasonably satisfactorily for all concerned through negotiations with either side emerging as the victor."

In sum, obvious advantages and disadvantages exist in the employment of negotiation as a means of pacific settlement. Dag Hammarskjold, former Secretary-General of the UN, stated as follows:

> This instrument (negotiation) has many advantages... But it has also weaknesses. There is the temptation to play to the gallery at the expense of solid construction. And there is the risk that positions once taken publicly become frozen making compromise difficult.[60]

This is very true. It needs only be added that whether negotiation should or should not be used in a given situation is a factor of the kind of dispute in question and the parties involved.

Inquiry

> In differences of an international nature... arising from a difference of opinion on points of fact, the signatory powers recommend that the parties who have not been able to come to an agreement by means of diplomacy should, as far as circumstances allow, institute an International Commission of Inquiry to facilitate a solution of these differences by elucidating the facts by means of an impartial and conscientious investigation.[61]

The usefulness of the institution of commissions of inquiry had been realised as far back as the time of the Hague Convention of 1899. Inquiry in a general sense encompasses all forms of search for information. In its specialised sense as a particular process of settling international disputes it is useful in that many disputes invariably stem from differences over facts. In that case; "[t]he commission's task is to find and report the facts of the situation, without evaluating

---

[59] *Ibid.*

[60] Hammarskjold quoted in Satow *op. cit.*, p. 350.

[61] Article IX of the Hague Convention, 1899.

them or drawing conclusions from them. The disputants can do with the report as they please."[62] Thus Article XIV of the Hague Convention of 1899 provides:

> The Report of the International Commission of Inquiry is limited to a statement of facts, and has in no way the character of an Arbitral Award. It leaves the conflicting Powers entire freedom as to the fact to give to this statement.

Following the reasoning in both the 1899 and 1907 Conventions the League of Nations and the UN have accepted this method of pacific settlement. For instance, the League of Nations appointed in 1932 the Lytton Commission of Inquiry to investigate the Japanese invasion of Manchuria. However, on this particular Commission a writer notes that it is an example of how such a commission of enquiry can be used to evade rather than live up to its responsibility; "... [i]n fact it served as a device for the members of the League to avoid taking protective action for China."[63]

The General Assembly of the UN in 1949 adopted a Resolution establishing the United Nations Panel for Inquiry and Conciliation to be directed by the Secretary-General and adopted rules for its composition and procedure.[64]

Also in 1967, the General Assembly concluded its consideration of an item concerning methods of fact-finding by adopting Resolution 2329 (XXII). Thus, the General Assembly recognised the usefulness of impartial fact-finding as a means towards the settlement of disputes as well as their prevention. Pursuant to this Resolution a register of experts on legal matters and other fields to whose services States, which are parties to a dispute may resort by agreement, was prepared by the Secretary-General.[65]

In speaking about inquiry as a means of settlement of international disputes one has the giddy feeling that it might not be any better in practice than the various commissions of inquiry rampant in municipal settings especially in Nigeria, where commissions of inquiry are veritable instruments of time wasting

---

[62] Levi, *op. cit.*, p. 294.

[63] *Ibid.*

[64] Satow, *op. cit.*, pp. 350-51.

[65] *Ibid.*, p. 371.

bureaucracy merely affording the government a cooling-off mechanism. Herein lies the greatest flaw of this method of pacific settlement.

Arbitration

Arbitration is among the oldest methods of pacific settlement. It involves, like the other forms apart from negotiation, decisions taken through third party participation. Arbitration became popular after the United States introduced it in its Jay Treaties, 1794.[66] Nevertheless, there was no widely agreed formalisation of the arbitration procedure until the Hague Conventions of 1899 and 1907.[67] These two conventions gave the definition of Arbitration as "...the settlement of disputes between States by judges of their choice and on the basis of respect for law." Hence arbitration could be by mixed commissions or by heads of third States or by any other agreed means.[68] In as much as there are similarities between arbitration and adjudication (or judicial settlement) there are certain basic dissimilarities. Whereas in judicial settlement the parties need not partake in the appointment of judges, in arbitration the parties chose the arbitrator(s). The basis of the decision must be respect for law, *but not necessarily the rules of law*. The parties to a dispute are also allowed to choose upon what principles the decision is to be made in so far as it does not violate the law. The decisions of arbitrators are thus known as "awards" while those of judges in adjudication are known as "judgements."[69] It suffices to state here that both are binding upon the parties, and both are final unless there emerge new facts of compelling nature, which decisively affect the decisions.

In the twentieth century other devices came into greater prominence, which call for third-party participation, but do not necessarily call for a commitment in advance by the contending parties to accept the eventual judgement. A limitation in this way of the initial commitment makes acceptance easier, but equally obvious

---

[66] Levi, *op. cit.*, p. 297.
[67] *Ibid.*
[68] Satow, *op. cit.*, p. 354.
[69] Levi, *op. cit.*, p. 297.

is the fact that it makes the prospect of ultimate decisions much less certain. In this situation the International Law Commission introduced into the General Assembly in 1958 a Convention on Arbitral Procedure based on what it called the 'Principle of Non-frustration." This principle attempted to ensure that once a country had agreed to arbitration, it could not later withdraw from that commitment. Debate over this proposition over the next five years reached no practical conclusion; on the contrary it revealed a deep difference of doctrine between those countries which were prepared to accept some such limitation on national freedom of choice at some stage in the arbitration proceedings and those (particularly the erstwhile Communist countries) who argued that at any moment in the discussion the autonomy of the national will of sovereign States could become paramount.[70]

Because the arbitral procedure must always be based upon respect for Law the generally accepted basic principles must be obeyed. Both sides must be given an opportunity to be heard; the arbitrator must be impartial; all proceedings must be fair. Within the limits set above the disputants have a wide choice on the procedure. They may agree on the power and jurisdiction to be given to the arbitrator, the composition of the arbitration tribunal, the delimitation of the subject matter which is to be considered by the tribunal, the basis for the award, even possibly the interpretation of the principles to be applied in the particular case and the alternative awards the arbitrator is allowed to make. All these details are to be agreed upon in a "*Compromis.*" *Without this Compromis* there can be no arbitration, even if the parties have a treaty obligation to submit their disputes to arbitration. Should any of the details of the *Compromis* be violated in the course of the arbitration procedure, the award is null and void,[71] "...though who decides such a violation if the parties cannot agree is an unanswered question."[72]

Chile and Argentina appealed to the United Kingdom for arbitration over certain frontier disputes, pursuant to an Agreement dated 17th April, 1896. Arbitration was also requested later to

---

[70] *Ibid.*

[71] Levi, *op. cit.*, p. 298.

[72] *Ibid.*

determine the Beagle Channel, many of the arrangements for Arbitration were inspired by those of the Permanent Court of Arbitration.[73]

Some United Nations specialised agencies have also interested themselves in arbitration as a method of peaceful settlement of disputes. The International Bank for Reconstruction and Development (IBRD) has established a Centre for the Settlement of Investment Disputes where questions can go to arbitration through the inquiry and conciliation procedures.[74] There was also set up in 1967, a UN agency, the International Centre for the Settlement of Industrial Disputes (ICSID). Any award accorded by this agency is to be given recognition and effect in Nigeria as if it were a Supreme Court Decision. All these point to the potency of the arbitration procedure. As a learned author notes:

> In short ...arbitration is not an obscure or difficult resource for states which require an answer to a specific question... Failure to settle does not suggest so much weakness in procedure as an absence of readiness to accept an unfavourable judgement.[75]

Conciliation

Conciliation as a procedure for the resolution of international disputes is conceived in different lights by various authors. For instance, while Levi says; "[c]onciliation is a composite of Mediation with Commission of Inquiry,"[76] Gore-Booth posits that, "this word (Conciliation) can be employed very generally as an aspect of good offices." Roling, the eminent Belgian jurist, concurs with this latter description. He states:
"... *I' essential de la conciliation est l'examen an fond ce qui, la differencie des bons offices (good offices) qui differencie conciliation et arbitage.*"[77]

---

[73] Satow, *op. cit.*, p. 355.
[74] *Ibid.*
[75] *Ibid.*
[76] Levi, *op. cit.*, p. 295.
[77] A.I.D.I. 49 (1961), Vol. 2, p. 227: Quoted *in Report on the Peaceful Settlement of Disputes*, Annex II, Para. 4 *in* Satow, *op.. cit.*

A commission of conciliation ascertains the facts of a dispute and on the basis of its findings, proposes its settlement. However, the proposal is a recommendation only and advisory.[78] Article 15 of the European Convention for the Peaceful Settlement of Disputes describes the tasks of a conciliation commission as:

> to elucidate the questions in dispute, to collect with that object all necessary information by means of enquiry or otherwise, and to endeavour to bring the parties to the terms of settlement which seems suitable to it and lay down the period within which they are to make their decision.

Against the advantages of the conciliation procedure Gore-Booth advances two arguments:

> First, there are in fact treaties which bind the participants in advance to accept the Conciliation Commission's views, creating the concept of a 'binding conciliation.' Secondly and more important, a decision arising out of what is basically a diplomatic procedure could well diverge in general or in an important particular from a judgement on a comparable matter given on a strictly legal basis.[79]

Despite these arguments, the Vienna Convention of 1969 on the Law of Treaties provides for "compulsory conciliation" as a means of settling certain classes of disputes about the interpretation of the larger bulk of part V of the Convention.[80]

Since 1918 several hundred conciliation commissions have been concluded and hundreds of conciliation commissions have been established. Writers have recorded almost no other cases of conciliation, except in the League of Nations and the United Nations, where it is used as part of their peace-keeping machinery. The Security Council in particular has established a number of conciliation commissions to help solve difficult disputes, as in the Netherlands-Indonesia dispute, the Greek Frontier incidents, the India-Pakistan dispute over Kashmir, and the Palestine issue.[81]

---

[78] Levi, *op. cit.*

[79] Satow, *op. cit.*, p. 354.

[80] *Ibid.*

[81] Levi; *op. cit.*, p. 295.

Good Offices

The use of Good Offices in the settlement of international disputes entails the intercession of a third party (a state, an international organisation or even a private person) in a dispute between parties who refuse to negotiate with the aim of bringing such parties into direct negotiations.[82] To Darwin, "Good Offices are sometimes held to mean the action taken to bring about or initiate, but without active participation, the discussion of the substance of the dispute."[83]

Thus it is clear that Good Offices will prove more important when the disputants are already at war or are on the delicate brink of one with each side not yet fully appreciative of a negotiated - settlement. Instances of such situations abound; the Roosevelt role in the Israel - Egypt war in 1973; France in the US - North Vietnam war; France in the Dogger Bank crisis between Great Britain and Russia.[84] On the use of Good Offices a learned author observes that:

> Any party to a dispute may ask for good offices and no party has to accept proffered good offices. Nobody has the duty to offer good offices, even when asked to do so. The offer is always advisory, never binding and cannot be considered an unfriendly act. Presumably for this reason, the dispute continues, unaffected in any way by the offer. But an outside nation might consider the good offices services as 'meddling' in other peoples affairs, as China did regarding American attempts in South Africa and Rhodesia and Soviet attempts in Lebanon in 1976.[85]

It is to be understood that special agreements in treaties may alter the voluntary nature of good offices. For instance, the League of Nation's Covenant and the Charter of the UN state that members must settle by peaceful means, at least those of their disputes "... the continuance of which is likely to endanger the maintenance of international peace and security." Thus it is proffered that such action would as a minimum include that Good Offices be offered and accepted.

---

[82] *Ibid.*, p. 292.

[83] Darwin as quoted in Satow, *op. cit.*, p. 353.

[84] *Ibid.*

[85] *Ibid*, p. 293.

Mediation

There appears tc be a grey area between the definition of mediation and that of good offices. This is moreso because "[t]he rules relating to mediation are essentially the same as those applying to good offices."[86] However, the confusion as to what the two terms means seems to have been resolved by the wording of General Assembly Resolution 186/5/11 of 14th May, 1948 which invited a committee of the Assembly to "...appoint a representative of local and community authorities in Palestine who would use his good offices ...to promote adjustment of the future situation in Palestine."[87] The aim of mediation is the reconciliation of the opposing views of the disputants and the appeasement of their feelings of mutual resentment. The difference between mediation and conciliation lies in the fact that while a mediator deals with the substance of the dispute and is under the obligation to suggest possible (though not binding) solutions; the organisation or individual offering "good offices" is more or less only obligated to provide every possible facility including advice on procedure; proposals must come from the parties to the dispute themselves.

H.G. Darwin thinks of mediation thus: "Mediation as a method of peaceful settlement of international disputes means the participation of a third State or a disinterested individual in negotiation between States in dispute."[88]

The UN. tried a number of times especially in the early years of its existence to use mediation in settling highly contentious questions.[89] In the case of Palestine, Count Folke Bernadotte of Sweden was appointed Mediator; after his assassination Dr. Ralph Bunche (who was later to become Senior Under Secretary-General) took over as Acting Mediator.

Under the UN Charter it would appear that mediation though used on a number of occasions is not fully exploited because a dispute must have reached the point where its continuance "is likely to endanger the maintenance of international peace and security"

[86] *Ibid.*

[87] Satow, p. 352.

[88] *Report on the Peaceful Settlement of Disputes*, p. 72, para. 1.

[89] *Op. cit.*

(Article 33) before organs of the United Nations can go into action. By that time, more often than not the positions of the disputants would have become rigid, and public mediation effort by the United Nations becomes difficult. The practice has therefore developed that the Secretary-General or his representative engages quietly and discretely in mediation efforts when they are merited by the parties--whether States or Liberation Movements.[90]

From all these it can be submitted that an alternative method of which the UN can make use would be that, before a conflict of interests or opinion becomes a "dispute", it should be dealt with while it is a "situation" which might lead to international friction or give rise to a dispute (Article 34). But the possibilities of dealing with a situation are fewer and less effective and do not necessarily include--if they do not actually exclude--the afore-discussed means of pacific settlement.[91]

Administrative Tribunals

Within the UN System disputes that occur from time to time are not limited to those between member states, nor do they necessarily fall into the classifications given earlier. Certain disputes emanate and exist between workers of the organisation and the organisation itself. Such disputes are equally amenable to judicial settlement and this function is performed by the various administrative tribunals that exist within the UN. Examples of these include: the ILO Administrative Tribunal and the UN Administrative Tribunal.

Rosenne rightly proclaims that the proceedings in the Tribunal are contentious proceedings between the staff member and the organisation. The result of these proceedings is a judgment, which is, subject to the procedure of recourse, final and executory. The recourse is not an appeal, that is, just a further stage of contentious procedure, but it is an advisory process for which the statute of the court lays down a certain set of conditions.[92]

---

[90] Levi, *op. cit.*, pp. 293-4.

[91] This idea is originally Levi's but we totally identify with it. See *Ibid*, 293.

[92] Rosenne, *op. cit.* p. 488.

The United Nations Administrative Tribunal is "competent" to hear and pass judgement upon applications alleging non-observance of contracts of employment of staff members of the Secretariat of the UN or of the terms of employment of such staff members. (The words "contract" and "terms of appointment" are used here to encompass all pertinent regulations and rules in force at the time of the alleged non-observance, including the staff pension regulations).[93] The Tribunal just as the ICJ itself has *competence de la competence*. As it is put in Article 2(3) of the Statutes and Rules of the Administrative Tribunal of the United Nations,[94] a dispute as to whether the Tribunal has competence must be settled by the decision of the Tribunal itself so long as the cause of the complaint arose after January 4, 1950. That the Tribunal is a judicial body performing judicial functions and not a mere subordinate committee of the General Assembly is clear in the various articles of its Statute. Articles 1 and 2 establish the Tribunal and give it competence to hear and pass judgement upon applications from affected applicants in respect of a dispute between a staff member and the organisation. Article 10 provides in paragraph 2 that the judgements shall be final and without appeal and paragraph 3 makes it clear that the judgements must state the reasons on which they are based. A further testimony to the judicial powers of the Tribunal lies in the Staff Rules II, part 1 of the UN Administrative Tribunal which provides *inter alia*:

> There are no provisions attributing an advisory character to the Tribunal's functions nor those in any way limiting the independence of the Tribunal's activity; its independence is guaranteed by Article 3 paragraph 5 which provides: No member of the Tribunal can be dismissed by the General Assembly unless the other members are of the unanimous opinion that he is unsuited for further service.

In the case, the Effect of Awards of Compensation made by tne United Nations Administrative Tribunal the ICJ was of the view that

---

[93] Taslim Olawale Elias, *United Nations Charter and the World Court: Law Series No. 1* (Ibadan: Nigerian Institute of Advanced Legal Studies, 1989), p. 15.

[94] As adopted by the General Assembly by Resolution 351A (IV) on 24 November 1949 and amended by Resolution 782B (VIII) on 9 December 1953 and by Resolution 957 (X) on 8 November 1955.

the Tribunal has been established not as an advisory organ or a subordinate committee of the General Assembly but as an independent and truly judicial body pronouncing final judgements without appeal within the limited field of its function. The Court further held that following a well established and generally recognised principle of law a judgement that is rendered by such a judicial body is "*...res judicata* and has binding force between the parties to the dispute."[95]

Nonetheless it is important to note the special relations which exist between the Tribunal and the Court. The latter's jurisdiction is limited to acting as a review body and not as a court of appeal--a role which it has performed commendably well in many instances.[96] The wealth of reasoned replies to the questions put to it by the Tribunal goes a long way to improving the rule of law within the UN system.

[95] *ICJ Reports*, 1954, p.47.

[96] *See* our discussions later particularly Tables XV and XVI.

Chapter 2

Role and Functions of the International Court of Justice

Before a critique can be written on the work of the ICJ it is necessary to examine the goals which the Court has set out to achieve. However, it must be said that in the last resort recourse to International Justice depends on the will of governments and on their readiness to submit for legal decision their disputes with other States. As has been said by a former President of the Court: "As for the Court it means to accomplish to the full the duties incumbent upon it and it is hoped that it will not weaken in that resolve."[1] The main concern of the Court is that disputes brought before it shall be settled in accordance with the Law as expeditiously and as amicably as possible.[2]

Every legal system, it is said, belongs to the integrating functions of a society, i.e., controlling deviations from existing social norms.[3] For the ICJ this is also true and like other legal systems the large social system (in this case the international community) delegates to the UNO its tasks or (input) that become the projected output of this sub-system.[4] Unfortunately, however, as regards exactly what these tasks are, there exists no small measure of controversy and misunderstanding. This is even so among the jurists of the International Court. It is clear, as Prott notes, that:

> How an I.C.J. judge views the function of the International Court depends on his conception of his own role. His training in particular

[1] Judge J. Gustạvo Guerrero, President of the PCIJ (1936-45) and of the ICJ 1946-49 on December 1939, quoted in S. Rosenne, *The World Court: what it is and how it works*. 3rd ed (Dobbs Ferry, N.Y.: Oceana Publications, 1973) p. 9.

[2] Zafrulla Khan, in *ICJ Yearbook*, 1971-1972, p. 137.

[3] Lyndcll V. Prott, *The latent Power of Culture and the International Judge* (Great Britain: Billing and Sons Ltd., 1979) p. 873.

[4] *Ibid.*

> system of national law has significantly, sometimes even decisively moulded his conception of his role.[5]

The many roles and functions that have been perceived as falling under the court's ambit include: the judicial role, the political role, diplomatic role, the cooling-off function, arbiter among nations, guardian of international morality, etc. There is no doubt that in some ways and to various extents the Court performs all these roles. Debatable as what constitutes the entire functions of the ICJ are, there are certain obvious functions which can be readily identified.

International Conflict Resolution

> Do not all States in contention claim to have the Law on their side? Why then should they not test that before the Court? Nagendra Singh, President ICJ.

Judicial settlement of international disputes constitutes the primary and most important task of the ICJ. The Court itself has this to say of its duties:

> The function of the Court is to state the Law, but it may pronounce judgement only in connection with concrete cases where there exists at the time of the adjudication an actual controversy involving a conflict of legal interests between the parties. The Court's judgement must have some practical consequences in the sense that it can affect existing legal rights or obligations from their legal relations. No judgements on the merits in this case could satisfy these essentials of the judicial functions.[6]

It is clear so far that the Court concerns itself only with disputes in which some legal issues are present and which are suitable for judicial settlement. For this reason Prott rightly concludes that the Court's concern also ends where such disputes end or when their character changes considerably.[7]

The words of Sir Gerald Fitzmaurice in *the Northern Cameroons Case* and the Court's pronouncements on the *Interpretation of Peace Treaties and Nuclear Test Cases (Australia v. France)* lend credence to this view. Fitzmaurice believes that:

---

[5] *Ibid*, p. XIX.
[6] *The Northern Cameroons Case, ICJ Reports* (1963) p. 33-34.
[7] *Ibid.*

> ...Courts of Law are not there to make Legal pronouncements in *abstracto,* however great their scientific value as such. They are there to protect existing and current legal obligations, to afford concrete reparation if a wrong has been committed, or to give rulings in relation to existing and continuing legal situations.[8]

Therefore, according to this view any legal pronouncements that emerge are necessarily in the course and for the purpose of doing one or more of these things. Otherwise they would serve no purpose falling within the proper function of the court of law as a judicial institution.

The Court itself insists that "the dispute brought before it must therefore continue to exist at the time when the Court makes the decision. It must not fail to take cognisance of a situation in which the dispute has disappeared because the object of the claim has been achieved by other means".[9] It cannot be denied that the existence of disputes is the primary condition for the Court to exercise its judicial function; nevertheless it is not sufficient to ignore other collateral functions which the Court serves. In any case, whether there is a dispute or not is a matter for objective determination of the Court itself.

Cooling-Off Function

In the performance of conflict resolution among States the ICJ also has what can be called a therapeutic function to fulfil to parties in a dispute.[10] The Rules of Court ensure the parties a "cooling off period." Judges Tanaka and Lachs note the fact that because of the time that passes between the various stages of submission of a case to the Court and the pronouncement of a judgement, parties to any dispute are sort of quietened down.[11] Countries are known to have exploited this therapeutic effect by submitting disputes which have generated huge domestic public opinion calling for immediate drastic and radical action to the ICJ, in order that frayed nerves might be cooled by the lengthy judicial process. Another way in which countries can exploit judicial settlement by the ICJ is that a

---

[8] See Fitzmaurice, *Northern Cameroons Case*, ICJ Reports (1963) pp. 98-99.
[9] *Nuclear Tests Case*, (*Autralia v. France*) ICJ Reports (1974) pp. 270-271.
[10] Prott, *op.cit.*, p. 75.
[11] *Ibid.*

government will more enthusiastically agree to the submission of a case to the Court if it is known or felt that the Court will most probably hand down a rational and dispassionate judgement which would be different from the radical and bandwagon feeling articulated by their domestic public opinion. For example the near hysterical public interest generated in the frequent military skirmishes between Nigeria and Cameroon over Bakassi has conveniently (for both governments) disappeared. For the major part of the populace, the entire conflict is shielded away behind the dignified mystery of the International Court. The war songs emerging from both sides of the border have quietened. Governments can now think. The matter in any case lies before the Court and no government can be accused of chickening out or bowing to pressures. There is nothing inherently bad with this sort of situation since, importantly, lives are inevitably saved and the scourge of war is at least postponed and hopefully averted.

Another aspect of the therapeutic effect generated by the Court's work in its conflict resolution lies in the use of sober well measured and well delivered speech. This is also connected with the Court's general disposition to judicial settlement which is "on the whole, done ... in as conciliatory a manner as possible."[12] An example of this is the *Right of Passage Case* between Portugal and India. Among the findings of the Court on this case are that Portugal had a right of passage to the extent necessary for the exercise of Portuguese sovereignty over certain enclaves in question and subject to the regulation and control of India, in respect of private persons, civil officials and goods in general. However, the Court noted that Portugal did not have in 1954 such a right of passage in respect of armed forces, armed police and ammunition. The Court thereby found that India had not acted contrary to its obligations resulting from the right of passage of private persons, civil officials and goods in general. With this kind of "judgement of Solomon," the Court was able to achieve what Rosenne records thus: "Although both sides could cry victory -- an important factor from the point of view of prestige -- there is little doubt India is the substantial victor in this case and that if Portugal did obtain from the Court formal

[12] *Ibid.*

recognition of Portuguese sovereignty over the territories in question, the judgement effectively deprived Portugal of the means of enforcing that sovereignty."[13]

In the *Asylum Case* the Court found it legally incorrect for Columbia to grant diplomatic asylum to a Peruvian politician on an alleged rule of unilateral and definitive qualification of the offence. Columbia and Peru were unable to come to an agreement on the basis of the sentence laid down and the Court was requested to determine the manner in which effect should be given to its judgement and whether Columbia was, or was not, bound to hand over Haya De La Torre (a Peruvian politician). In a judgement delivered on June 1951, the ICJ concluded that: "... the asylum must cease, but that the Government of Columbia is under no obligation to bring this about by surrendering the refugee to Peruvian authorities."[14] This instance also affords a good example of the Court's therapeutic, conciliatory and weighted judgement.

Though the court itself realises that it can serve a "Cooling-Off" function, it will appear to be rightfully on guard to prevent an abuse of its judicial process. Where a State seeks to clearly manipulate proceedings in order to slow down the process of international sanctions or hinder active consideration of an issue before another competent UN institution the Court will not allow the scheme. In the Lockerbie case,[15] for instance, Libya's request for provisional measures was turned down. Libya wanted the Court to restrain the UK and USA "from taking any step that might aggravate or extend the dispute, as would surely happen if sanctions were imposed against Libya or force were employed." Three days upon the closure of oral hearings on this request, on March 31, 1992 the Security Council explicitly invoked Chapter VII of the Charter, which deals with "action with respect to threats to the peace, breaches of the

---

[13] Rosenne, *op.cit.* p. 117.

[14] Nascimento E. Da Silva, *Diplomacy in International Law* (Leiden, A.W. Sijohoff, 1972) p. 105. See also J.B. Syataow, *Decisions of The International Court of Justice.A. Digest* (Leyden: A.W. Sijthoff; Dobbs Ferry, NY: Oceana Publications, 1962) p. 51

[15] Questions of Interpretation and Application of the 1971 Montreal Convention Arising from the Aerial Incident at Lockerbie (Libya v. U.K.; Libya v. US) Provisional Measures 1992 ICJ Reports 3,114 (Orders of April 14).

peace, and acts of aggression." This resolution provided *inter alia*, that on April 15, 1992, all States would adopt, under Article 41, certain coercive measures (commercial, diplomatic, and economic) against Libya should it not comply with Resolution 731, including the surrender of two terrorist suspects to the US or U.K.

Now to have granted Libya's request would have given reprieve to a State which was facing the peril of Security Council sanctions for its recalcitrance based upon rights claimed under the 1971 convention for the suppression of Unlawful Acts against the Safety of Civil Aviation.[16] Whereas, Article 103 of the Charter (Including Security Resolution 748), prevail over any other international agreements (such as the Montreal Convention).[17]

Diplomatic Function

The use of the Court is increasingly assimilated into the diplomatic process in international relations. This is a role many commentators on the Court's work will only grudgingly admit. Indeed it is a role completely unimaginable to earlier scholars of the adjudicatory process in international matters. But in recent times the procedures of the Court have proved useful in assisting Governments to solve inter-state problems. This in no way derogates the system of international adjudication. Neither should it be considered an abuse of the judicial process. It is quite usual even in domestic systems for settlement to be eventually made out of court, ordinarily at some stage before the case comes on for hearing. The institution of

[16] Sept. 23, 1971, 24 UST 564;10 ILM 115, 1971 (also known as the Montreal Convention).

[17] Some scholars criticize the refusal of the Court to grant the provisional measures. Basing their arguments on dissenting opinions of Judges Ajibola, Bedjaoui. Weeramantry and El Kosheri, they insist that the Court could have asserted its legal and inherent power to indicate provisional measures *proprio motu* for example by calling on the parties to prevent the aggravation or extension of the dispute. Judge Bedjaoui also introduced a distinction between the effective exercise of the Court's power to indicate provisional measures which he considers as fully justified by the facts of the case and its effect which he believes was nullified by Resolution 748. See 1992 I.C.J. Prep. at 48 - 49, 158 -57 (Bedjaoui) 70 - 71 , 181 (Weeramantry) and 88 - 90, 193 - 95 (Ajibola). See also Vera Gowland - Debas, "'The Relationship Between The International Court Of Justice And The Security Council In The Light Of The Lockerbie Case". *AJIL* 199 vol.88, pp. 643-648.

proceedings in such circumstances is not necessarily a waste of time and resources. Rather, it may be that the imminence of a judgement, which may indeed go either way, may offer the impetus for genuine negotiations. Situations may alśo arise where a case may be withdrawn in response to changes in the relevant socio-political equation. In other words the eventual solution may be devoid of the influence of the pendency of the matter before the Court. Such instances are not necessarily negative.

An initial pointer to this role can be found in the 1969 *North Sea Continental cases*. After the Court decided upon a particularly knotty legal issue, normal negotiations became more focused and the dispute was thus settled. In I992 Finland and Denmark in the *Passage Through the Great Belt* achieved settlement of their dispute just within hours of the commencement of the oral proceedings. In an earlier phase of the matter, the Court had itself encouraged the parties to negotiate a settlement. They duly proceeded to negotiate but failed to agree at that stage. So litigation continued on course. Extensive written pleadings were submitted on the substantive issues of fact and law. However, the parties then resumed discussions, and this time succeeded at the last moment. It is a reasonable inference that the parties participation in the Court's proceedings relating to the production and exchange of full written pleadings, together with the imminence of trial of the action if negotiations did not succeed, helped in some way to generate a momentum which eventually brought the negotiations to a successful head.

There are other instances, where the Court encouraged negotiations and, accordingly, allowed a period for negotiations before fixing time limits for written pleadings in the case. Parties may also ask for an extension of the time allowed for negotiations. In an unusual manifestation of this function the Court decided regarding the fight over the Danube between Hungary and Slovakia, that Hungary was wrong to suspend and then in 1989 to abandon its obligations to a common dam project as spelled out in a 1977 treaty binding both States. But the Court also found that Czechoslovakia (from which Slovakia emerged after the collapse of communism) had proceeded illegally when it diverted the river through the dam in 1992. The two countries were thus ordered by the Court to proceed to negotiate in "good faith."

In short, the Court is beginning to be employed in closer relationship with normal diplomatic negotiation. No longer is the Court a "last resort" to be employed when all else has failed. As a President of the Court convincingly put it, the Court procedures can sometimes form part of, and be a vector in, diplomatic negotiations. The two processes are, of course, juridically distinct, but in practice they may be employed complementarily, and not necessarily on a basis of mutual exclusivity. It is the constant jurisprudence of the Court that judicial settlement is only an alternative to friendly settlement by the parties themselves. Whenever the Court or its procedures can help in this way, the Court is, in an important sense, still productively at work.[18]

Arbiter Among Nations/Guardian of International Morality and Legality

The role of the ICJ as an arbiter between nations is strengthened by instances where heads of government express a belief in the impartiality of the Court. Such an occasion arose in Col. Muammer el Qadaffi's call for the trial of the two Libyan officials suspected to have masterminded the bombing of Pan Am flight 103 over Lockerbie to take place at the Hague by the ICJ. The Libyan government remains unimpressed by the plans of the Secretary-General to send two experts to inspect the Scottish legal system with the hope of defusing Libya's criticism that its citizens would not receive a fair trial in the UK.

In an effort to defuse Arab and African criticisms that the Libyans wanted for trial in Scotland would not get a fair trial there, the British Government opened the Scottish legal system to inspection by three international organizations and extended invitations to the Arab League and the Organization of African Unity. It would, however, appear that nothing short of a trial by the ICJ would satisfy scholars and governments from the developing nations. President Mandela of South Africa also insists that nothing short of an ICJ trial of the Lockerbie dispute will be impartial. A trial by a special chamber of the Court preferably using the summary

---

[18] See the addresses of the President of the Court, Sir Robert Jennings at the 47th and 48th Session of the General Assembly; *The Yearbook of the ICJ 1992-1993*, vol. 47, pp. 249-251; *Yearbook of the ICJ 1993-1994*, vol. 48, pp.219, 220.

procedures would therefore seem more appropriate. Unfortunately, Libya has failed so far to convince the Court that it should assume jurisdiction.[19]

Increasingly, there are calls made upon the Court to assume jurisdiction over international criminals even though crimes against humanity are not normally considered to be within the jurisdiction of the ICJ since the Court rules on disputes between nations .The Khmer Rouge, for instance, made several offers to hand over erstwhile despot Polpot to the International Court of Justice for trial involving crimes against humanity.[20] This is yet another indication of the growing popularity of the Court's contentious jurisdiction and a measure of the moral authority it possesses in the minds of statesmen and politicians.

Advancing Jurisprudence and Elaboration of the Law

Apart from the central role of conflict resolution or perhaps in the course of achieving that aim, the Court must engage in the development of the law. There are broadly two main approaches possible in this task whether in the international field or elsewhere. There is the approach which conceives it to be the primary if not the sole duty of a judge to decide the case in hand, with the minimum of verbiage necessary for this purpose and to confine himself to that. The other approach conceives it to be the proper function of the judge, while duly deciding the case in hand, with the necessary supporting reasoning, all the while not unduly straying outside the four corners of the case, to utilise those aspects of it which have a wider interest or connotation, in order to make general pronouncements of law and principle that may enrich and develop the law.[21]

While the latter position might be more beneficial, one must not forget that in theory courts of law interpret the law and do not make it. Indeed judges are themselves loath to admit the increasingly popular notion that they in a way perform a law-creating role. Nevertheless as a writer notes that "in practice... the law is complete

[19] See *New York Times,* October 29, 1997 p. 2; See also "Mandela presses for Neutral Nation trial of Lockerbie suspects" *New York Times* Oct. 26, p. 6.

[20] See Elizabeth Becker, "On it's last legs,the saddest Cambodian Army," *New York Times,* Oct.20, 1997. p. 4; see also *New York Times* June 22, 1997, p. 8.

[21] G. Fitzmaurice, in "Hersch Lauterpacht - The Scholar as a Judge" BYIL Part 137 (1961) pp. 14-15.

only after the judge defines what it means and that therefore the judge is part of the law making process."[22] We can also make reference to Article 38 (1d) of the Statute to help define what the law means. The article provides for the application of "... judicial decisions and the teachings of the most highly qualified publicists of the various nations." Of course this includes World Court Judges and Jurists of other International Tribunals. Article 38(2) also unequivocally confers on the Court the power... to decide a case *ex aequo et bono*, if the parties agree thereto. In that case the Court need not confine itself to applying the existing law but could, if it deemed the existing law to operate harshly, inefficiently or unjustly, give a judgement which aligns more with the essentials of equity and justice.

In as much as there are such strong arguments in favour of the proposition that the Court performs the function of law development we must not fail to acknowledge a limitation in this direction embodied in the provisions of Article 59, which states: "The decision of the Court has no binding force except between the parties in respect of a case."

In other words the International Court is specifically bound from applying precedent or the doctrine of *stare decisis* in its decisions. Its decisions are to serve only as evidence for the existence of international law.[23] Levi, however rightly notes that:

> Nevertheless, the fact is that all courts and tribunals - international courts, municipal courts, -- rely upon and cite each other abundantly in their verdicts. Decisions, especially repetitive similar decisions, acquire an authority affecting the formulation of legal norms in subsequent cases. They are not merely evidence of existing law; they often become the creators of law, especially customary law, by becoming part of international practice.[24]

Sir G. Fitzmaurice also correctly remarked that international courts had recognized the development of law as an essential part of their function.[25] Sir Hersch Lauterpacht thinks it may well be an exaggeration to assert that the Court has proved to be a significant instrument for maintaining international peace, but it has at least

---

[22] Werner Levi, *Contemporary International Law: A Concise Introduction* (Boulder. Colorado: West View Press, 1979) p. 53.

[23] *Ibid.*

[24] *Ibid.*

[25] Fitzmaurice, *op.cit.*, p. 15.

made a tangible contribution to the development and clarification of the rules and principles of international law.[26] Lauterpacht refers to this phenomenon as "a heterogeny of aims… where… institutions set up for the achievements of definite purposes grow to fulfil tasks not wholly identical with those which were in the minds of their authors at the time of their creation…"[27]

Prott developed a hypothesis describing how development of the law is an expectation, which is directed at the ICJ by various "role transmitters." He arrived at this position using many methods including interviews with ICJ judges and he found out that "... more espoused the 'broader' than the 'narrower' interpretation of the judicial function."[28] Fitzmaurice remarking on the *Barcelona Traction Case* wrote

> ...There are a number of particular matters, not dealt with or only touched upon in the judgement of the Court, which I should like to comment on. Although these comments can only be in the nature of *obiter dicta* and cannot have the authority of a judgement, yet since specific legislative action with direct binding effect is not at present possible pronouncements of one kind or another constitute the principal method by which the law can find some concrete measure of clarification and development.[29]

This view we share with him. Indeed there is strong opinion in favour of the view that separate opinions and to some extent dissenting opinions, if they must be continued in the practice of the Court, would be worth it only if they are valuable in helping to clarify and elaborate the law.

Brownlie in a similar vein believes that:

> (i)n certain respects the court has been influential viz, in the development of international law as a whole as a result of its jurisprudence and in the giving of advisory opinions on the interpretation of the United Nations Charter and other aspects of the law of international organisations.[30]

Examples where this is evident include *the Reparations Case* and the *Competence of the General Assembly Case.*

---

[26] *Ibid.*

[27] M. W. Janis, *International Courts for the Twenty-First Century.* (Leiden: Kluwer Academic Publishers, 1992), p.30.

[28] Prott, *op .cit.* p. 78 *et passim.*

[29] Fitzmaurice, *Barcelona Traction Case*, Sept. 1964 quoted in Prott p. 78.

[30] Brownlie, *op.cit.* p.731.

The jurisprudence of the Court also has a profound effect on other international courts and trib ˜ .ls. In 1986 the ICJ found that the US committed violations such as mining Nicaraguan ports and arming and financing the Contras. But the court decided that the Contras acts could not be construed as acts of the US because it did not have total control. Obviously following the precedent of this decision the UN Tribunal at The Hague ruled similarly that acts of Bosnian Serbs cannot be construed as acts of Belgrade without proof of Belgrade's total control.

What surprises one then is the vehemence with which the ICJ refuted this law development role in the *South West Africa Cases*:

> If on a correct legal reading of a given situation, certain alleged rights are found to be non-existent, the consequences of this must be accepted. The Court cannot postulate the existence of such rights in order to avert those consequences. This would be to engage in an essentially legislative task, in the service of political ends the promotion of which, however desirable in itself, lies outside the function of a court-of-law... The Court is not a legislative body. Its duty is to apply the law as it finds it, not to make it.[31]

This question then is -- why on this particular case and instance did the court, using such strong terms, shirk from repeating its practice of development of the law?[32] Echoes of such undue conservatism still emerge from the Court's bench in recent times. Roberts Jennings claims that

> now that the Court has a relatively considerable waiting list of waiting cases there might be something to be said for giving somewhat less importance to the law developing function of the Court and rather more to its task of the effective and correct disposal of the particular case before it.[33]

In reality no such thing is required of either the Court or indeed any other international court. Neither rules nor customary international law can be mechanically applied. In the last 50 years or more the ICJ has rendered hundreds of judgements, orders and advisory opinions. To close ones eyes to the obvious law creating function of the Court is to disregard reality. To canvas a cessation of this function is unproductive.

---

[31] *South West Africa Case* 1966, and *South West Africa, Second Phase 1966* I.C.J. Reports, 6 pp. 36,48.

[32] For a full understanding of our conclusions on this issue. see infra.

[33] Jennings, *op. cit.* p. 498.

Chapter 3

Contentious Jurisdiction Of The International Court of Justice

Jurisdiction and Seising

The concept of the Court's seising -- or state of being seised of a dispute--may tend to be confused with that of its competence to hear and determine the dispute. In the *Nottebohm Case* as well as several others the Court has made a distinction between its jurisdiction to deal with the case, and the validity of the formal step by which the proceedings were instituted--termed the seising of the Court.[1] In the *Nottebohm Case*, the Court expounded that seising depended on the carrying out of the correct procedural steps for bringing the dispute before the Court, as prescribed by the Court's Statute and Rules. It is true that if the Court has not been duly seised it is incompetent to hear the case; but it does not follow that after the Court has been seised (therefore possessing the seising of a case) it has on that account substantive jurisdiction and competence to hear and determine that case on its merits.

What seising gives is the ability to determine if it possesses substantive jurisdiction and competence. Fitzmaurice writes on the distinction:

> Seising might therefore be said to confer jurisdiction or competence on tribunal in the procedural sense. But substantive jurisdiction and competence will necessarily depend on other factors. It is clear however, that without the measure of procedural competence which only a valid and regular seizing can confer but which such a seising when effected does of itself entail would the tribunal be able to determine its substantive jurisdiction if in question or otherwise uncertain ; and the inherent power of international tribunals to

[1] Shabtai Rosenne, *The International Court of Justice: An Essay in Political And Legal Theory* (Leyden: A.W. Sythoff, 1961) p. 257.

> determine their own jurisdiction (the *competence de la competence*) would be nullified.[2]

We also subscribe to his argument. This same distinction between jurisdiction and seising constitutes the basis of the whole jurisdiction by *forum prorogatum* since the validity of seising is unaffected by the existence or non-existence of substantive competence at the time of seising. Thus jurisdiction can be perfected after the seising by virtue of the principle of *forum prorogatum*. Rosenne correctly notes that:

> The ability of the seising to produce intended effects however depends not on its formal validity but upon the title of jurisdiction existing or brought into existence (*forum prorogatum*) between the parties which in a concrete case may make it impossible for the Court to decide the case, even though it has been regularly and validly seised. On the other hand, the cases indicate that the mere seising does not affect the substantive right of the parties and it only produces effects within the limit of the law in force between them.[3]

Jurisdiction of the Court in Contentious Cases

Broadly speaking, the expression "jurisdiction" refers to the power of the Court to do justice between litigating States, that is, to decide the question before it with binding force.[4] The jurisdiction of the ICJ falls into two distinct parts--its capacity to decide disputes between States and its capacity to give advisory opinions when requested to do so by the qualified specialised agencies and institutions. Article 34 of the Statute of the Court declares that only States may be parties in cases before the Court. Therefore private persons and other unqualified international organisations are prohibited from having recourse to the Court. Basically, the Court's jurisdiction in contentious cases in accordance with article 36(1) of its Statute encompasses all cases referred to it by States who are parties to a dispute and regarding all matters specially provided for in the UN Charter or treaties or conventions in force. Of great importance in extending the jurisdiction of the ICJ is article 36(2) of the Statute,

---

[2] Fitzmaurice, "The Law and Procedure of the International Court of Justice: 1951-54 Questions of Jurisdiction, Competence and procedure" BYIL (1958) p.15.

[3] *Ibid.*, p. 258.

[4] Rosenne (1957) *op.cit*. p. 253. See also Rosenne (1973) *op.cit*., p. 65.

known as the optional clause. This clause confers upon States parties to the Statute the rights to declare at any time that they recognise as compulsory and without special arrangement in relation to any other State accepting the same obligations, the jurisdiction of the Court in specific legal disputes.

However, before we further define the jurisdiction of the Court we must recall the general principle of International Law that no State can be compelled to litigate against its will. We must, therefore, always seek as the basis of the jurisdiction of the Court, the consent of the litigants, given either generally and in advance or ad-hoc and upon the occurrence of the dispute.[5]

As Oppenheim has rightly observed: "International society has not reached as national societies have the point at which any creditor or party injured can summon his debtor before a court without the latter's consent to go there."[6]

In fact a great number of the judgements given by the Court so far have been in one form or the other, concerned with a plea to the jurisdiction of the Court namely, with a contention that the jurisdictional clauses invoked by a plaintiff State did not actually confer such jurisdiction upon the Court.[7] The Court has upheld the consent principle on numerous occasions.

In the *Corfu Channel Case* (Preliminary objection) the Court expressly acknowledged that: "the consent of the parties confers jurisdiction on the Court."[8] In the Reparations Case it said: "An international claim is dealt with by means of negotiation and cannot in the present state of the law as to international Jurisdiction be submitted to a tribunal except with the consent of the States concerned."[9] In the *Peace Treaties Case* it held that: "The consent of States, parties to a dispute is the basis of the Court's jurisdiction in contentious cases."[10] In the *Anglo-Iranian Oil Co. Case*, the Court pronounced that "unless the parties have conferred jurisdiction on

[5] L. Oppenheim, *International Law: A Treatise Vol. II Disputes War and Neutrality*. H. Lauterpacht (ed.) 7th Ed. (London: Longmans, Greens and Co. Ltd., 1952) p. 57.
[6] *Ibid.*
[7] *Ibid.*
[8] Corfu Channel Case (Preliminary Objections) *ICJ Reports*, (1988) p. 27.
[9] Reparations Case, *ICJ Reports* (1950), p. 71.
[10] Peace Treaties Case, *ICJ Reports* (1950), p. 71.

the Court in accordance with Article 36, the Court lacks such jurisdiction."[11] In the *Ambatielos Case* (obligation to arbitration) it was held that the court is not departing from the principle that a State may not be compelled to submit its disputes to arbitration without its consent."[12] In the *Monetary Gold Case*, the Court reaffirmed this view by denying that it had jurisdiction. It held that to adjudicate upon the international responsibility of Albania without her consent would run counter to a well-established principle of international law embodied in the Court's Statute: namely that the Court can only exercise jurisdiction over a State with its consent.[13]

It is to be noted that the consensual element does not merely refer to consent of the two States involved in the dispute but also any State whose legal position vis-a-vis any of the parties is likely to be affected. Lack of consent by such a State may lead the Court to decline jurisdiction even though from the formal point of view all the parties appearing before it have consented to the jurisdiction. As a result of this practice of the Court, learned writers such as Oppenheim and Rosenne have concluded that, there lies a difference between the formal validity of duly constituted proceedings and their essential validity.[14] This distinction constitutes the inability to decide the merits of the *Monetary Gold Case* in which the Court said: "Where, as in the present case, the vital issue to be settled concerns the international responsibility of a third State, the Court cannot without the consent of the third State give a decision on the issue binding upon any State either the third State or any one of the parties before it."[15]

The withdrawal of the US in the case concerning *Military and Paramilitary Activities in and Against Nicaragua* however was unsuccessful and the Court went ahead to establish its jurisdiction. Though this decision generated a lot of controversy among scholars, it established that the court would render null and void unreasonable

---

[11] Anglo-Iranian Oil Co. Case, *ICJ Reports* (1952), pp. 102-3.

[12] Ambatielos Case (obligation to arbitration), *ICJ Reports* (1953), p. 19.

[13] Monetary Gold Case, *ICJ Reports* 1954.

[14] See Oppenheim *op.cit.*, p. 883 and Rosenne (1961) *op.cit.*, p. 261. Cf. M.N., Shaw International Law, 3rd ed. (Cambridge: Grotius, 1991) pp. 674-675.

[15] *Ibid.*

reservations to its jurisdiction.[16] However, the Court remains the only organ operating within the UN which is shielded and which shields itself from the deleterious consequences which come from making decisions on matters when one of the parties has not truly consented.[17]

We may new proceed to discuss the various modes of conferment of jurisdiction having established that underlying all possible means of conferring jurisdiction on the Court is the consensual element.

We must observe that legal writers are not in agreement as to classification of the various ways of conferring jurisdiction on the Court. Rosenne "thinks there are two basic ways and many variations by which jurisdiction to decide contentious cases is conferred on the Court."[18] To Gore-Booth there are "...three ways in which a case may be brought..."[19] Brownlie on his part identifies up to five jurisdictional heads.[20] Lissitzyn breaks it into three heads, i.e. (1) Optional clause with or without limitation (2) by an undertaking with respect to a class of existing or future disputes, or (3) express or tacit agreement to submit a particular dispute to the Court.[21] Without prejudice to the classifications already proffered by various writers, it is the position of this study that jurisdiction or competence of the ICJ on a given dispute emanates from either one or a combination of three modes of consent. They are: Consent *ad hoc*; Consent *post hoc* and Consent *ante hoc*.

Consent Ad Hoc

Consent *ad hoc* refers to jurisdiction by special agreement and unilateral application. Once a dispute already exists the consent of the parties may be given *ad hoc* to the exercise of jurisdiction by the Court. Usually this consent is written in the form of a "*compromis*" (special agreement). For example, in the *North Sea Continental Shelf*

---

16 We shall deal with the issue of reservations to the Court jurisdiction below.

17 The I.C.J., *The International Court of Justice* (The Hague: ICJ, 1986), p. 37.

18 Rosenne (1961) *op. cit.*, p. 260; See also Rosenne (1973) *op. cit.*, p. 68.

19 Satow, *op. cit.*.

20 Brownlie, *op.cit.*, p. 138.

21 Lissitzyn, *The International Court of Justice: Its Role in the Maintenance of International Peace and Security*, (New York: Octagon Books, 1972) p. 61.

Cases, jurisdiction was based on such *ad hoc* agreements between Denmark and the Federal Republic of Germany and between the Netherlands and the Federal Republic of Germany.[22] Also in the *Kasikili/Sedudu Island (Botswana/Namibia)* the case was submitted to the Court by the parties Special Agreement of February 15, 1996, which was transmitted to the Court on May 9. It is worthy of note that as long as the necessary consent is really present, the Court is not particularly concerned with the form. As the PCIJ. said in the Case of the Minority Schools in Upper Silesia: The acceptance by a State of the Court's jurisdiction in a particular case is not under the Statute subordinated to the observance of certain forms. Citing this decision the ICJ. in the *Corfu Channel Case* (Preliminary Objection) said: "Furthermore there is nothing to prevent the acceptance of jurisdiction, as in the present case, from being effected by two separate and successive acts, instead of jointly and before hand by a special agreement."[23]

Apparently the Court is of the opinion that consent *ad hoc* may arise where the plaintiff State has accepted the jurisdiction by a unilateral application followed by a separate act of consent by the other party, either by communication to the Court or by taking part in the initiation of proceedings.

Jurisdiction Post Hoc (Forum Prorogatum)

In international law as we have repeated several times, jurisdiction by international courts only arises with the consent of the States concerned. In this sense one may be excused if the claim is made that all jurisdiction in international cases is in a sense prorogated jurisdiction. But speaking particularly on the principle of *forum prorogatum* as it pertains to the Court, it needs be recorded that this form of consent is often invoked by the unilateral act of the parties. The plaintiff by application seises the Court of jurisdiction and waits for the respondent. Consent to jurisdiction is often inferred from conduct of the respondent. If the respondent subsequently files a defence on the merit, that signifies submission to the Courts jurisdiction. For example in the *Asylum Case* the Court said:

---

[22] Rosenne (1961) p. 252.

[23] PCIJ Series A, No. 15 (1948) p. 15.

> The parties in the present case consented to the jurisdiction of the Court. All questions submitted to it have been argued by them on the merits and objection has been made to the decision on the merits. This conduct of the parties is sufficient to confer jurisdiction on the Court.[24]

However to fully explain this form of the conferment of jurisdiction we wish to mention and highlight three possible propositions. The first proposition is that a formal agreement conferring jurisdiction upon the Court can be made at any stage up to the conclusion of the hearing. It may not even necessarily be made before the Court but may be made extraneously.[25] This principle was clearly established in the Mavrommatis judgement of the PCIJ.[26] The important thing to note here is that an application will not be inadmissible simply because at the time it is brought no such formal agreement existed. If for instance the respondent State pleads to the merits without raising an objection to the jurisdiction of the Court then the principle of *forum prorogatum* may confer jurisdiction on the Court. From this it follows that the latest date by which a formal agreement should be made is the date for the filing of the counter memorial or preliminary objection by the respondent State.[27]

The second proposition refers to informal agreement by successive acts. Jurisdiction may be conferred upon the Court by an informal agreement between the parties reached by successive acts. For instance, in the *Right of Minorities Case* in which Poland had first raised objections to jurisdiction in the second written pleading (its rejoinder) after having argued the case on its merits in its first written pleading (its counter memorial) the Court said: and there seems to be no doubt that consent of a State to the Court may not only result from the express declaration but may also be inferred from acts conclusively establishing it...[28]

Another suitable instance is the *Corfu Channel Case* (Preliminary Objection). Here the successive acts were the application followed by a letter to the Court by the Deputy Minister for Foreign Affairs of Albania, in which the respondent State

---

[24] *ICJ Reports* (1948) p. 15 pp. 7-15.
[25] *ICJ Reports* (1951) p. 15.
[26] See Rosenne (1961) *op.cit.*, p. 291.
[27] *Ibid.*, p. 292
[28] *Ibid.*

indicated that not withstanding certain irregularities, it was prepared to appear before the Court in the Case. This was held to have perfected the jurisdiction *ratione personae* and *ratione materiae*.[2]

Agreement in course of pleading relates also to the principle of *forum prorogatum* and constitutes the third proposition. The ICJ. and the PCIJ. have in several cases held that jurisdiction can be deduced from their conduct in pleading to the merits of a claim (including a counter claim) without raising the question of jurisdiction. Thus this tacit consent is clearly distinguished from the second form of proposition, i.e. informal agreement. The characteristic feature of this aspect of the *forum prorogatum* principle is that, for the Court to assume jurisdiction, it has to be satisfied that there is the absence of conditions of equivocation on the part of the respondent and this may necessitate a more extended examination of its conduct and intentions than is necessary where formal consent exists.[30]

However, in considering whether jurisdiction has been conferred by the tacit consent of the respondent, the Court will have regard to the whole of its conduct, and not merely to isolated phenomena and it will refuse to exercise jurisdiction if the whole of that State's conduct in the case is consistently that of refusal to submit itself for judgement.[31]

For instance, the fact that a State puts up appearance does not *ipso facto* signify consent. Consent in this sense must be reasonably clear, and free from ambiguity. In the *Anglo-Iranian Oil Case*, the Iranian government filed additional papers to fortify her defence, but throughout the case maintained that the Court lacked jurisdiction. On the submission of the United Kingdom to the Court to hold, that the act constitutes submission to jurisdiction of the Court, it was held that:

> The principle of *forum prorogatum* if it would have to be applied in the present case would have to be based on some conduct or statement of the Government of Iran which involved the jurisdiction of the Court. Having filed a preliminary objection, for the purpose of disrupting

---

[29] *Ibid.*, p. 292.
[30] *Ibid.*, p. 296.
[31] The ICJ, *op. cit.*, p. 180 (Supra note 64)

jurisdiction. and having throughout maintained that objection... no element of consent can be deduced from such conduct.[32]

Jurisdiction Ante Hoc (Compulsory Jurisdiction)

Another means by which the Court possesses jurisdiction over a case is through the application of compulsory jurisdiction (otherwise known as the optional clause). This kind of head of jurisdiction entails consent *ante hoc* and is a noteworthy advance in the techniques of conferring jurisdiction on the Court. It was introduced by the Statute of the PCIJ. and maintained by the Statute of the ICJ.[33]

The Optional Clause as embodied in Article 36, paragraph 2 of the Statute states that the parties to the Statute may at any time declare that they recognise as compulsory *ipso facto* and without special agreement (in relation to any other State accepting the same obligations) the Court's jurisdiction in all legal disputes concerning: (a) the interpretation of a treaty ,(b) any question of international law, (c) the existence of any fact which if established would constitute a breach of an international obligation, (d) the nature or extent of the reparation to be made for the breach of an international obligation.

Such an acceptance is made by unilateral declarations which are deposited with the Secretary-General of the UN [34] and are made unconditionally or subject to reservations which are not to be incompatible with the purposes of the optional clause. The ICJ Statute does not prescribe any given form as declaration accepting the compulsory jurisdiction of the Court. In practice, declarations are made in the form of official notifications signed by the President, the Prime Minister, the Minister for Foreign Affairs, the ambassador or the permanent representative at the UN. The scheme is usually as follows:

1. Preamble (rarely)
2. Clause withdrawing a previous declaration (relatively rarely)
3. Reference to Article 36(2) of the ICJ Statute (indirectly or directly)

[32] Rosenne (1961) *Op. cit.*, p. 298.
[33] Rosenne (1973) *op. cit.*, p. 71.
[34] Brownlie (1973) *Op. cit.*, p. 723 (supra note 50).

4. **Reference to the condition of reciprocity**
5. **Initial date of effectiveness of the new declaration (rarely)**
6. **Reservations (in most declarations)**
7. **Formal conditions (in most declarations)**
8. **Date; signature.**[35]

The aim of this provision was to facilitate as much as possible, the acceptance of the Court's compulsory jurisdiction and at the same time to preserve the sovereignty of States with regards to matters which they feel should not be brought before the Court. Therefore Nigeria in its acceptance declared that "...the Federal Republic of Nigeria recognises as compulsory *ipso facto* and without special agreement ... on the sole condition of reciprocity, the jurisdiction of the International Court of Justice in conformity with Article 36, paragraph 2 of the Statute of the Court." While Rosenne noted that as at 1973 the bulk of contentious cases of the Court fell within declarations made under this Article 36(2) of the Statute,[36] the utility of the optional clause has been in recent times largely under-exploited.[37]

Reciprocity, therefore, is the key word in this system and the effect of the declaration is a joinder of consent to the jurisdiction on the part of two States which accept in advance the same obligation. These declarations are unilaterally made, vary in their terms and seldom have precisely the same field of application. Thus on the principle of reciprocity, the lowest common factor in the two declarations is the basis for jurisdiction; therefore a respondent may take advantage of a reservation or conditions in the declarations of the applicant State.[38] Jurisdiction exists only to the extent that declarations coincide. The independent declarations are binding in that "they can only be withdrawn in accordance with the law of treaties and operate with a suspensive condition, *viz*,., the filing of an application by a State with a coincident declaration."[39]

---

[35] Renate Szafarz, *The Compulsory Jurisdiction of the International Court of Justice*, The Hague: Martinus Nijhoff, 1993, pp. 64-5.

[36] Rosenne, *op. cit.*, p. 73.

[37] Infra

[38] Brownlie, *op. cit.*, p. 273.

[39] Leo Gros (ed) *The Future of the International Court of Justice*, Vol.2 (New York: Oceana Publications, 1976) p. 727.

Condition of reciprocity does not mean that the declaration must be framed in identical words. To require identical declaration or equivalent reservations would lead to the nullification of the system of compulsory jurisdiction. According to M. O. Hudson" two states may be bound *inter se* even though their obligations are not in all respects co-extensive, but they will be bound only to the extent that they have accepted the same jurisdiction."[40]

Though authors like Rosenne, Brownlie, Hudson, Elias, Shaw and a host of others point to a steady increase in the number of subscribers to the optional clause as a positive development, there is no absolute certainty that real progress has been made. Robert Y. Jennings wrote on one hand in 1992 that he welcomed the continuing enlargement of the compulsory jurisdiction of the court, with significant additions to the number of optional clause declarations, and further withdrawals of reservations to the jurisdictional clauses of treaties. Movement is steady; but it is progress and not the persistent decline which marked an earlier period.[41] However, later in 1995 he was of the counter opinion that, "The optional clause remains an underused and less than satisfactory method for augmenting the competence of the Court."[42] In as much as this may be, the significance of the compulsory jurisdiction ought not to be measured solely by the number of States which have accepted it, or by the number of instances in which it was used. The chief importance of the system is psychological. It is a useful instrument for the dissemination of the idea that judicial settlement of international disputes is both possible and desirable.

---

[40] M. O. Hudson, "The Twenty-Ninth Year of the World Court", in *British Yearbook of Int. Law*. (1958) p. 89.

[41] R. Jennings. "The Role and Functioning of the Court" in *ICJ Yearbook* (1993) *op.cit.*, p. 249.

[42] R.Y. Jennings, "The United Nations At Fifty: The International Court of Justice After Fifty Years," AJIL 89 (1995), p. 495. Jennings, seeming equivocation here may be due to the fact that in the first instance in 1992 he was writing as an optimistic President of the Court whereas in the latter instance he writes with the dispassionate severity of a jurist and commentator on the Court's work.

Treaties In Force

"Treaties in Force'' as a form of jurisdictional head falls under jurisdiction *Ante hoc* and is a conventional mode of conferring jurisdiction on the ICJ. It derives its statutory basis from Article 36(1) of the Statute, by which "the jurisdiction of the Court comprises ... all matters specially provided for in the Charter of the United Nations or in treaties and conventions in force." Thus the consensual element here exists in the treaties States have put into force between themselves. Usually they would have at the time of the drafting (or after that) agreed anticipatory to confer jurisdiction on the Court in respect of any dispute arising under that treaty. The effect of this principle is to confer jurisdiction on the Court whenever a treaty or convention in force between the parties to the treaty provides a reference to the ICJ. at least in a *prima facie* sense and any of the parties may call on the Court to adjudicate in accordance with its terms.[43]

The Court rejected the preliminary objection to its jurisdiction raised by the United States in the case concerning *Oil Platforms* (Iran v. United States) finding that it had jurisdiction to deal with the case on the basis of the Treaty of Amity, Economic Relations and Consular Rights between the United States and Iran signed in Tehran on 15 August 1959, which entered into force on 16 June 1957. The Court also found that the destruction of the Iranian oil platforms by the United States was capable of having an effect upon the export trade in Iranian oil and consequently upon the freedom of commerce guaranteed in paragraph 1, Article X of the Treaty. Therefore, the legality of that destruction could be examined in relation to that paragraph.

In the classic type of this jurisdictional head there is a special agreement in existence. For instance in the *Ambatielos Case*, the Anglo-Greek Commercial Treaty of 1926 provided expressly for reference to the Court of all disputes as to the interpretation or application "...of any of the provisions of the present treaty."[44] On the basis of this clause the Court assumed jurisdiction. Using this

---

[43] Rosenne (1957) *op. cit.*, pp. 277-278.
[44] Rosenne (1961) p. 278. See also Rosenne (1957) p. 277.

method States have also been referring particular and defined matters to the Court for adjudication. The distinguishing feature of the special agreement as a title of jurisdiction lies in that jurisdiction is conferred and the Court is seised of the concrete case by the mere notification to the Court of the agreement.[45] During the period of existence of the PCIJ eleven cases were instituted by special agreement. Under the ICJ, the *Minquiers and Echrehos Case*[46] and the *Corfu Channel Case*,[47] are two of many instances this mode of conferment of jurisdiction was used.

Another type of this jurisdiction head and the more common one is jurisdiction conferred by a compromissory clause in a multilateral or bilateral treaty. The effect such a clause will have is to establish the jurisdiction of the Court, between the parties to the extent already specified in the compromissory clause. A pertinent example can be found in Article 37(1) of the ILO Constitution which states: 'Any question or dispute relating to the interpretation of this constitution or any subsequent convention shall be referred for decision by the ICJ."

Agreement may in principle exist to have recourse to the Court on a concrete dispute without a specification of the precise terms of reference. An example of this is the Act of Lima of 31st August 1949, upon which the proceedings of the *Asylum Case* were based. An agreement can also be reached in the course of the diplomatic correspondence prior to the institution of the proceedings.[48] These later forms of agreement can be said to be borne out of recent State practice. To conclude; it has to be understood that the invocation of jurisdiction under the head "treaties in force" is subject to the conditions that: (1) at the time the dispute arises, there must be in force the treaty in question between both parties; (2) where a dispute arises and one of the parties does not take any step for arbitration till the expiration or termination of the treaty, the party cannot subsequently invoke this provisions to vest jurisdiction on the Court.

---

[45] *Ibid.*

[46] Minqueirs and Ecrehos Case (United Kingdom/France) (1952) *ICJ Reports.*

[47] Corfu Channel Case (Preliminary Objections) (1948) *ICJ Reports.*

[48] Taslim Elias, *The International Court of Justice and some contemporary Problems: Essays on International Law* (The Hague: Martinus Nijhoff Publishers, 1983) pp. 33-35.

Transferred Jurisdiction

This head of jurisdiction is conferred by virtue of Articles 36(5) and 37 of the ICJ Statute which refer to treaties concluded before 1945. The Statute of the Permanent Court had provisions for jurisdiction on the basis of compromissory clauses in conventions and treaties.[49] At the creation of a new Court, the Statute of the PCIJ was amended to form that of the new Court and it recognised that:

> In substance if not in form, the new Court is a continuation of the old; the Statute is virtually the same, jurisdiction under instruments referring to the old Court has been transferred to the new; and there is continuity in the jurisprudence of the Court.[50]

Article 37 specifically provides that:

> Whenever a treaty or convention in force provides for reference of a matter to a tribunal to have been instituted by the League of Nations, or to the Permanent Court of International Justice, the matter shall, as between the parties to the present Statute be referred to the International Court of Justice.

For this article to be operative certain conditions must be fulfilled. First the treaty must be "in force," that is, binding on each of the litigating States in relation to each other. On the question whether this means in force on 26th June 1945, the date of signature, or the day upon which the proceedings are instituted, Rosenne states persuasively that, the latter is the most probable interpretation.[51] This is in accordance with the general rule that the jurisdiction of the Court and the effectiveness of seising are determined by the law in force between the parties on the date upon which the Court is to make that determination. Secondly, the treaty or convention thus in force must provide for a reference to a tribunal to be instituted by the League. Thirdly, all parties to the dispute must be parties to the old Statute.

Incidental Jurisdiction of the Court

"Incidental Jurisdiction" is a term which we must not fail to mention in contradistinction to "Principal Jurisdiction" because it mitigates

---

[49] Brownlie (1979) *op.cit.*, p. 713.
[50] *Ibid.*
[51] *Ibid.*; Rosenne (1957) *op. cit.*, p. 280.

the severity of the consent doctrine. The term, "Principal Jurisdiction" may be defined as the jurisdiction of the Court to adjudicate on the merits of the case. The formulation of issues or questions put to the Court constitute the merits of the case. However, once there has been a submission to the jurisdiction of the Court there are by necessary implication certain consequences which can be called the incidental powers. This refers to "all other matters with which the Court may be called up to deal in connection with or derived from the decision on the merits."[52] These powers do not depend on the willingness of the parties but flow from the Statute. The existence of this differentiation is also recognized by the Security Council and indeed the phrase "Incidental Jurisdiction" appears in one of the reports of that body's Committee of Experts.[53]

Matters Specially Provided for in the Charter

Article 36(1) of the Statute might be taken as an interesting innovation compared with the Statute of the PCIJ. It contains an express reference to "all matters specially provided for in the Charter of the United Nations." This stipulation would seem superfluous when coupled with the expression "treaties and conventions in force," in the same Article. The UN Charter is undoubtedly also a treaty in force. Moreover as noted by many writers a close examination of the Charter reveals no "matters specially provided for" in regard to the jurisdiction of the Court. Anand explains this stipulation recalling that it was drafted by a Committee of Jurists in Washington in the Spring of 1945, before the Charter was adopted in San Francisco.[54] It is stated in the report of the Committee of Jurists that "this text reproduces Article 36 of the Statute with an addition in

[52] *Ibid.*, p. 264.

[53] The Committee of Experts consists of one representative of each member of the Security Council and is established *ad hoc* to deal with various matters, usually of an organisational character, placed before it. It works with greater informality than is possible in the Council itself. The title 'Committee of Experts' is in reality a misnomer as the members of the Committee are not required to be 'experts' in the matters on the agenda. See Rosenne, *op.cit.*, pp. 228-264.

[54] R. P. Anand, *Compulsory Jurisdiction of the International Court of Justice* (New Delhi: Asia Publishing House, 1961) p. 131.

case the UN Charter should make some provision for compulsory jurisdiction."[55]

However, it is sure now that the idea of compulsory jurisdiction in the way it was first thought of has not seen the light of day. This in our view is unfortunate and a fine opportunity thus missed to make judicial settlement of disputes unassailably and irreversibly entrenched in international relations. As convincingly put by Anand the words "all matters specially provided for in the Charter," do not add anything substantial to the Courts jurisdiction.[56]

Multiple Jurisdiction

Jurisdiction may sometimes result, or appear to result from more than a single source, and there may as a result be conflict between these different sources. The question that may be asked is, how are such conflicts to be resolved? It seems reasonable to assume that multiplicity of sources is intended to have cumulative effect, and an application will not necessarily fail because it is brought in reliance on one, when it might have been brought under another source.[57] This principle was applied, in fact, by the PCIJ in the *Electricity Company of Sofia and Bulgaria Case*, where the parties relied both on the declarations of Belgium and Bulgaria accepting the jurisdiction of the Court under the optional clause and Treaty of Conciliation, Arbitration and Judicial Settlement of June 23, 1931. The question that arose was whether the Treaty simply reinforced the obligations resulting from one optional clause for the duration of the treaty. The Court observed thus:

> ... The multiplicity of agreements concluded accepting the compulsory jurisdiction is evidence that the contracting parties intended to open up new ways of access to the Court rather than to close old ways or allow them to cancel each other out with the ultimate result that no jurisdiction would remain in accordance with Article 36 of the Statute. The Treaty cannot be adduced to prevent those declarations from exercising their effects and disputes being thus submitted to the Court.[58]

The Court then went ahead to explain that only if objections to the Court's jurisdiction could be made under both instruments and

---

[55] UN CIO Doc, Vol. XIV, p. 668.
[56] Anand, *op. cit.*
[57] *Ibid.* p. 125.
[58] *Hudson's World Court Reports*, vol. IV, p. 403.

were held to be well-founded, would the Court decline to entertain the Case.[59] It therefore seems clear that when the parties manifest a general intention to confer jurisdiction on the Court, the multiplicity of sources will not be allowed to defeat the intention.

Jurisdiction To Decide *Ex Aequo Et Bono*

In its role in the judicial settlement of disputes, the Court can decide a case *ex aequo et bono*. From the wording of paragraph (1) of Article 36 it seems that notwithstanding the nature of the dispute the Court is entitled and, indeed, bound to entertain and adjudicate upon any dispute which the parties have in fact agreed to refer to it.[60] However, certain international lawyers express the view that the Court is not competent to entertain a purely political dispute and that the words "all cases" and "all matters" in Article 36 must be taken to mean all cases and all matters which are susceptible of solution by application of legal rules and principles set forth in Article 38 and no others.

According to Anand it is only when neither party relies upon any legal right and desires that the Court decide solely on the basis of policy and expediency, that the Court must decline jurisdiction unless the last paragraph of Article 38 is brought into play.[61] This article provides that previous enumeration "shall not prejudice the power of the Court to decide a case *ex aequo et bono* if the parties agree thereto." The object of this last paragraph of Article 38, is to meet the eventuality of a case where the issues are unsuitable for decision on strictly legal grounds, yet the parties desire to have recourse to the Court and obtain from it a binding decision arrived at according to equity and good conscience.

Judge Lauterpacht also believes that the wording of Article 38(2) of the Statute militates so strongly in favour of the view that there is nothing to prevent the Court form deciding *ex aequo et bono*, if the parties so desire so long as the Court does not arrogate to itself the right of deciding *ex aequo et bono*, but acts in this capacity at the express wish of the parties. That function we join him in viewing as not fundamentally different from that envisaged in Article 38,

---

[59] Anand, *op. cit.* p. 125.
[60] *Ibid.*, p. 127.
[61] *Ibid.*, p. 122.

paragraph (1) where the Court is authorised to apply "international conventions, whether general or particular, establishing rules expressly recognised by the contesting States."[62] Given such an agreement Lauterpacht explains the decision rendered would be a decision given in accordance with rules agreed upon by the parties. It is of no juridical importance that they contain an authorisation to depart from the law as it existed before the *ex aequo et bono* agreement was made. The will of parties is law. Lauterpacht in fact goes a step further to say that even if Article 38 did not contain its present last paragraph the Court would still be at liberty to render, at the will of the parties, decisions *ex aequo et bono* by virtue of a proper interpretation of other provisions of that article.[63]

It may, however, be pointed out that the issue of propriety is likely to loom large in questions of jurisdiction *ex aequo et bono*, because as Judge De Visscher has remarked, notwithstanding the provision in the Statute of the Court, the task ill befits an agency whose functions are essentially judicial.[64] It cannot, therefore, be assumed as Anand seems to have done that because States are agreed to seek a decision *ex aequo et bono*, the Court will necessarily undertake to give such a decision. To authorise the Court to decide *ex aequo et bono* is not to authorise it to depart from the essential rules governing its activity as a Court.[65] That seems to be sufficient to prevent such a process from being abused.

The Non Ultra Petita Rule

The rule means simply that a tribunal will not decide and will not award by way of compensation remedy more than it is asked to award. Thus the ICJ in its role of judicial settlement is bound by the terms of the parties' submission, and where it deviates, then to the extent of that deviation, it lacks jurisdiction. Consequently, any finding based on such frolic venture will be null and void. In the *Corfu Channel Case* (supra) the Court having appointed experts to look into the claim came out with a finding higher than the UK

[62] Lauterpacht, *The Function of Law in the International Community* (London; 1933) pp. 315.

[63] *Ibid.*, p. 316.

[64] *Ibid.*

[65] *Ibid.*

claimed, but the ICJ nevertheless restricted itself to the claim by the British Government.

The jurisdictional element in this rule being that it is derivative from the consensual principle the fact that parties have consented to the Court's jurisdiction does not confer on the Court a "roving commission" in respect of the case.[66] The Court is confined not only to decide that case alone but also to decide the points submitted and no others. Similarly, where the objects of the dispute submitted to the ICJ disappear before the final decision by the Court, then the Court lacks any basis for its decision and must thus discontinue with the hearing of the matter. The Court had this to say in the *Nuclear Test Cases*: "The existence of a dispute is the primary condition for the exercise by the Court of its judicial function to the extent that the dispute must continue to exist at the time the Court makes its decision."[67]

Interim Measures

Some disputes before the ICJ at times are of such a special and ongoing nature that it might be considered appropriate to enact interim measures designed to ensure that the parties to the dispute refrain from taking any action "which might aggravate or extend the dispute or prejudice in respect of the carrying out of whatever decision the Court may render in a case."[68] Article 41 specifies this jurisdiction to indicate such provisional measures. It has been pointed out that, though Article 41 is contained in the chapter on procedure it really relates to a matter superceeding procedural importance.[69]

The Article reads thus:

> 1) The Court shall have the power to indicate, if it considers that circumstances so require, any provisional measures which ought to be taken to preserve the respective rights of either party.

---

[66] M.H. Mendelson, "Interim Measures of Protection." *BYIL* (1922-23) p. 259.

[67] *Ibid.*

[68] *Nuclear Test Cases, ICJ Reports*, (1973), pp. 93 and 135, at pp. [illegible] respectively.

[69] Satow, *op. cit.*, p. 365.

2) Pending the final decision, notice of the measures suggested shall forthwith be given to the parties and to the Security Council.

To indicate interim measures, the Court must be satisfied that there is a substantial and imminent danger of steps being taken which might prove prejudicial to the effectiveness of an ultimate decision on the merits, whether in favour of the plaintiff or the defendant. The measures may be indicated on the request of either party, or the Court's own motion. In practice, however, it has always been the plaintiff who makes such requests.[70]

This remedy is analogous to the common law interlocutionary injunction whereby the parties to a dispute may be joined *pedente lite* from acting in a manner prejudicial to the effectiveness of the judgement which may ultimately be given. Similar, but not always as extensive, remedies are to be found in many civil law systems.[71]

Throughout the period of existence of the PCIJ it indicated interim measures only twice -- in the *Case Concerning the Denunciation of the Treaty of November 2, 1865 between China and Belgium*[72] and in the *Electricity Company of Sofia and Bulgaria Case.*[73]

The ICJ in the first quarter of a century of its existence received only two requests for interim measures. The United Kingdom's request for the remedy was granted in 1951 in the *Anglo-Iranian Oil Company Case*. Iran, however, refused to comply on the grounds that the Court had no jurisdiction over the merits of the case, and the measures were in fact subsequently revoked when the Court accepted an Iranian preliminary objection.[74] Another possible result of an application for interim measures can be found in the example of the invocation of Article 41 by Switzerland in the *Interhandel Case*. The Court here refused indication of provisional measures because it decided there was insufficient danger to the applicant's rights to justify provisional measures.[75]

---

[70] Infra. See for instance the Cameroonian request for such measures in the Land and Maritime Dispute between Cameroon and Nigeria, *ICJ Reports*, 1996, p. 105. See also Mendelson, *op. cit.*, p. 259.

[71] *Ibid.*

[72] PCIJ Series A No. 8 (order of 8 Jan. 1927).

[73] PCIJ A/B No. 79 (order of 5 Dec. 1939).

[74] *ICJ Reports*, (1952), p. 93.

[75] *ICJ Reports* (1957), p. 105.

Thus, if the request for interim measures is preceded by a determination as to the Court's jurisdiction over the merits (substantive jurisdiction) there would not be any problem. If the decision is that the Court is without competence, the case would be struck off its list, and proceedings in connection with which interim measures might be sought will not be allowed. If on the other hand the Court has already determined it possesses competence to determine the merits of the case then there would be nothing to stop the indication of interim measures, provided other conditions for their indication were met.

The real difficulty arises if the request for interim measures is made before the Court has had the opportunity to determine its jurisdiction on the case. Here the Court would have to steer the delicate course between Scylla and Charybdis, in that there are two possibilities. First, because of the precious time that may be consumed during proceedings on preliminary objections, and the urgency which characterises interim measures, the Court may indicate interim measures only to discover later (with great damage to its authority and image and a lot of unfairness to the respondent) that it lacks jurisdiction. Secondly, the Court may refuse to indicate provisional measures in time only to establish jurisdiction over merits of the case later with the resultant effect of the rights of the applicant being so prejudiced that it will be unable to derive any, or any adequate, benefit from the eventual judgement.[76]

What is important to note is that requests for interim measures according to the current rules of the Court have priority over all other cases. In practice the Court accords due deference to such requests. For instance, during the judicial year 1993-94 when the ICJ had one of its busiest period of activities with 11 cases at various stages of procedure, it received two requests of a complicated and lengthy nature in relation to the case brought by Bosnia and Herzegovina against Yugoslavia (Serbia and Montenegro) concerning the Genocide Convention. In accordance with its rules the Court abandoned all competing business and with dispatch dealt with the requests. The first was handled in some three weeks, and the second in only a little longer time -- that period including in both

[76] See also Satow, *op. cit.*, p. 365.

instances time for an oral hearing in which both parties were heard and for the study of several written observations.

It is therefore a pity that despite the great importance the Court attaches to the mechanism of interim measures its ultimate utility is marred by the very poor record of compliance with provisional measures granted. Indeed, it would appear that interim measures are in reality treated as advisory and are not regarded as judgements on the merits of the case. [77] The fact is, once the Court has satisfied itself that the provisions invoked by the applicant appear *prima facie* to afford a basis upon which the jurisdiction of the Court may be founded, there is no plausible reason why provisional measures granted should not enjoy the status of a "judgement within a judgement." This sort of interpretation best serves the cause of justice. If for instance non-compliance leads to the continuance of genocide, or to the removal of the subject matter from jurisdiction (as in continuous mining of minerals in an area subject to dispute) or to the problem of *res extincta* then it becomes difficult to see how the eventual victor on whose behalf interim measures were granted would appreciate the differentiation between a judgement and a mere interim measure. The real benefits of the victory would have disappeared.

Whereas, assuming the dispute over rights is eventually resolved by the Court's judgement in such a way as to prove that the interim measures were never required the remedy of costs remains open to the injured party[78]

Chambers of the Court

Chamber of Summary Procedure

It has been correctly noted that one of the most positive signs of life in the International Court is the emergence of special five-judge chambers to settle disputes submitted by compromise between States. The Statute (Article 29) provides that, with a view to the speedy dispatch of business, the Court shall form annually a Chamber composed of five judges which, at the request of the

[77] Shaw, *op. cit.*, p. 671.

[78] The Court has the general power to award costs, although the normal principle is that each party bears his own costs. Statute Article 64 Rules Article 81.

parties, may hear and determine cases by summary procedure. The Court also selects two judges for this Chamber to cover the exigencies of one or more judges who may, at a particular time find it impossible to sit. Under Article 15 of the Rules of the Court, the President and Vice President are members of this Chamber *ex officio*, the other members and the substitutes being elected. The Chamber of Summary Procedure has never as yet been called upon to meet in the over 50 year experience of the Court. This fact is not too flattering according to observers of the Court's work. It raises the question of a probable lack of trust in the ability of the Court to render such a specialised service in relation to the sensitive disputes States refer to it.

Chambers Provided for in Article 26, Paragraph 1 of the Statute:
The Court may from time to time form one or more chambers, composed of three or more judges, as the Court may determine, for dealing with particular categories of cases, for example, labour cases and cases relating to transit and communications. Cases are heard and determined by these chambers if the parties so request (Statute Article 26, paragraph 1).

For a long time the Court considered the question of the possible formation of a chamber to deal with environmental matters. The view initially amongst members of the bench was that it was not really necessary to set up a standing chamber. The thinking was that the Court was able to respond rapidly to requests for the constitution of a so - called "ad hoc" chambers (pursuant to Article 26, paragraph 2, of the Statute) which could deal also with any environmental case. Eventually as a result of international developments in the field of environmental law and protection which have taken place in the last few years, and considering that it should be prepared to the fullest possible extent to deal with any environmental case falling within it's jurisdiction, the Court in 1993 deemed it appropriate to establish a seven-member Chamber for Environmental Matters. composed of judges (elected by secret ballot) who have expressed a special interest in such matters. They are as follows: Judges Schwebel, Bedjaoui, Evensen, Shahabuddeen, Weeramantry, Ranjeva and Herczegh.

Chambers Formed under Article 26, Paragraph 2, of the Statute:
The Court may form a chamber for dealing with a particular case, the number of judges constituting such a chamber being determined by

the Court with the approval of the parties (Statute Article. 26, paragraph. 2). Chambers of this kind have been formed at the joint request of the parties to deal with four cases. They are as follows:

1. Delimitation of the Maritime Boundary in the Gulf of Maine Area (Canada/United States of America) : constituted on 20 January 1982. The Judges were Odo Ago (President), Gros, Mosler, Schwebel; and Judge (ad hoc) Cohen.
2. Frontier Dispute (Burkina Faso/Republic of Mali) : constituted on 3 April 1985. The Judges were Bedjaoui (President). Lachs, Ruda; Judges (ad hoc) Luchaire, and Abi `Saab.
3. Eletronica Sicula S. p. A. (ELSI) (United States of America/Italy): Constituted on 2 March 1987 with the following composition:- Judges Nagendra Singh (*President*),.Oda Ago, Schwebel, and Sir Robert Jennings. As a result of the death of Judge Nagendra Singh the Court, on 20 December 1988, elected President Ruda to succeed him in the capacity of member and (*ex officio)* President of the Chamber.
4. Land, Island and Maritime Frontier Dispute (El Salvador & Honduras/Nicaragua (as from 13 September 1990 intervening): constituted on 8 May 1987 with the following Judges: Oda, Sette-Camara, Sir Robert Jennings; Judges (ad hoc) Valticos and Virally. The Chamber elected Judge Sette-Camara to be its president. With the death in office of Judge Virally, Mr. Torres Bernadez was chosen to sit as Judge (ad hoc) in his place, and on 13 December 1989 the Court declared the Chamber to be composed as follows: Judges Sette-Camara (president), Oda, Sir Roberts Jennings; Judges (ad hoc) Valticos and Torres Bernadez. On 7 February 1991 Judges Sir Robert Jennings and Oda exchanged places in the order of precedence within the Chamber owing to their election as the Court's President and Vice-President respectively.

The provision in the Rules relating to Chambers are contained in Articles 15-18 and 90-93. In practice, the two most important changes in the 1978 Rules over the old Rules are the provision for consultation with the parties as to the composition of the Chamber and to ensure that judges appointed to any particular Chamber can continue as members despite the fact that they may leave the full Court.

Chapter 4

The Problem of Reservations to the Court's Jurisdiction under the Optional Clause

With minor exceptions all Governments which are now bound by the Optional Clause have attached more or less wide reservations to the Court's jurisdiction in this respect. The practice of making reservations was already widely used in the days of the League of Nations. PCIJ cases such as *Electricity Co. of Sofia* (1939)[1] and *Phosphates in Morrocco*[2] point to this.

A reservation as correctly defined by Levi is:

> The exclusion or modification of the legal effect of certain provisions of a treaty... it is the equivalent by the reserving party or in other words a change in the nature of its consent, therefore requiring a corresponding change in the consent of other parties to produce a concordance of wills.[3]

It would prove quite instructive to examine some general points about the drafting of Article 36, paragraphs (1) (2) and (3) of the Statute (i.e., the Optional Clause) in particular. Article 36(2) which provides that States parties to the Statute may at any time declare that they recognise as compulsory and without special agreement, in relation to any other State accepting the same obligation the jurisdiction of the Court in all legal disputes concerning the matter under consideration. Article 36(3) also states that the declarations so made can be given "... unconditionally or on condition of reciprocity on the part of several or certain states, or for a certain time." In paragraph (1) of Article 36, jurisdiction is conferred on the Court in "all cases" and "all matters" (referred to it by the parties. When this is compared with paragraph (2) which refers specifically to "all legal disputes" we see that the former is not restricted to disputes while

---

[1] PCIJ Series A B N 77, p.82.

[2] PCIJ Series No. 74 p. 33.

[3] Levi, *op.cit.*, p. 222.

the latter is surely a limitation. Therefore we wish to conclude here that the optional clause itself--i.e., 36(2)-- is well delimited and really requires no further qualification and reservation. Moreover Article 36(2) has been severely qualified with the words "in relation to any other State accepting the same obligation." Taking all this into consideration, we consider paragraph 3 of Article 36 superfluous. Its reference to a condition of reciprocity is unnecessary and its provision that declarations could be made conditionally only serves to hinder the positive legal effect of the optional clause.

Therefore it is not surprising that strange and ill-advised reservations have been concocted by a lot of States. As a writer notes:

> The reservations attached by the United States in 1946 ... go much further in the direction of reducing the acceptance of the Clause to the vanishing point of legal obligation... It is clear that an obligation the extent of whose application is left to the interested party is a legal obligation in name only.[4]

Multiplied in effect by their reciprocity these escape devices are capable of limiting the acceptance of compulsory jurisdiction of the Court to a pitiful and absolute minimum of actual commitment. We are rightly warned that the existing regime of reservations presents the danger that "... the attitude of States may degenerate into one of pure opportunism,declarations being made and cancelled and varied as the immediate interests of each State may dictate."[5]

Reservations to the Court's jurisdiction have come in many forms. There are Reservations as to Reciprocity as contained in Article 36(2) and (3). The condition of reciprocity has been worked out in such a way that a State may always invoke a provision in its opponent's declaration for the purpose of excluding a particular dispute from the application of the optional clause jurisdiction.[6] Thus like a double edged sword a reservation works both ways -- not only in favour of the State which made it, but also in favour of its opponent. Therefore the Portuguese reservation which asserts a right to qualify the acceptance of compulsory jurisdiction at any time bv

---

[4] Oppenheim, *op. cit.*, p. 63.

[5] *Ibid.*

[6] Waldock, "Decline of the Optional Clause" in *British Yearbook of Int. Law.* (1955-6) p. 276.

notifying a new reservation has the effect of conferring upon every State adhering to the clause the right, *vis-a-vis* Portugal, to qualify its acceptance of compulsory jurisdiction by notifying a new reservation. The *Norwegian Loans Case* presents a clearer picture of the working of this reservation. In this case an action was brought by the French against Norway under the optional clause. The French declaration contains the following reservation: "This Declaration does not apply to differences relating to matters which are essentially within the National Jurisdiction as understood by the French Republic." A similar reservation is not found in the Norwegian declaration, but Norway subsequently and successfully invoked the provision of the French declaration.[7]

There are reservations stating "time limits" i.e., *Ratione Temporis*. Here the reservation is conditioned by reference to time. Reservations in this sense are made by declarations, which are expressed to last for a certain term of years. The period of time found in such declarations actually varies. It could range from six months, or six years to decades or even immediately on notice to the Secretary General of the UNO.[8] The power to terminate the declaration on notice is a highly controversial one. Brownlie says, "... whilst a power of termination immediately on notice weakens the system of compulsory jurisdiction, it would seem to be compatible with the Statute of the Court."[9] However, it is with a good measure of relief that we note the judgement of the Court on the preliminary objections of the *Right of Passage Case*, which stated that the ordinary meaning of the words "with effect from the moment of notification" used in the "third condition" (of Portugal) was that the notification applied only to disputes brought before the Court after the notification. The Court thus concluded that this "third condition" (time limit reservation) introduced no degree of uncertainty into Portugal's Declaration. This shows that the extent to which this reservation weakens the compulsory jurisdiction is not great.[10] Once the Court is seised of a case on the basis of the declarations in force

---

[7] *Ibid.*
[8] Rosenne (1957) *op. cit.*, p. 261.
[9] Brownlie, *op.cit.*, p. 726.
[10] Rosenne, *op.cit.*, p. 88, 89; Anand, *op. cit.*, p. 228

at the date of application, any subsequent termination either by unilateral immediate termination or expiry of term affects in no way the jurisdiction of the Court in that case.

Reservations have also been made excluding "Past Disputes." Anand correctly notes that as a general rule, the declarations are made to apply only to disputes subsequently arising. There are two main reservations of this kind. The Belgian and Australian reservations are fairly wide. The Australian reservation for example exempts the Court's jurisdiction "... in all legal disputes arising after August 18, 1930, with regard to situations or facts subsequent to that date,"[11] This form of reservation has been employed by some other States such as Canada, Columbia, Finland, France, India, Luxembourg, New Zealand, South Africa, Sweden and the United Kingdom. Whereas, a smaller group of States (Netherlands, USA, Belgium, Pakistan, Turkey) have employed another formula as expressed by the United States of America: "... in all legal disputes hereafter arising." In as much as we are tempted to reason that the object of this kind of reservation clause is to remove the threat of the revival of old disputes the situation or facts of which date from a period when the State whose action is impugned was unable to foresee the legal proceedings or even laws to which these facts and situations give rise or flout; the objectivity of reasoning in Professor Brierly's comment on the British reservation to the Geneva Convention is better appreciated. He wrote:

> Why do we propose to lay on our successors in respect of the disputes which we bequeath to them, procedure which we are unwilling to apply to the disputes which have been bequeathed to us? Can the thought behind the reservation be that our predecessors have done certain questionable things, which we should not care to defend, whereas our own conduct is so exemplary that our successors have nothing to fear from arbitration? The explanation seems to be too cynical to be accepted; but is there another?[12]

The duplicity reported here, we posit is a common factor running through all such declarations made by States.

---

[11] *Ibid.*

[12] Brierly, "British Reservations to the General Act" *British Yearbook of Int. Law*, 8 (1931) p. 133.

The Domestic Jurisdiction Clause is a common mode of declaration imposing severe restriction on the jurisdiction of the ICJ in contentious cases. Proposals to give the World Court obligatory jurisdiction received strong support both at the time of the drafting of the PCIJ Statute in 1920 and at the time of drafting of the new Statute in 1945, but were rejected on both occasions. Such proposals were favoured largely by majority of the Third World States, but the opposition of the Soviet Union and the United States led to the retention of the principle of jurisdiction based on the consent of the parties and of the optional clause. The interests and policies of the Soviet and the capitalist States were viewed as being basically opposed and irreconcilable in such a way that impartial adjudication of disputes of any importance between them was believed to be virtually impossible.[13] As S. B. Krylov, one of the Soviet delegates at San Francisco and subsequently the Soviet member of the Court, tersely puts it, "the USSR was guided by the necessity of defending the interests of the socialist State, the United States was apprehensive of opposition in the Senate to the ratification of the Charter and the Statute."[14]

Thus, someone like M. Litinov fearfully declared that, "it was necessary to face the fact that there was not one world but two -- a Soviet world and a non-Soviet world. Because there is no third world to arbitrate... only an angel could be unbiased in judging Russian affairs."[15]

Already Article 2(7) of the UN Charter implicitly excludes from the Court's jurisdiction matters which are essentially within the domestic jurisdiction of States. The UN also does not require members to submit such matters to settlement under the Charter. There is, therefore, no way the principal judicial organ of the UN can adjudicate upon matters essentially within the domestic jurisdiction of a State. Reservations, which exclude from the Court's jurisdiction disputes with regard to matters which by international

---

[13] O. J. Lizzitzyn, *The International Court of Justice: Its Role in the Maintenance of International Peace and Security* (Westport, Connecticut: Greenwood Press Publishers, 1970) p. 61.

[14] *Ibid.*, p. 63.

[15] T. A. Taraconzio, *The Soviet Union and International Law* (New York: Macmillan, 1985) p. 296.

law fall essentially within the domestic jurisdiction of the State, are merely repetitive of Article 2(7) of the Charter. The superfluity of this kind of reservation is comparable to reservations as to reciprocity.

The Special Problem of Self Judging or Automatic Reservations

The fear of the US delegation that a provision from the obligatory jurisdiction of the Court would encounter difficulties in the Senate was partly borne out in 1946 when the Senate attached reservations to the United States declaration of acceptance of the compulsory jurisdiction of the Court under the "optional clause." In that particularly significant Declaration of 14th August, 1946 it was stated that:

> The United States of America recognises as compulsory *ipso facto* and without special agreement, in relation to any other State accepting the same declaration, the jurisdiction of the International Court of Justice in all legal disputes hereafter arising with regard to matters which are essentially within the domestic jurisdiction of the United States of America as determined by the USA.[16]

The U.S.A. also exempted "disputes arising under a multilateral treaty, unless (1) all parties to the treaty affected by the decision are also parties to the case before the Court, or (2) the United States of America specifically agrees to jurisdiction."[17] The first form of reservation described is the *Connally Reservation/Connally Amendment* after the name of the senator who suggested the formula to the US Senate. Such reservations are also known as "automatic" or "self judging" reservations. A similar reservation based on the domestic jurisdiction clause is the French declaration which states that: "This declaration does not apply to differences relating to matters which are essentially within the National Jurisdiction as understood by the French Republic."[18] Among the reasons advanced for these reservations were that, it would be reckless to proceed

---

[16] U. S. declaration of 14th August, 1946 accepting the jurisdiction of the ICJ under Article 36, paragraph 2: UNTS Vol. 1, p.9.
[17] *U. S. Department of State Bulletin*, XV (1946) p. 452.
[18] French Declaration of March 1, 1949; see *ICJ Yearbook*, 1946-47, p.219.

precipitately since "(t)he Court has yet to win the confidence of the World community and that international law has not yet developed the scope and definiteness necessary to permit disputes generally to be resolved by judicial, rather than political tests."[19]

The problems raised by this so-called "automatic reservation" to declarations accepting the jurisdiction of the International Court under Article 36, paragraph 2 of the Statute are among the most discussed issues in the literature of the Court.[20] Unfortunately following the footsteps of the US and other developed States many developing States have also employed this device. They include Liberia,[21] Mexico,[22] Philippines,[23] Sudan[24] etc. This reservation is automatic in the sense that by virtue of it, the function of the Court is confined to registering the decision made by the defendant government. The declaration thereby creates a mere illusion of compulsory jurisdiction, because when the chips are down jurisdiction conferred on the Court is voluntary and can be eliminated at will.

The Court itself has seriously shirked its responsibility to pronounce the Connally reservation as illegal and of no effect. In reality however, the potency of this particular reservation as a jurisdictional weapon is very weak.[25] Indeed, scanning through the jurisprudence espoused by the Court indirectly through the individual and separate opinions of the judges it is incontrovertible that self judging clauses of the Connally reservation genre are ineffectual if not out rightly illegal.

The *Norwegian Loans Case*[26] presented the first instance where the Court could have considered the Connally type of reservation

---

[19] US Congress, Senate Committee on Foreign Relations, Compulsory Jurisdiction, International Court of Justice, Hearings... on Senate Res. 126..., 11,12 and 15 July 1946, pp. 43-45.

[20] James Crawford, "The Legal Effect of Automatic Reservation to the Jurisdiction of the International Court" in *British Yearbook of Int. Law,* 36 (1979) p. 63.

[21] Declaration of 12th December, 1966.

[22] Declaration of 28th October, 1947.

[23] Declaration of 18th January, 1972.

[24] Declaration of 2nd January, 1958.

[25] See C.A. Ogan, "Potency and Weakness of a Jurisdictional Weapon: The Odyssey of the Connally Reservation" in *Justice*, 21 (1991) pp. 55-62.

[26] *ICJ Reports* 1957, p. 9.

and declare it illegal. France had brought an application against Norway. However, while the Norwegian declaration relied upon by France contained no provision similar to an automatic reservation, the French declaration in force at the material time did. Relying on the reciprocity principle, Norway challenged the competence of the Court to entertain the French application. In its judgement reference was made by the Court to this proviso and it agreed with Norway. Nevertheless, the Court decided it lacked jurisdiction, without enlightening us on the legality of the French reservation.[27] It stated that "the Court does not consider that it should examine whether the French reservation is consistent with the undertaking of a legal obligation and is compatible with Article 36, paragraph 6 of the Statute. The validity of the reservation has not been questioned by the Parties..."[28] In his dissenting opinion, however, Judge Encore made it clear that by the fact that France reserved her right to determine herself the limit between her own national jurisdiction and the Court's jurisdiction, "France renders void her main undertaking."[29] Judge Lauterpacht in his individual opinion correctly said of such reservations,

> It is for the reason of the later qualification an instrument incapable of producing legal effects before this Court and of establishing its jurisdiction. This is for the reason that (a) it is contrary to the Statute of the Court (b) the existence of the obligation being dependent upon the determination by the Government accepting the optional clause. The acceptance does not constitute a legal obligation. The declaration of acceptance cannot accordingly, provide a basis for the jurisdiction of the Court.[30]

He further noted that, not only are such reservations contrary to one of the fundamental principles of international and national jurisprudence according to which it is within the inherent power of a tribunal to interpret the text establishing its jurisdiction; but that it is also contrary to a clear specific provision of the Statute of the Court as well as to the general Articles 1 and 92 of the Statute and the

[27] Ogan, *op. cit.*, p. 51.
[28] *ICJ Reports*, 1957.
[29] *Ibid.*, p. 68.
[30] See the individual opinion of judge Lauterpacht, Norwegian Loans Case *ICJ Reports*, 1955.

Charter respectively which requires the Court to function in accordance with its Statute.[31]

The second occasion, and some say the best, in which the Court could have determined the legality of the Connally reservation presented itself in the *Inter-handel Case.*[32] Here dispute arose from the taking of the property of a Swiss Company by the US. The US objected to the Court's jurisdiction *inters alia* because it claimed the matter was essentially within the domestic jurisdiction of the US. Here the legality of the Connally reservation was clearly at issue.[33] Yet the Court decided that it lacked jurisdiction not because of the Connally clause (it infact did not pronounce its legality), but because Switzerland had not exhausted all available local remedies before instituting proceedings. However, many judges seized the opportunity to take this clause to the cleaners. Significantly, Judge Klarestad who was then President of the Court, suggested that the Connally reservation be severed from the rest of the US declaration of acceptance to avoid making the whole of the declaration invalid.[34]

Again in the *Aerial Incident of July 27, 1955*[35] the matter could have been settled. Bulgaria invoked the Connally reservation in the US declaration insisting that the subject matter of the dispute was essentially within the domestic jurisdiction of Bulgaria as understood by Bulgaria. The US, however, on May 13 requested discontinuance of the proceedings and this was granted by ICJ Order of May 30, 1960.

Without actually raising the Connally Reservation in the Military and Paramilitary Activities in and against Nicaragua,[36] the US still made frantic efforts to prove that the Court had no jurisdiction. The US sought to show in its Counter Memorial that Nicaragua never accepted the Court's compulsory jurisdiction and therefore could not take advantage of the reciprocity principle. It also invoked the multilateral treaty reservation referred to earlier (the

---

[31] *Ibid.*

[32] *ICJ Reports*, 1959, p. 6.

[33] Ogan, *op. cit.*, p. 57.

[34] *Ibid.* See also D.J. Harris *Cases and Materials on International Law*, Third Ed. London, 1983, pp. 730-731.

[35] *ICJ Reports,* 1960, p. 146, (Order of May 30)

[36] *ICJ Report* 1986, p. 14.

so-called Vandenberg reservation). In further desperation the US hastily forwarded to the Secretary-General of the UN a note purporting to modify the 1946 Declaration of Acceptance. Through this, it sought to exclude from the Court's jurisdiction immediately and for two years running all disputes with any Central American State arising out of or related to events in Central America.[37]

On January 18, 1985 the US notified the ICJ of its withdrawal from the proceedings in the case concerning military and paramilitary activities in and against Nicaragua. In its notice the US alleged that the Court lacked jurisdiction and competence. It contended that the Court's decision of November 26, 1984 finding that it has jurisdiction is contrary to law and fact. The allegation invoked the venerable tradition in international arbitration and adjudication of the consequences of the exercise of excess jurisdiction by an international tribunal.[38] This instance has elicited varied and diverse response from legal scholars. Michael Reigman for instance believes that:

> The U.S. by its withdrawal of January 18, 1985 has not helped the Court. Nor will the Court be helped by the termination of the US declaration and probable emendation of the declarations of other States now made necessary by the novel and expansive jurisprudence implicit in the judgement of November 26, 1984. But before condemning the US for what appears to be a retreat from international adjudication, international lawyers might do well to read the judgement again in the light of the classic theory of public international jurisdiction. For it is an affirmation and not a repudiation of law to reject a decision by a tribunal that had no jurisdiction to make such a decision.[39]

We do not entirely share this view. The fact is, the egregiousness of the violations by the US of international legal rules was such that to fail to have established jurisdiction in that case the Court would have removed any possible role for itself as a credible adjudicator of future international disputes.[40] With the Connally type reservation States may brandish in the Court's face a "magic wand." After taking

---

[37] 123 ILM 670 (1984).

[38] Michael Reigmann "Has the International Court Exceeded Its Jurisdiction," *British Yearbook of Int. Law*. 80 (1986), p. 128.

[39] *Ibid.*

[40] See M.J. Gbennon, "Protecting the Court's Institutional Interests: Why not the Marbury Approach." *AJIL* 22 (1987).

a close look at the facts of any Case if a declarer reasons that the Court's decisions may be unfavourable it can simply make the Court's jurisdiction disappear into thin air in negation of the system of compulsory jurisdiction. Thus, a State with such a subjectively worded optional clause purports to possess just as in fairy tales, "the wish of all wishes." It can simply wish any trouble away. To use the words of Bin Cheng, a declarant (and in turn his opponent) have the opportunity to accept the ICJ's compulsory jurisdiction "only in relation to disputes which [it] can afford to lose." Being a self judging exercise it does not take much legal acumen to discover that it runs foul of that basic principle of natural justice -- *nemo judex in causa sua*.

What the US managed to achieve in the Nicaraguan case was to rob most scholars of the Court, particularly those from the developing world off the satisfaction of establishing their conviction of the impotence about all Connally type reservations. As C.A. Ogan put it, if the US had invoked the Connally reservation "the ICJ would have seized the opportunity to demystify this type of scarecrow once and for all."[41]

Reservations 'Properly so called' and 'Improperly so called'

Much of the controversy surrounding the Court's decision on whether to accept or refuse a reservation stems from a misunderstanding of what is and what is not a reservation within the meaning of the Court's Statute and for the purposes of litigation before the Court. Thus, we make the distinction between "reservations properly so called" and "reservations improperly so called." In the first place, it appears that much of what has been paraded as reservations under the optional clause are reservations "improperly so called." Even among the reservations "properly so called," there can be a further distinction separating their legality on the one hand, and their propriety on the other hand.

The question of the legality of reservations on one hand and the propriety of reservations on the other hand may be raised to the

[41] Ogan, *op. cit.*, p. 59.

extent that while certain reservations are legal their propriety can be nullified by their superfluous nature. On the other hand, many of the reservations, which have been concocted by States, lack both legality and propriety. What can one say of such purported formula as the Israeli "reservation" which exempts all disputes which "involve a legal title created or conferred by a Government or authority other than the Government of Israel or an authority under the jurisdiction of that government" except to pronounce it strange to say the least.

Apart from the category exempting matters solely within domestic jurisdiction which is a Charter provision, there can be strictly speaking only three sets of reservations which are legal according to the pertinent clauses of Article 36 of the ICJ Statute. They are declarations made barring (a) non-legal disputes (36(2)); (b) reservations "on condition of reciprocity' (36(3)) and (c) reservations "for a certain time" (36(3)). With regards to non-legal disputes any further reservation made on this ground is superfluous since both the Charter and the Statute are replete with provisions specifying that the principal judicial arm of the UN will deal only with legal disputes. Besides, it falls squarely within the Court's competence to decide whether the case submitted to it concerns a legal dispute or not. The condition as to reciprocity (*ratione personae*) we have concluded is already explicitly recognised in the Statute (36(2)), i.e., in relation to any other State accepting the same obligation. Without further reference to it in any declaration as a separate reservation, it can be invoked by any State accepting the Optional Clause. Therefore the only new thing added as a possible ground for reservation under 36(3) which directly prescribes forms of permissible reservations is the reservation *ratione temporis*. The propriety of including this kind of reservation is another issue on its own and would depend on the reasons for involving it in each particular instance.

All other forms of reservations would therefore appear to be reservations "improperly so called" at least in relation to the provisions of Article 36 of the Statute. This includes reservations *ratione Fori*, i.e., exempting disputes in regard to which the parties thereto have agreed or shall agree to have recourse to some other method of settlement. This again is a superfluous reservation.

Articles 33 and 95 of the UN Charter already give legal recognition to the right of States to pursue settlement of disputes in various other peaceful ways. Furthermore, a distinction can be made between reservations and formal conditions. As pointed out earlier, reservations are restrictions relating to the content of the commitments entered into in a particular declaration; formal conditions on the other hand pertain to the duration, termination, and modification of a declaration.[42] This distinction was followed by the ICJ in the jurisdictional judgement in the Nicaraguan case. Here, the Court stated that: "The notion of reciprocity is concerned with the scope and substance of the commitments entered into including reservations, and not with the formal conditions of their creation, duration or extinction."[43]

While a similar distinction is made in doctrine, different terms are used. Thus for some, it is assumed that formal conditions are simply a variation of reservations *ratione tempories*.[44] The third condition in the Portuguese declaration is for instance, listed as a reservation. This strange condition runs thus: "The Portguese Government reserves the right to exclude from the scope of the present declaration, at any time during its validity, any given category or categories of disputes, by notifying the Secretary-General of the United Nations and with effect from the moment of such notification."[45]

It may prove instructive for us to examine and compare the various current declarations to the optional clause and the very few past declarations withdrawn by some States, notably the US declaration. This exercise reveals that some States are more sincere in their acceptance of the optional clause than others. While most States riddle their declarations with all sorts of reservations to serve as impediments to would be litigants there are a few commendable acceptances of the optional clause such as those of Nigeria and Haiti

---

42 See Szarfarz, *op. cit.*, p. 46.

43 *ICJ Reports* 1984, p. 419, para. 62. See also the Court's pronouncement, p. 418.

44 See M. Iwanejko, *Miedzynarodowy Trybunal Sprawiedliwosci Krakow*, 1969. See also Leo Gross `Compulsory Jurisdiction under the Optional Clause: History and Practice in L.F. Pamrosch (ed.) *The International Court of Justice at a Crossroads*, New York Dobbs Ferry: Oceana, 1987), p. 23.

45 See *ICJ Yearbook*, 1989-90, p. 90.

which give much hope for the future of compulsory jurisdiction. In sharp contrast with this we find such declarations as those of India and Malta which leave one at a loss as to whether there was infact any intention to accept compulsory jurisdiction at all.

Table 0: Patterns of Reservations to the Optional Clause in Current and Past Declarations

Country	Rationae Materiae			Ratione Decidendi	Ratione Personae	Riatione Fori	Riatione Temporis	Formal Conditions
	Objective Domestic Jurisdiction Clause	Subjective Domestic jurisdiction Clause	Other matters					
Australia						x		x
Austria						x		x
Barbados	x		x		x	x		x
Belgium					x	x	x	
Botswana	x					x		
Bulgaria							x	x
Cambodia	x					x		x
Cameroon								x
Canada	x				x	x	x	x
Columbia							x	
Costa Rica								x
Cyprus	x				x			x
Denmark								x
Dominican Republic								
Egypt								
El Salvador	x		x	x		x	x	
Estonia						x	x	x
Finland					x	x		x
Gambia	x							
Greece			x					
Guinea-Bissau								x
Haiti								
Honduras	x		x			x		
Hungary	x		x					
India	x		x	x	x	x	x	x
Japan						x	x	
Kenya	x		x			x	x	x
Liberia		x				x		x
Liechtenstein								x
Luxembourg							x	x
Madagascar						x		
Malawi		x	x			x		

Malta	x		x	x	x	x		x
Mauritius	x		x		x	x	x	x
Mexico		x						x
Nauru						x		
Netherlands			x			x	x	x
New Zealand					x	x		x
Nicaragua								
Nigeria								
Norway								x
Pakistan	x			x		x		x
Panama								
Philippines		x	x	x	x	x		x
Poland	x		x		x	x	x	x
Portugal								x
Senegal	x					x		x
Somalia					x			x
Spain					x	x	x	x
Sudan		x	x				x	x
Suriname			x			x	x	x
Swaziland	x					x		x
Sweden							x	x
Switzerland								x
Togo								x
Uganda								
UK and N. Ireland					x	x		x
Uruguay								
USA		x	x					
Zaire								x

In sum, however, apart from the permitted reservations under Article 36 of the Statute and the implicit recognition of matters within domestic jurisdiction, all other strange and ill-advised reservations (improperly so called) or conditions attached by States to their acceptances under the Optional Clause do not derive their legality from the Statute of the Court and lack propriety in all instances. To summarise our arguments therefore, it is necessary to state that the system of attaching reservations to acceptances under the optional clause needs to be overhauled. When the much-needed review of the Statute of the Court takes place, it is hoped that provisions allowing reservations to the Court's compulsory jurisdiction, particularly in Article 36(3) will be trimmed down if not entirely discarded. The only reservation that may be retained is that which allows reservations for a certain time. It may be necessary to allow this in order that States may not have the feeling that they are entering a commitment from which they can never get out. In that case, States may be allowed to make declarations for fixed period, of say five years, ten years or more subject to renewal. Even here, it must be made clear that reservations "for a certain time" pertain only to fixed periods of acceptance and not the present lax interpretation adopted by States by which they simply exempt past disputes. The jurisdiction of the Court must be left as wide as possible in the interest of international peace and stability.

A suggested redrafting of the Article 36(3) of the Statute reads thus:

> The declarations referred to above may be made unconditionally and acceptance may be made indefinitely or for a fixed period of time renewable at the option of the State making the declaration.

The retention of the principles of domestic jurisdiction (in the Charter), of reciprocity and the requirement of "in all legal disputes" under Article 36 and in Charter provisions will continue to guarantee the protection of States. The major advantage of this suggested change is that it will bring certainty and clarity to an area fraught with confusion. The existence of scores of reservations of doubtful purpose interjecting each other *inter se* and amplified in conjunction with the principle of reciprocity has turned the existing system of compulsory jurisdiction of the ICJ into a severely perforated vessel incapable of holding water. Indeed the existence of these reservations may well account for the stunted growth of the compulsory jurisdiction of the Court. As Jennings wrote; "States may well decide that there is some advantage in remaining outside a system which permits States to join more or less on their own terms at an opportune moment."[46]

[46] Jennings (1995), *op. cit.*, p. 495.

Chapter 5

Proceedings in Contentious Cases

Procedure in the Court is regulated by a combination of provisions sometimes appearing in the Statute and sometimes in the Rules of Court (1978) over all of which lie a thick layer of practice and Jurisprudence.[1] Rules appearing in the Statute are mandatory, while the others possess inherent flexibility as recognised in Article 101 of the Rules which states: "The Parties to a case may jointly propose particular modifications or additions to the Rules which may be applied by the Court or a Chamber if the Court or the Chamber considers them appropriate." Thus while the principles found in the Statute are obligatory those found in the Rules are to an extent facultative.[2] Among the mandatory provisions of particular relevance is the requirement in Article 43, paragraph 1 of the Statute that the procedure shall consist of two parts, written and oral; that the written proceedings shall consist of the communications of memorials and counter-memorials and, if necessary, replies and that the oral proceedings consist of the hearing by the Court, in principle in public (Statute, Art. 46), of the witnesses, experts, agents, counsel and advocates of the parties. Generally speaking the procedure of the ICJ follows closely that of the PCIJ. That procedure, the informal Inter-Allied Committee thought, had worked satisfactorily in practice and called for little change.[3] Nonetheless, there are some discernible changes. An attempt to try and draw parallels between the proceedings before the International Court and those of municipal

---

[1] Rosenne, *op .cit.*, p.73.

[2] The flexibility of the Rules is quite noticeable and of particular significance is the pronouncement of the PCIJ in the Free Zones Case: "In contradistinction to that which is permitted by the Rules (Article 32 and Article 31) the Court cannot on the proposal of the parties depart from the terms of the Statute;" PCIJ Series, No. 22, p. 12; Rosenne (1961) *op. cit.*, p. 283 see also the following: *Pleading*, Vol. V, pp. 134-5; Nottebohm Case, 1952.

[3] Rosenne (1961), *op. cit.*, p. 379.

courts will definitely be fraught with difficulties. This is because the conduct of proceedings before the International Court bears little beyond superficial resemblance to the conduct of proceeding in municipal courts. As a learned author notes:

> Strange as it may seem, the International Court is with all its solemnity, and with all the complexity of the issues brought before it, a body of great informality. One of the most important factors is the continuous co-operation of the two parties and the Court, especially in the stage of the oral hearings. The published volumes of pleadings are full of demonstrations of the reality of this even in the most hard-fought cases.[4]

It should also be pointed out clearly that the proceedings have as their primary objective the systematic and contradictory presentation of facts by agents of the parties upon which the respective cases rest and upon which the decision of the Court will be pronounced. This informs the sharp division of the proceedings into two distinct phases -- the written and the oral proceedings. It has been pointed out that the maintenance of these two phases for the merits of contentious cases, is an essential part of the judicial process, and is based on Article 43 of the Statute. On the other hand, also, some latitude is allowed to the parties, subject to the control of the Court, in so far as concerns the extent to which they will avail themselves of their statutory right to make use of the two phases.[5] The Statute and Rules of the ICJ cannot be said to contain much detailed instruction regarding the method by which a case should be tried.

Preliminary Steps

After the institution of proceedings and the transmission of necessary documents to the parties, the first step by the Court is for the President to ascertain the views of the parties with regards to questions of procedures. For this reason he may summon the agents to meet him as soon as they have been appointed (1978 Rules Article 31).[6] Instances exist in which the agent is represented by a

---

[4] *Ibid.*

[5] *Ibid.*

[6] This corresponds to Article 40, paragraph 1 of the 1972 rules and Article 37, paragraph 1 of the 1946 rules.

diplomatic agent at the Hague.[7] Alternatively the Court may be notified by the parties of their views in writing.[8] The non-designation of an agent as a representative by the respondent state will not stop the Court from deciding on the next step as it did in the Corfu Channel Case.[9] Where the Court is properly seised of a case (in the light of the information obtained by the President under Article 31) the Court will make all necessary interlocutory orders fixing time-limits and prolonging them after giving the respondent a reasonable opportunity to comment. The term "fixing time limits" is here used as defined in Article 48 of the 1978 Rules of the Court which defines it as "assigning a specified period...indicate definite dates" for the completion of the various steps in the proceedings. In the *UN Administrative Tribunal Case* the United States government indicated that it did not consider sufficient time had been allowed by the Court's President for the filing of written statements. In its response the Court turned down the request for an extension, the President being of the view that a period of three months was long enough, having regard to all the circumstances of that case as well as arrangements made for other pending cases.

Written Proceedings

This is the first substantive phase through which a case before the ICJ passes. Written proceedings as described by the 1978 Rules in Articles 45-46, consist of communications (a) to the Court and (b) to the parties as well as memorials, counter-memorials and, if necessary, replies as well as all documents in support. The memorial which is the first written pleading of the plaintiff State, is supposed to contain (a) a statement of all relevant facts, (b) a statement of law

---

[7] That is, the person in whose hands is entrusted the formal representation of a party in international litigation. He may be assisted in the pleading by counsel and other experts as may be required. No particular formal qualifications exist for the position of Agent, however States usually either appoint a high-ranking member of its diplomatic service such as their ambassador to the Netherlands or the legal adviser (or any of his subordinates) in the foreign service. However this is not invariable. It does happen that a practising lawyer may be appointed.

[8] Asylum Case (Pleading), P.181, see *ICJ Reports*, 1951 at p.5.

[9] Rosenne (1973) *op. cit.*, p. 108.

and submissions, and (c) copies of all relevant documents. The counter-memorial, the first written pleading of the defendant State on the merits of the case, contains (a) an admission or denial of the facts stated in the memorials, (b) additional facts if any, (c) observations concerning the statement of law in the memorial, (d) a statement of law in answer thereto and submissions, (e) annexed copies of relevant papers.[10]

The second round of written pleading on the merits consists of a Reply and a Rejoinder by the plaintiff and the defendant respectively. No rules govern their contents, and their purpose is essentially to amplify the case as presented in the Memorial and Counter-Memorial (Rules of Court Articles 45 (2) and 46 (2)). The Reply and Rejoinder shall not merely repeat the parties contentions but shall be directed to bringing out the issues that still divide them (Article 49 (3)). It frequently occurs that the issues are not all fully brought out until the Counter-Memorial is filed, for example, when that document contains a counter claim. Even if it does not it is only when the argument and submissions of the Memorial and those of the Counter-Memorial are compared that it is possible to see what the case really is about, for only then does its presentation cease to a unilateral one. This is the reason why the Reply and the Rejoinder are considered important stages of pleading in the International Court.[11]

Article 45 of the 1978 Rules reproduces Article 44 of the 1972 Rules which is itself an amended version of Article 41 of the 1946 Rules. Article 46 of the 1978 Rules is a slightly revised version of Article 45 of the 1972 Rules which is also an amended version of Article 42 of the 1946 Rules. The constant practice of the Court until the 1972 amendments was based upon the assumption that the question of whether Replies and Rejoinders were necessary was a subjective matter for the parties. The Court for a long time found two rounds of written pleadings necessary except where the parties agreed otherwise. In the event of disagreement between them the Court would not diminish the number of pleadings envisaged in the

---

[10] *Ibid.*

[11] See Rosenne (1983) *op. cit.*, p.105 - 106. See also our recommendations on rationalising the procedure of the Court *infra*.

1946 Rules. By its revised Articles 45 and 46 the Court now prescribes as the general rule in cases instituted by applications one round of written pleadings, filed consecutively, and in cases instituted by special agreement two rounds of written pleadings, filed simultaneously unless otherwise provided. The right to allow replies would appear to rest upon the Court. Article 45 (2) reserves the right of the Court to decide *proprio motu* if a reply or rejoinder is necessary. In cases introduced by special agreement the Rule in Article 46 (2) is framed in more categoric terms: "The Court shall not authorise the presentation of replies unless it finds it necessary." If one considers this Provision together with that of Article 44 (4) which gives the Court power to decide upon matters of written pleadings where consultation required under Article 31 reveals persistent disagreement between the parties, then the effect is that no State has a right to file a reply.[12] Articles 50 - 53 of the 1978 Rules lay down some general conditions applicable to all written pleadings -- including documents instituting interlocutory or derivative proceedings and interlocutory applications as well as observations. There shall be annexed to the original of every pleading certified copies of any relevant documents added in support of the contentions contained in a pleading (Article 50(1)). The documents annexed must be "certified copies," although no indications are given in the Rules as to what the expression means...[13] The original of each pleading is to be signed by the Agent and filed in the Registry. It shall be accompanied by a certified copy of the translations, for communication to the other party in accordance with Article 43, paragraph 4 of the Statute as well as by the number of additional copies required by the Registry, but without prejudice to any increase in number should need later arise (Article 52(1)).

---

[12] *Ibid.*

[13] The Court has sometimes demanded the original text of a document. In the Corfu Channel Case the Court requested the applicant to produce such documents, but this was refused without consequences on the grounds of state secrecy. A similar rule applies in the case of request for advisory opinions. Thus, in The Legality of the Use by a State of Nuclear Weapons in Armed Conflict, the letter of the Director-General of the World Health Organisation (WHO) transmitting the request to the Court was sent along with copies of the English and French texts of resolution WHA 46.40 by which the body's Assembly made the request.

The Court may decide that copies of the pleadings and documents annexed should be made available to any State entitled to appear before it which requests it. It may also decide that such copies be made accessible to the public on or after opening of the oral proceedings (Article 53). In the *Continental Shelf Case (Tunisia/Libya)* a number of governments requested copies of the pleadings. Upon the objection of one of the Parties the President decided it would not at that time be released to non-Parties. The consequence of this was that Malta's request for permission to intervene was presented and argued before the Court without Malta's appraisal of the contents of the pleadings as they stood at that stage.[14] In any event it is usual that the original pleading is accompanied by from 50-100 copies for the members of the Court as well as other persons and governments authorised to receive them.[15] This is in accordance with Rules, Article 53, paragraph 2. Thus, for instance, in the Case concerning *Maritime Delimitations and Territorial Questions between Qatar and Bahrain* (*Qatar v. Bahrain*) the Court, after ascertaining the views of the Parties, decided that the pleadings on questions of jurisdiction and admissibility, and the documents annexed thereto, should be made accessible to the public as from the opening of the oral proceedings.[16]

Closure of Written Proceedings

In the light of the provisions of Article 54 of the Rules, at the closure of the written proceedings (i.e., upon the filing of the last pleading or the expiry of the time-limit the case is in the technical position of being "ready for hearing." This means that the criterion for the taking by the Court of oral proceedings is established and introduction of further documentary evidence is highly restricted. Presentation of new documents is regulated by Statute, Article 52; Rules, Article 56 and 74, para. 3. According to Article 56 of the Rules; after the closure of the written proceedings no further

---

[14] Rosenne (1983) *op. cit.*, p. 118.
[15] Cf. Rosenne (1961) p. 385; Rosenne (1973) p. 106 and Rosenne (1977) p. 388.
[16] *ICJ Yearbook* (1993-94) pp. 212-213.

documents may be submitted to the Court by either Party except by the consent of the other Party or, after argument, with the consent of the Court. For this purpose a special interlocutory procedure is established. The Party wishing to produce a new document is to file the original or a certified copy in the Registry, which will be responsible for communicating it to the other Party and for informing the Court.[17] If permission to produce the document is granted (by the other party and/or the Court) the other party is given the opportunity of commenting upon the new document and even of submitting comments upon the new document.[18] In the case concerning *Maritime Delimitation and Territorial Questions between Qatar and Bahrain (Qatar v. Bahrain)*, supplemental documents were filed by one of the Parties after the closure of the written proceedings. The other Party indicated that it had no objection to the production of the documents, reserving the right to comment thereon, and submitted documents under Article 56, paragraph 3, of the Rules of Court.

In the case concerning *Application of the Convention on the Prevention and Punishment of the Crime of Genocide (Bosnia and Herzegovina v. Yugoslavia (Serbia and Montenegro))*, the Applicant submitted a series of documents to the Court up to the eve of the oral proceedings, and even during those proceedings. The Court considered that such submission was incompatible with the orderly staging of the proceedings and respect for the principle of equality of the Parties. Nevertheless, referring to Article 74, paragraph 3, of the Rules of Court and to the urgency and other prevailing circumstances, the Court deemed it possible to accept the documents in question as constituting in that instance "observations" presented to it in accordance with that provision, since they concerned requests for the indication of provisional measures.

The Oral Proceedings

The oral hearing is the second major phase in the life of a contentious case before the ICJ. Unlike the written pleading the oral

[17] Cf., Rosenne(1961) p. 385; Rosenne (1973), p. 106 and Rosenne (1977)p. 388.

[18] Rosenne (1961) *op. cit.*, p. 388.

pleading is in principle conducted in public and in an atmosphere of impressive and dignified solemnity.[19] Only on very rare occasions does the Court hold parts of hearings *in camera.* This was done in two politically charged cases. The first was on 15 and 16 March, 1965 in connection with the composition of the Court in the *South West Africa Case* and the second 27 January, 1971 in connection with the composition of the Court in the *Namibia Case*. It may prove instructive to delve a bit into the time honoured setting of the Court during oral proceedings.

The members of the Court and the Registrar in their Judicial robes, are seated at a long table on a raised dais; the President sits in the centre and other members in descending order of precedence, placed alternatively to his left and right. Immediately below sit the staff on duty, including the secretaries, interpreters and official recorders. The speaker's rostrum faces the President a short distance from his seat and is of easy access to the Bar where agents and counsel (all suitably robed in either their professional or academic garb) are seated. Behind them are the reserved places for members of the diplomatic corps and other distinguished visitors including the general public. At the appointed hour the Chief Usher gives the time honoured cry, "La cour!" as in the English equivalent, "Court"! (meaning, "all rise"). The judges in silent procession proceed with measured and dignified steps to their places. The President gives a sign for them to be seated. The others present follow suit and the sitting begins.[20] Roseanne has the following to say of the Court at this stage:

> The atmosphere is subdued and forensic. The Great Hall of Justice is bigger than many courtrooms. Discreetly placed microphones easily carry the voices to all the corners... While, clearly, there is no room for histrionic advocacy sometimes encountered in Jury trials, the effect of command of language and mastery of complicated situations of fact and law, and where appropriate a touch of humour or drama, is conceded in the lifeless printed versions of the oral proceedings.[21]

---

[19] Rosenne (1961) *op. cit.*, p. 394.
[20] *Ibid.*
[21] *Ibid.*, 395.

It is to be understood that the oral hearing is not just a continuation or repetition of the written pleadings. The written pleadings lay down the foundations of the case (of fact and of law) on which the oral pleading is to be based. The oral pleading has been described by many authors as strenuous. The Rules however require that the oral statements shall be as succinct as possible and very much within the limits of what is requisite for the adequate presentation of that Party's contention at the hearing. The oral pleading should be directed to the essential issues dividing the Parties and is not expected to traverse the whole ground covered by the written pleadings nor should it simply repeat facts and arguments contained in the written phase. The Court could even indicate the specific points or issues to which the parties should address themselves (Rules (1978) Article 61, amendment of the Rules (1972) Article 57, and Rules (1946) Article 52). This is done to obviate prolixity and repetitiousness in the oral phase. The Court may during the hearing, put questions to the agents and advocates and may ask them for explanations (Statute, Article. 45; Rules, Article. 61 and 72). Each judge has a similar right, but before exercising it he should make his intention known to the President who is responsible for the control of the hearing. In the case concerning *Application of the Convention on the Prevention and Punishment of the Crime of Genocide (Bosnia and Herzegovina v. Yugoslavia (Serbia and Montenegro))*, during the hearings on the further requests for the indication of provisional measures, a Member of the Court and one of the judges *ad hoc* put questions to both Parties. Another Member of the Court put a question to one of the two Parties. The reply to the latter question was given during the oral proceedings; the replies to the other questions were given in writing after the closure of the oral proceedings.

During the hearings in the case concerning *Maritime Delimitation and Territorial Questions between Qatar and Bahrain (Qatar v. Bahrain)*, the Vice-President of the Court put questions to both Agents. The replies were given in writing after the closure of the oral proceedings under Article 61, paragraph 4, and Article 72 of the Rules of Court, and each of the Parties submitted written observations on the other's reply.

The normal order for addressing the Court is that the applicant State presents its oral argument first, then the respondent State. This is followed by the Oral-Reply and Oral-Rejoinder, delivered in the same order. During the oral phase witnesses and expert witnesses can be called and the Court has retained a general right to determine in each case how and when evidence shall be taken

Submissions and Closure of Oral Proceedings

As earlier said of the written proceedings, oral pleadings too have to contain "submissions." In the course of the oral proceedings, the Agents of the Parties are expected to present to the Court their ultimate and final submissions. Of this practice it has been rightly observed that:

> So important are these that it is obligatory for the Court's judgement to set forth the parties' submissions. A submission is an extremely concise statement of what a party wants from the Court and it should be drawn up in such a way as not to recapitulate the arguments. Each submission indicates what that party considers should be the language of the operative part of the judgement (as opposed to the pleading, which explains the party's view on relevant reasons of facts and of law in support of its submission). It shows what the party is asking the Court to decide concretely.[22]

The submissions should be worded in the form of a positive statement. As a statement of what a Party thinks the decision should be, they should not contain a series of arguments or propositions of support. Furthermore, the submissions should stand in direct relation to the original statement of claim as it appeared in the application (or preliminary objection). Submission in the oral phase should be read by the Agent and written copies signed by him, should be communicated to the Court and the Party against whom they are filed who always has the chance of commenting on them, even if that entails a modification of that Party's own final submission.

At the completion of the presentation of the case by both Parties, the President formally declares the hearing closed. He may do this at the termination of the last hearing devoted to the case, or he may wait a few days, depending on the circumstances. Once oral

---

[22] Rosenne (1973), *op. cit.*, p. 99.

proceedings are closed, no further evidence or pleading may be submitted by either Party (unless the Court calls for it) and the Court withdraws to consider the judgement. As Rosenne wittily comments, "The parties can now relax and the initiative passes to Court."[23]

Deliberation of the Court

It may be noted that the Court's deliberation represents a crucial phase in the process of adjudication of a case referred to the Court. The process of this deliberation has undergone a long history of modification and review, beginning with the resolution guiding the Court's judicial practice adopted by the PCIJ in 1931.

After the termination of the written phase and just before the oral pleadings, the judges of the Court exchange views, normally in a private meeting of the Court. This is done to bring out any issue raised in this first phase in regard to which there may be need to call on the Parties for explanation during the oral hearing. A similar exercise takes place after the first round of oral pleadings. By the time the oral proceedings are completed and the judges have had sufficient period of time to study the case, a deliberation is held. The purpose of this is to examine the case as it presents itself after the hearing and to bring out questions that need to be resolved. Proposing and debating solutions is not indulged in. It is the duty of the President of the Court to outline the issues which in his opinion will require subsequent discussion and decision by the Court. Other judges of the Court have the right to comment or to call attention to any other issue or question which they may in their individual capacities consider relevant.

At the completion of this deliberation, each judge prepares a written note which is then circulated to all the other judges. It contains the judge's views on the numerous questions or issues raised including his tentative answers and conclusions. After this stage another deliberation takes place. When the judges are called upon to speak not in the order they request as in the earlier deliberation, but in an order of inverse precedence. At this deliberation they must declare their views. After this, a drafting committee is appointed by

---

[23] *Ibid.*, p. 103.

secret ballot. Two judges are elected from the members of the Court whose statements and notes have most closely and effectively reflected the Court's opinion as a whole. The President is a member of the drafting committee in the capacity of *ex officio* unless he happens not to share in the majority opinion as it appears then to exist in which case his place is occupied by the Vice-President. The Vice-President could actually also be ineligible to be a member of the committee if he does not share the opinion of the majority. In such an event another member of the Court is elected, and the senior judge will preside in the drafting committee.

The committee's preliminary draft of the decision is circulated, and the judges may submit amendments. After these amendments have been considered, a draft decision is submitted by the drafting committee for discussion in the Court in the form of the "first reading." After the first reading, the texts of separate or dissenting opinions are circulated after which an amended draft is submitted for "second reading."

The final decision is based on conclusions concurred to after a final discussion by the judges who vote in inverse order of precedence. Understandably at this stage only an affirmative or a negative vote is permitted; absentations are disallowed. If the issues are separable, separate voting is allowed. It is to be noted that no detailed minutes are prepared throughout the Court's private deliberations and apart from the judges and assessors, if any, only the Court's Registrar is allowed to be present. Such minutes as may be taken are restricted to the subject of the debates, the votes taken, names of those voting for or against and statements which are made expressly for the record (1978 Rules, Article 21). A judge may for instance insist that his words on a particular topic be recorded. Article 56(1) of the Statute makes it mandatory for the Court to state the reasons on which judgement is based. Also Article 55(2) of the Statute gives the President the casting vote in the event of a tie.

When the final decision is ready the parties are notified of the date of the public meeting at which the judgement will be delivered, in accordance with Article 58 of the Statute which provides: "The judgement shall be signed by the President and by the Registrar. It shall be read in open Court, due notice having been given to the agents." Translations of the operative clause of such judgements are sealed and are handed over to the Agents. A copy is sent to the archives of the Court and the Registrar of the Court sends officially one copy each to every member of the United Nations. This serves to justify the saying that, "Justice must not only be done but must be seen to have been done." The procedure of the Court has been well developed thorough deliberations and is based on an enviable historical evolution. However, the time consumed in the adjudication of a case and the effect it has on the costs of litigation are factors which point to a need to re-examine certain aspects of the Court's procedure.[24]

Effectiveness of the Judgements of the World Court

Judgements of international judicial bodies are the final decisions on international legal disputes. Ultimately it may be said that the rendering of judgements is the essence of the existence of an international court. Thus we must consider the general nature and effectiveness of an ICJ judgement. In accordance with Article 39, the official languages of the Court are French and English; therefore, the Court's judgment will be delivered in either language, if both Parties are in agreement. Parties to a case including (it appears) successful intervenors may address the Court in its pleadings in the language of their choice, but the Court must give judgment in English and French, stating which of the two texts is to be considered as authoritative.[25]

[24] *Infra.*

[25] Elias (1989) *op. cit.* p. 124. The fact that the Court sticks to two languages translates into a significant economic advantage in comparison with other major organs of the UN which operate in five major languages. Thus the Court views recent slashes in its budget by the General Assembly as unjustifiable and unacceptable. (See Chapter IV of the Court's Report to the General Assembly for 1 August 1995 to 31 July 1996 (official Records of the General Assembly, Fifty-first Session Supplement No. 4 (A/51/5) reproduced in *ICJ Yearbook* (1996) pp. 257-262.) We cannot but view with horror such cuts in the funds available to the Court. The price of dispensing justice on the international plane may be tremendous but the price of lack of justice in international relations has proved very often in this century alone to be much more greater. The thought of entering the next century with an impaired International Court is unthinkable.

It has been stated that the ICJ, like other international courts and tribunals does not have as its purpose the making of law. Indeed, as stated earlier international courts are not bound by their previous decisions as to the law they apply. Thus, a judgment of the ICJ according to Article 59 of the Statute is binding on the Parties alone and it imposes obligations on them only in respect of the particular case. Harris thinks this character attaches to both the decisions of the full Court and the Court in chambers. Therefore the common lawyer has to continuously remind himself that as regards the ICJ and other international Courts cases do not make law. In other words, the World Court, as any other international court is by no means the mechanical recorder of law as most lay men may see it.[26]

However, this is not to say that every judgement of the Court is entirely new or not predicated upon some settled law. The absence of *stare decisis* in the practice of the Court does not dictate this. A perusal of the practice of the Court will reveal to the discerning mind a remarkable consistency in its judgments. If this were not so then the writing of such a book as this would not only be many times more difficult but might in fact be unnecessary. The settlement of international disputes *via* the judicial method would also become a game of chance, a form of Russian Roulette which would scare away prospective litigants. It suffices to say then that ICJ judgements are clothed with great political, moral and legal aura by virtue of which they are consistent, coherent and persuasive.

Ideally, the Court as the principal judicial organ of the UN should represent the most authoritative pronouncement not only on international law but also on the resolution of legal disputes between States.[27] Seen from this view point, it is a great pity that the record of compliance with the Court's judgements is considered dismal. It remains true though, that the prevailing situation, at least as regards non-compliance, is not the fault of the Court but is largely a fall-out of the general lack of genuine political will of States in respect to the adjudicatory process. The Court on its own part is fairly well equipped to adjudicate on disputes referred to it by judgements constituting a judicial decision which, under the Statute of the Court,

[26] C. J. Harris, *op. cit.* p. 55.

[27] Terms of Reference, Guidelines and Rules of the Secretary - General Trust Fund to Assist States in the Settlement of Disputes through the International Court of Justice. Para. 2.

is binding only upon Members of the UN. Article 94, paragraph 1 of the Charter significantly declares that each member of the UN undertakes to comply in any case to which it is a party with the decision of the International Court of Justice.

In fact, the Court fully aware of the responsibilities imposed upon it, constantly bears in mind the necessity of ensuring that its procedure is commensurate with the expectations of those States and international organisations entitled to resort to it. For instance, using the legal means at its disposal, it revised its Rules both in 1972 and 1978 enabling *inter alia* a new impulse to the machinery of *ad hoc* chambers. It is probably as a result of these efforts that we can still speak of a general effectiveness of the Court's judgements to the extent of clarifying by some of its judgements the position of international law in a manner which transcends the direct effect of the decision upon the parties to a case.

Thus, it is ironical that whilst States apparently display an interest in the case law of the Court as is evident from their adoption of General Assembly resolution 44/22[28] they are frequently unwilling to comply with judgements and decisions awarded against them. The position of the law is however clear on the issue, if the party concerned fails to perform the obligations imposed upon it under a judgement of the ICJ, the other party may have recourse to the UN Security Council, which may, if it deems it necessary, make recommendations or decide upon measures to be taken to give effect to the judgement (Article 94, Charter). Nonetheless, instances of shameful non-compliance abound doing great harm to the moral and actual authority of the principal judicial arm of the UN.

In the *Corfu Channel Case*, for example, Albania has for more than four decades refused to pay Court ordered reparations to Great Britain for damage done to British warships by Albanian mines in international straits.[29] In the *Anglo-Iranian Oil Company Case*, Iran disregarded the Court's order to refrain from nationalising a British corporation, pending a final judgement of the Court or agreement between the parties. In the *Fisheries Jurisdiction Case* Iceland

---

[28] See Letter of 27 August, 1990 to the Secretary-General of the U.N. from the President of the ICJ ,His Excellency Mr. J.M. Ruda. Translated in *ICJ Yearbook* (1991) Appendix, p.186.

[29] Not until 8 May, 1992 was a Memorandum of Understanding signed between both Governments involved to settle the outstanding issues. See reprint *ICJ Year Book* (1996) *op.cit.* Appendix, pp. 257-258.

refused to obey an order not to enforce a 50 - mile fishing zone until the Court ruled on the suits instituted by the UK and West Germany. In the *United States Diplomatic and Consular Staff in Tehran Case*, the International Court rendered a unanimous interim order granting provisional measures in favour of the US. The US Embassy in Tehran had been occupied forcefully by Iranian "revolutionaries" and at least 50 diplomatic and consular staff were held hostage. Yet Iran failed to comply with the Court's order and even refused to argue the case before the Court.[30] Similar refusal to comply with the Court occurred in the Nuclear Test Cases.[31]

In the light of all these, would it not amount to sheer naivety to simply conclude as Umezurike did that compliance is assured since "(P)arties to the UN Charter and the Statute of the Court agree to comply with its decisions"? While it may be true that the vast majority of judgements have been followed, the record of non-compliance threatens to escalate if drastic changes are not implemented. A basic problem is the fact that the Court has no control whatsoever over the execution of its judgements and no other body is specifically charged with monitoring and enforcing compliance in all cases. Thus enforcement may come circuitously through self-help, co-operation of third States, recourse to municipal Courts and action by international institutions.[32]

What then, if anything, is gained by a State which litigates before the Court at great monetary expenses only to get a judgement that is not respected by the other Party? It may well be that the real benefit gained will be the use of the Court as a public forum. Thus, for instance, throughout the *Diplomatic and Consular Staff Case*, the United States admitted the use of the Court as a means "to maintain support for the American position by the vast majority of nations on Earth."[33] The mere fact of a well publicised victory in the litigation is enough satisfaction for some States. Thus in the *Fisheries Case (UK v. Norway)* the judgement of the Court that the method of maritime delimitation employed to cause a Norwegian Decree of

---

[30] See M. W. Jainis, "The International Court," in M. W. Jains (ed) *International Courts for the Twenty-First Centrury* (The Hague: Kluwer Academic Publishers, 1992) p. 22-25.

[31] *ICJ Reports* (1960) p. 6.

[32] See Schacter, "The Enforcement of International Judicial and Arbitral Decisions," *AJIL* 54 1960, p. 1.

[33] Janis , *op. cit.*, p. 27.

1935 is not contrary to international law was sufficient for Norway to forget monetary compensation. In the pleadings and during oral arguments, Norway had reserved the right to claim compensation for damages resulting from the British refusal to recognise Norway's sovereignty over territorial waters. By a letter of February 1st, 1952, the Agent for the Norwegian Government notified the Court that his Government did not intend to avail itself of this right.[34]

However, some insist that no matter how much such use of the Court as a Public Forum helps States, there are possible questions as to whether such non-compliance by recalcitrant States does not unduly injure the Court's already battered reputation. Janis thinks that: "It may be the prospects for the Court would be brighter if States turned to it only in those situations when it seemed likely that the Court's decision, if rendered can be effectively enforced." The question then is how can a State effectively make such an *a priori* decision? Indeed is it fair that States always have to make such *a priori* judgement before prosecution of their claims or before resorting to judicial settlement? The simple fact is that no litigant deserves the deplorable fate of gaining a judgement the execution of which depends on the will and caprice of the loser in the action. If *a priori* determination of the possibility of eventual compliance were to be the crucial issue, then all a difficult State (and there are many of them) would have to do is to immediately raise the spectre of a possible refusal to respect Court judgements at the beginning of a crisis in order to avoid pacific settlement via the judicial method. Such a state of things would ultimately be subversive of international peace and security.

The only discretion that should be allowed States in matters of submission to the authority of the ICJ is that which is already allowed (i.e., the primacy of State consent as basis for the Court's jurisdiction). Once the Court's judgement emanates from the due exercise of jurisdiction based upon consent of the parties given *ante, hoc, ad hoc, or post hoc*, it becomes imperative that compliance must follow unless the Court by some equivocation exempts a party from specific performance.[35]

---

[34] See International Court of Justice, *Background Note,vi, Collected Unofficial Summaries of Decisions Concerning the Law of the Sea*, 1996 - 1986, pp. 20 - 21.

[35] Such an instance was discussed with respect to the *Asylum Case*.

A possible formula to prevent further dilution of the Court's effectiveness by recalcitrant States is to give true meaning to the provision of Article 94 of the Charter. This can be done by interpreting that Article in such a way that the Security Council is always empowered to deal with cases of failure to perform obligations incumbent upon a State under a judgement, whether or not the victor complains. The mere fact that contentious litigation was pursued up to the end with no withdrawal of proceedings in order to resort to negotiated settlement (as States are allowed if not encouraged to do) is enough reason to protect successful litigants from non-execution of the Court's judgement. If need may be, Article 94 may among the many others targeted be amended for that purpose in the near future. The amended version may be to the effect that all judgements, orders and opinions of the ICJ must be communicated to the Security Council which would, if any State refuses to comply within reasonable time, make recommendations or decide upon measures to be taken to give effect to the judgement. The powers of the Security Council to act in this wise may be placed under the procedural matters referred to in Article 27 (2) of the Charter. Thus decision on these matters would require only the affirmative votes of any seven members of the Council. Through this means, the Court's judgement which usually takes a long time to appear will not be subject again to the veto power of the permanent members of the Security Council. In like manner, those States with the veto will not be in position to subject the Court's judgement to another trial in accordance with their own interests.

In the final analysis it should be stated that ultimately the effectiveness of the Court's orders , interim measures, decisions or judgements, lies in the overall political will of States to give effectiveness to the Court. They formed the Court and the Court continues to exist because they need it. Thus, any State which disobeys the Court's judgement may be inadvertently shooting itself in the leg. The rule of law on the international plane is better than the rule of force. Ineffectiveness of an ICJ judgment in any given case would only encourage more recalcitrance. This would translate into a further step towards the abyss of the rule of force, to the consequences of which any State may fall victim at any time.

Chapter 6

Advisory Jurisdiction of the World Court

Definition of Advisory Opinions

It is only proper that before we discuss the advisory regime of the ICJ at length in this chapter, we attempt at least a perfunctory definition of the term "Advisory Opinion." This task has not been made easy by the fact that the term "advisory opinion" has not been defined either in the League's Covenant or the Statute and Charter of the United Nations. However, advisory opinions have been considered by States as well as International Organisations to be authoritative statements of law. Ian Brownlie defines "advisory opinions" from a functional point of view. In his words, "The uses of the advisory jurisdiction are to assist the political organs in settling disputes and to provide authoritative guidance on points of law arising from the functions of organs and specialised agencies."[1]

The Court itself in the *Certain Expenses Case* defined advisory opinion by comparing it with the term "judgment." It noted that advisory opinions are not judgments but "merely opinions and merely advisory."[2] Thus it is clear that advisory opinions have slightly different judicial characteristics from judgments in the contentious jurisdiction of the Court. Indeed the main difference from the procedural point of view between the two is that in the advisory jurisdiction of the Court there are technically no "Parties" and no binding "decisions." The individual State's role in advisory cases is essentially that of supplying "information," *an amicus curiae* function so to speak.[3]

---

[1] Brownlie, *op. cit.*, p. 728.

[2] *ICJ Reports* (1962), p. 168. See also Dharma Prataap, *The Advisory Jurisdiction of the International Court* (Oxford: Clarendon Press, 1972) p. 230.

[3] Rosenne (1973) *op. cit.*, p. 81.

As Prataap bluntly puts it "... advisory opinions are not binding."[4] In our view then, an advisory opinion is an authoritative statement of law and fact, given by the ICJ in response to a request from an authorised body on specific issues.

It is worthy of note that the Court has assimilated its advisory procedure to its contentious procedure as closely as practicable.[5] This is because the origin of many requests lies in actual disputes, and the very nature of the judicial function has given a contentious aspect to advisory proceedings.[6]" Thus Article 68 of the Statute makes applicable to advisory procedure the provisions of the Statute relating to contentious cases "to the extent to which it recognises them to be applicable." Article 102 of the 1978 Rules contains a corresponding provision that enables the application of the contentious procedure.

The Development of the Advisory Procedure

The evolution of the advisory procedure of the ICJ is a gradual one which developed from the practice of the PCIJ which had been given advisory jurisdiction by Article 14 of the Covenant of the League of Nations. Before then, several international bodies were conferred with this advisory jurisdiction. And even after the inception and conferment of the function on the PCIJ by Article 14 of the League's Covenant, such international bodies still performed this function.[7] These bodies' advisory opinions were technical in character and at variance with that of the PCIJ. So when the Court started functioning, there was uncertainty about the nature and scope of its

---

[4] Prataap, Dharma, *The Advisory Jurisdiction of the International Court.* (Oxford: Clarendon Press, 1972) p.231.

[5] Sloan, "Advisory Jurisdiction of the International Court of Justice," *California Law Review,* 38 (1950), p. 848.

[6] Brownlie, *op. cit.*, p. 729.

[7] Such bodies included: International Bureau of the Universal postal Union (UPU). Under Article 15 of the UPU: Convention of 9th October, 1874, this provision has been maintained in the later Conventions of the Union; International South American Postal Bureau under Article 12 of the Montevideo Convention of 2 February, 1911; the International Commission for Air Navigation under Article 34 of the Aerial Navigation Convention of 13 October, 1919; and a host of others. For more details, see Hudson, *op. cit.*, p. 484-5 and Prataap, *op. cit.*, p. 1.

jurisdiction in this area as to whether it would be obligatory or discretionary, and there was the problem of what procedure should be followed. These and other problems were taken into consideration in drafting Article 14 of the League's Covenant. By giving this jurisdiction to the PCIJ it was intended to assist the Council and the Assembly "in the discharge of their duties of conciliating and reporting upon disputes submitted to them" by giving authoritative opinions on points of law arising out of these disputes, and upon which those bodies requested the Court's opinion. There were subsequent revisions of the Article until the UN Charter came into force having six organs with the ICJ as the "principal judicial organ."[8]

Thus, Article 96 of the UN Charter provides:

> 1. The General Assembly or Security Council may request the International Court of Justice to give an advisory opinion on any legal question.
>
> 2. Other organs of the UN and specialised agencies, which may at any time be so authorised by the General Assembly, may also request advisory opinions of the Court on legal questions arising within the scope of their activities.

The first paragraph of the Article reproduces the substance of the provisions relating to advisory opinion in Article 14 of the League Covenant. The Statute of the ICJ, which forms an integral part of the Charter, deals with advisory opinions under a separate Chapter 4. The provisions included therein are similar to those contained in the Statute of the PCIJ as revised in 1929. There are also a few variations which are of a minor character, except for a new paragraph which has been added to Article 65 and which now gives express recognition to the discretionary powers of the International Court of Justice in the exercise of its advisory jurisdiction. Article 65 of the Statute of the ICJ thus provides:

> 1. The Court may give an advisory opinion on any legal question at the request of whatever body that may be authorised by or in accordance with the Charter of the UN to make such a request.

---

[8] See Article 92 of the UN Charter.

2. Questions upon which the advisory opinion of the Court is asked shall be laid before the Court by the means of a written request, and accompanied by all documents likely to throw light upon the question.

Other proceeding Articles in Chapter 4 as regards the advisory procedure are Articles 66, 67 and 68. It suffices to mention here briefly that the drafting and expansion of the advisory provisions and the Statute are traceable as far back as the informal Inter-Allied Committee, which in 1943-4 considered proposals for the reorganisation of the PCIJ and offered proposals on advisory matters. The Committee's report, which included its proposals regarding advisory matters under a separate chapter 8 said that the advisory jurisdiction should be retained and ought to be enlarged for reasons it gave.[9]

There are various other proposals and suggestions such as that of the International Labour Organisation (ILO),[10] the Dumbarton Oaks Proposals (all of 1944), the UN Committee of Jurists (1945), the Washington Committee of Jurists and others all of which the San Francisco Conference considered before drafting what is now Chapter 4 of the Statute of the ICJ.[11] The provision as now put to use is still being tested.

This is in a nutshell the background of the advisory procedure provision as contained in Chapter 4. And with that background in mind, we shall how consider how and who institutes or sets the advisory proceeding machinery into operation.

The Jurisdiction of the Court in Advisory Cases

The question which arises after an organ or agency has complied with the provisions of Article 65 of the Statute of the Court is that of jurisdiction. The issue of advisory jurisdiction of the Court has raised a number of problems such as issues of propriety, the nature of questions and their involvement in political issues and the duty of

[9] "Report of the Informal Inter-Allied Committee on the Future of the PCIJ 10th Feb. 1944," *AJIL* 39, (1945,) pp. 20-3 referred to in Prataap, *op. cit.*, p. 235.

[10] Communication of the Acting Director of ILO to governments of member States of the UN, 13 April *ILO Official Bulletin* 26, No. 2 (Dec. 1st 1944), pp. 194-6.

[11] See *UN Year Book*, 1946-2, p. 17.

the Court as the principal judicial organ, which have not all been solved.

The Court has power to determine its own jurisdiction. And in doing this, the guiding rule has been, as contained in Article 68 of the Statute of the Court which provides: "In the exercise of its advisory functions the Court shall further be guided by the provisions of the present statute which apply in contentious cases to the extent to which it recognises them to be applicable." The Court applies the practice as in contentious cases by analogy to advisory proceedings.

In addition to its right to determine its own jurisdiction, the ICJ also has a duty in every request for an advisory opinion to assure itself of its jurisdiction. It must examine its jurisdiction *proprio motu*, even if no objection is raised by the "interested" organisations and States; that is, irrespective of whether any of the interested bodies does not object or whether one which might have objected has failed to appear. For instance in the *ILO Administrative Tribunal Case* none of the interested organisations and States objected to the jurisdiction of the Court. Yet, the Court commenced its opinion by examining its right to exercise jurisdiction in the case. The Court said:

> The Court will consider at the outset whether it should comply with the request for an opinion. The question put to the Court is a legal question. It arose within the scope of the activities of UNESCO when the Executive Board had to examine the measures to be taken as a result of the four judgments. The answer given to it will affect the result of the challenge raised by the Executive Board with regard to these judgments. In submitting the request for an opinion the Executive Board was seeking a clarification of the legal aspects of a matter with which it was dealing.[12]

Interested organs and specialised agencies can also raise objections to the Court's exercise of its jurisdiction in advisory proceedings as in contentious cases. For a long time such objections were not raised by States. The objections may border on whether the question requested was not within the scope of work of the body

[12] *ICJ Reports* (1956), p. 84.

requesting, but pertained exclusively to the field of activity of the body making the objection.[13]

Two recent applications to the Court bear out the use of the Court's discretion in such matters. On December 20, 1994 the International Court of Justice received a request from the UN Secretary-General, made by the UN General Assembly through Resolution 49/75k of December 15, 1994, for an urgent advisory opinion on the question: "Is the threat or use of nuclear weapons in any circumstance permitted under international law?"[14] First, the Court determined that it had juridiction to reply to the General Assembly's request. The Court recalled that Article 65 of the ICJ Statute requires the body requesting an advisory opinion to be "authorized by or in accordance with the Charter of the United Nations to make such a request." Some States contested the General Assembly's right to request this particular opinion, because they believed the issue to be unrelated to the Assembly's work, but the Court confirmed the Assembly's broad competence to engage the Court, deriving from the UN Charter and the Assembly's long-standing activities regarding disarmament and nuclear weapons.

The Court next satisfied itself that the request related to a legal question within the meaning of the ICJ Statute and the UN Charter, i.e., the compatibility of the threat or use of nuclear weapons with international law. In this connection, the Court noted that the political nature of any motives inspiring the request , the political implications of any advisory opinion , and any political aspects of the legal question are irrelevant to the establishment of its jurisdiction to give an opinion.

Having established its competence, the Court considered whether it should exercise its inherent discretionary power not to give an opinion. The Court reaffirmed it's consistent jurisprudence, according to which only "compelling reasons" can lead it to refuse a request for an advisory opinion. It held that the fact that the question put to it did not relate to a specific dispute, or that it was couched in abstract terms, was not a compelling reason to decline to give the

---

[13] See Rosenne, *loc. cit.*

[14] Legality of the Threat or Use of Nuclear Weapons, Advisory Opinion, 35 ILM 809, 814, paras. 10-13 (Advisory Opinion of July 8, 1996).

opinion requested. The Court also confirmed the exclusive right of the General Assembly to determine the usefulness of an opinion in the light of it's own needs.

One significant matter the Court did not address is the question of whether the General Assembly adopted its resolution by the majority required by Article 18 of the UN Charter. The Court failed to point out -- but the dissenting opinion of Judge Oda recites at length in part I and table I -- that the vote in the Assembly on the resolution was seventy-eight for, forty-three against and thirty-eight abstentions.[15] Excluding the abstentions (as required by the Rules of Procedure of the Assembly),[16] the affirmative vote constituted only 64 percent of those voting for or against, several votes short of the two-thirds majority required by the Charter, Article 18(2) for decisions on "important questions."

The first point to consider, therefore, is whether the decision to present this particular question before the Court was an important one within the meaning of the Charter provision. If it was not, then Article 18(3) required only a simple majority (i.e., more affirmative than negative votes), because the Assembly had never decided (as it could have under the latter provision) that questions of this type should require a two-thirds majority even if they were not "important." This issue could not have been examined by the Court before, because each of the previous twelve resolutions by which the Assembly had requested advisory opinions had been adopted by a two-thirds majority.[17]

---

[15] There were also 25 absentees (including China), plus the Federal Republic of Yugoslavia (which was excluded from participation in the work of the General Assembly by its Resolution 47/1 of September 22, 1992). Having recited these facts, Judge Oda does not, however, use them to challenge the jurisdiction of the Court to reply, but only to suggest that the Court should have used its discretionary power (examined in paras. 14-19 of the opinion) not to do so.

[16] See UN Doc.A/520/Rev.15, Rule 86 (1985), which defines the Charter term "members present and voting" (appearing in paragraphs 2 and 3 of Charter Article 18) to exclude those that abstain.

[17] The only two instances in which this matter was considered by the General Assembly itself were: (1) A ruling by the President, confirmed by the Assembly, that a two-thirds majority would be required for an amendment proposed by South Africa to request an advisory opinion on the competence of the Assembly to consider the question of Indians in South Africa, UN Doc.A/PV.52 (I/2), at 1058-60 (1946); however, the proposed amendment did not receive even a simple majority. (2) A

Thus is the very fact of presenting a question to the Court pursuant to Charter Article 96(I) an "important" one? Or does that characterisation depend on the nature of the question posed? If we adopt the latter approach as advanced by a certain writers[18] then it would not have been difficult to hold that a question relating to the threat or use of nuclear weapons falls under Article 18(2) of the Charter since it relates to "recommendations with respect to the maintenance of international peace and security." If the subject of the question is not considered as determinative, and the mere fact of the activation of the Article 96(1) procedure is seen as the crucial factor, then the answer is perhaps more difficult since this procedure is not explicitly listed (as six other procedures are) in the second sentence of Article 18(2). Text writers are divided on whether to consider that listing as exhaustive because of the general wording of the first sentence and the introductory clause of the second.[19]

The second point is whether, even if strict observance of Charter Article 18(2) would have required that the draft resolution in question should have been considered rejected for lack of a two-thirds majority, the fact that, at the meeting of the Assembly at which the resolution was declared adopted, inexplicably no representative objected[20] necessarily means that any deficit in the

---

ruling by the President that the resolution relating to the South West Africa (Status) query was a "procedural" one requiring only a simple majority: UN Doc.A/PV.269 (IV), at 536 (1949); however, Resolution 338 (IV) of December 6, 1949, was adopted by more than a two-thirds majority, *idem* at 537. Thus, neither ruling was one that could be examined by the Court. See Paul Szasz, Addendum: "The Vote In The General Assembly" *AJIL* 91 (1997) pp.133-134.

[18] Blaine Sloan favors this approach in *Advisory Jurisdiction of the International Court of Justice*, CAL.L. Rev. (1950) 38 830, 836-38, as does Shabtai Rosenne, The Law and Practice of the International Court (2d rev.ed. 1985) 663-64. Other commentators have examined the sparse practice and remained neutral: Kenneth James Deith, The Extent of the Advisory Jurisdiction of the International Court of Justice (1971) 44-47; Paul C. Szasz, *Enhancing the Advisory Competence of the World Court*, in The Future of the International Court of Justice 2, 499, 504-05 (Leo Gross ed., 1976); Hermann Mosler, analysis of Charter Article 96, in *The Charter of the United Nations*: A. Bruno Simma, ed., (1994) Commentary 1011, para. 12.

[19] Szasz, *op. cit.*, p.134 See also Rudiger Wolfrum, "Analysis of Charter Article 18," in The Charter of the United Nations, *ibid.*, p. 320, para. 10, and 322-23, para. 19 and the other commentators he cited.

[20] UN Doc.A/49/PV.90 (1994), at 35-36.

vote was thereby cured, as it were by passive consent. That the Court is not precluded from examining whether another principal organ's procedure in adopting a resolution presenting a query to the Court complied with the Charter is suggested by its examination of the circumstances of the adoption of Security Council Resolution 284 (1970) presenting a question concerning Namibia.[21]

In view of the Court's practice in considering *proprio motu* every Charter-related issue that bears on its jurisdiction to render an opinion some have wondered if it would not seem that the Court, in perhaps unseemly eagerness to address what is evidently one of the most interesting and important current legal questions, has failed to consider the possibly most serious objection to its jurisdiction to do so. We would not, however, characterize the eventual exercise of jurisdiction as unfortunate. If the Court refused to render an opinion based on the above argument such a decision would be to say the least based on tenuous grounds and would surely have drawn the ire of the majority of commentators and writers. However, we must admit that the Court has missed an opportunity to clarify, except by any implications of its inaction, a significant, though only procedural, issue that is quite likely to recur in connection with future proposals to seek its advice as to other politically controversial legal questions.

In the determination of its jurisdiction in advisory matters the ICJ has in recent times shown it will in the case of specialised agencies adopt a strict interpretation of the purposes and functions of the requesting specialised agency in order to ensure that there is a genuine and sufficient connection between the request and those functions or purposes. Thus in the *Legality of the Use by a State of Nuclear Weapons In Armed Conflict* the Court ruled that it was unable to render the advisory opinion requested by the World Health Assembly because the request submitted by the WHO did not relate to a question arising within the scope of the activities of that

---

[21] Legal Consequences for States of the continued presence of South Africa in Namibia (South West Africa) notwithstanding Security Council resolution 276 (1970), 1971 *ICJ Reports* 16, 21-23, paras. 20-26 (June 21).

organisation as required by Article 96, paragraph 2 of the UN Charter.[22]

The Court's observation was that none of the twenty-two functions listed in Article 2 of the WHO Constitution expressly refers to the legality of any activity hazardous to health, or depends upon the legality of the situations in which that organisation must act. Article 2 states that the WHO discharges its functions "to achieve its objective," which Article 1 defines as "the attainment by all peoples of the highest possible level of health." According to the Court, the functions listed in Article 2 authorise the WHO to deal with the effects on health of the use of nuclear weapons, or any other hazardous activity, and to take preventive measures that are aimed at protecting the health of populations in the event such weapons are used or such activities engaged in.

Having found the request to relate not to the effects of the use of nuclear weapons on health, but rather, to the legality of the use of such weapons in view of their health and environmental effects, the Court held that there was an insufficient connection between the request and the functions of the WHO to support the Court's jurisdiction. In the Court's view, "the lègality or illegality of the use of nuclear weapons in no way determines the specific measures, regarding health or otherwise (studies, plans, procedures, etc.), which could be necessary in order to seek to prevent or cure some of their effects." It can only be hoped that the emerging doctrine of sufficient connection will not be inadvertently used as a tool to stifle the exercise of the right of specialised agencies to approach the Court for advisory opinions.

The last point to consider is the possibility of compulsory jurisdiction by means of advisory opinions. It would seem incongruous at first to refer to compulsory jurisdiction in connection

---

[22] The question put to the Court is: In view of the health and environmental effects would the use of nuclear weapons by a State in war or other conflict be a breach of its obligations under International Law including the WHO Constitution. A letter from the Director-General of the World Health Organisation officially communicating to the Court the decision taken by the World Health Assembly in its Resolution WHA46.40 of May14, 1993, was received in the Court's Registry on 3 September 1993.Resolution WHA46. 40 was adopted by a vote of 73-40, with 10 absentations. Forty-one States were absent from the voting.

with advisory opinions. However, authors such as Hudson, Goodrich and Hambro have attempted to make the connection. Hambro, for instance, submits that this term (i.e., compulsory jurisdiction) is properly used whenever there is an obligation to request an advisory opinion and provided, further, that the advisory opinion is binding on the parties. While it might seem strange to request an advisory opinion and to decide in advance that such an opinion shall be accepted as binding, such a procedure may nevertheless be very useful.[23]

Such a stipulation can be found in the constitution of the International Labour Organisation (Article 37, paragraph 2) which states: "Any applicable judgment or advisory opinion of the International Court of Justice shall be binding upon any tribunal established in virtue of this paragraph."[24] In the Convention on Immunities and Privileges of the United Nations (Section 30) it is stated clearly that "the opinion given by the Court shall be accepted as decisive by the parties."[25] Another intriguing example is that contained in the Charter of the International Trade Organisation (Articles, 9(2) and (5)):

> Any decision of the Conference under this Charter shall, at the instance of any member whose interest are prejudiced by the decision, be subject to review by the International Court of Justice by means of a request, in appropriate form, for an advisory opinion pursuant to the Statute of the Court.
>
> The Organisation shall consider itself bound by the opinion of the Court on any question referred by it to the Court. In so far as it does not accord with the opinion of the Court, the decision in question shall be modified.[26]

The Legal Basis of the Court's Advisory Jurisdiction

In the days of the PCIJ there was a controversy as to the Court's advisory jurisdiction because the original Statute of the Permanent Court did not expressly provide for the advisory function of the

[23] Hambro, "On Compulsory Jurisdiction and Advisory Opinions" in BYIL, p. 155.
[24] See *ICJ Yearbook*, (1946-7), p. 202.
[25] *Ibid.*, p. 229.
[26] See Hambro, *loc. cit.*, for more details on this novel idea.

Court. It was posited by some that Article 1 of the Covenant had by implication, incorporated the last sentence of Article 14 of the Statute which provides for the giving of advisory opinions by the Court. This position was also that of the Court as reflected in its pronouncement on the *Case Concerning Certain German Interests in Polish Upper Silesia.*[27] Whereas others such as Professor Wright and Judge Moors argued that the fact that the Statute was separate from the Covenant and was accepted by States independently of their association with the League of Nations, makes it imperative that the advisory jurisdiction of the Court must be located within the four corners of the Statute.[28]

Fortunately, in the case of the UN and its International Court the case is much clearer. Apart from the Statute being made an integral part of the Charter in 1945, both Article 96 of the Charter and Article 65 of the Statute of the Charter designate specifically the advisory function of the Court. Article 96 of the Charter designates those bodies within the UN which might request advisory opinions. The first paragraph in Article 65 of the Court's Statute empowers the Court to give advisory opinions at the request of anybody authorised by, or in accordance with, the Charter to make such a request.

These provisions are complementing and regulate the entire advisory regime of the Court. The Court can under Article 65 of the Statute give opinions to bodies which have been authorised under Article 96 to request such opinions. Prataap contends that, even if this express provision in Article 65 were not there, jurisdiction is implied in Article 96 of the Charter. He also notes that the statement made before Committee IV/I during drafting of the Statute that while the Statute of the Court was a part of the Charter, the Charter was not a part of Statute does not justify the repetition in the Statute of a provision laid down in the Charter, because the advisory opinions have to be given to the organs of the United Nations and not to the States.[29]

This reasoning undoubtedly suits those who claim that the PCIJ's Advisory Jurisdiction can be implied from its Covenant, though not

---

[27] Prataap, *op. cit.*, p. 115.
[28] See Wright "The Mosul Dispute," *AJIL*, 20, n. 28(1926), p. 459.
[29] *Op. cit.*, pp. 116-7.

expressly found in the Statute. In as much as this reasoning may be true, it has been noted that in the absence of an express provision relating to advisory cases, it is difficult to see how jurisdiction would have been exercised under Article 30 of the Statute.[30] The Court itself has had cause to state that its power to give opinions is derived from Article 65 of the Statute.[31]

Seising the Court (Advisory Opinions)

There happens to be a divergence of views by various writers on the nature of authority to request advisory opinions. The late Judge Hudson in his work on the PCIJ used the expression "power" to describe the authority of the body that seeks to request an opinion of the Court.[32] Brownlie also speaks in terms of "power" to request advisory opinions.[33] In a later work by Hudson he employed the word "capacity."[34] On Rosenne's part: "The right to request advisory opinions should be retained by organs of international organisations."[35] He had explained in an earlier work that since the term "right" implies a corresponding duty on the Court's part to give an answer to the request, it is under a duty to give an answer to such a request though not necessarily to give the opinion requested.[36] Prataap on his own part disagrees, submiting that it would appear that if a body has a right to request an opinion, then the Court is bound to give it just as it is bound to give judgment in a contentious case, but he contends that the Court is not bound to give an opinion because under Article 65 of the Statute, the Court has discretion in the matter and thus may refuse to give an advisory opinion in certain

---

[30] *Ibid.*, p. 117.

[31] *Expenses Case*, ICJ Reports (1962), p. 155. But in earlier cases the Court appeared to have regarded its advisory jurisdiction as being derived from Article 96 of the Charter and Article 65 of the Statute. See *Admissions Case*, ICJ Reports (1947-8, p. 61 *and Competence of the General Assembly Case*, ICJ Reports (1950), p. 6.

[32] M. O. Hudson, *The Permanent Court of International Justice, 1920-1942* (New York, 1943), p. 84.

[33] Brownlie, *op. cit.*, p. 728.

[34] M. O. Hudson, "The Effect of Advisory Opinions of the World Court." AJIL, 4 (1948) p. 631.

[35] Rosenne (1973), *op. cit.*, p. 81.

[36] Rosenne, *The International Court of Justice* (Leyden, 1957) pp. 443, 464.

circumstances.[37] The construction of Article 65 actually agrees with this reasoning in that it reads: "The Court may give an advisory opinion..." Thus he further submits that authorisation given to a body only enables the body to submit questions of its discretion to the Court. The body on its own part is also not bound to make any request at all, but can do so if it so desires; and the Court is bound to entertain the request, but may refuse to render opinions at its discretion. He concludes his arguments by suggesting that the word "competence" might as well be used to designate this capacity of the requesting organ and perhaps it would be better employed in this context, rather than to describe the Court's jurisdiction to entertain a request and give an opinion.

A correct reading of Article 65 will show that there are five essential criteria which must be satisfied to elicit an advisory opinion from the ICJ. They are:

1. The questions must be legal questions;
2. They must be requested by duly authorised bodies;
3. They must be put to the Court by way of a written request;
4. The request must contain an exact statement of the question;
5. The request must be accompanied by all documents likely to throw light upon the question.

It will be only proper for us to examine one after the other some of these criteria in an effort to see how advisory proceedings are instituted.

Legal Questions

A request for an advisory opinion from the Court must have as its subject matter a legal question; and moreover be within the terms of the authority granted to the body making such request. The question then is -- what is a legal question? Vischer says it is "any question that can be answered in terms of law." To Lissitzyn, a legal question must be capable of being adequately answered by the application of judicial techniques within the existing framework of law.[38] It would seem then that it belongs in the first instance to the requesting organ,

---

[37] Prataap, *op. cit.*, p. 230.

[38] Lissitzyn, "The International Court of Justice" *op. cit.*, p. 30, in Prataap, *ibid.*

to determine if its request is legal and within its competence. Thus one would agree with Elias who wrote:

> It should be noted that the point about the point being legal is important in contrast to its being political in that if the question were predominantly political the Court should normally refuse the request. Where however the question is legal but also involves a factual element or basis the request may be answered by the Court after disentangling its really legal kernel.[39]

In the first and second Admissions Cases, the Court, without attempting to define what a legal question consisted of, indicated that questions of interpretation were necessarily and always legal questions, irrespective of the motives behind the request in interpretation: "To determine the meaning of a treaty provision... is a problem of interpretation and consequently a legal question." Again it was said that: "The Court cannot attribute a political character to a request which, framed in abstract terms, invites it to undertake an essentially judicial task, the interpretation of a treaty provision. It is not concerned with the motives which may have inspired this request..."[40]

In the *Legal Consequences for States of the Continued Presence of South Africa in Namibia South West Africa, notwithstanding Security Council Resolution 276 (1970)* the Court observed:

> In the view of the Court, the contingency that there may be factual issues underlying the question posed does not alter its character as a 'legal question' as envisaged in Art. 96 of the Charter. The reference in this provision to legal question cannot be interpreted as opposing legal to factual issues. Normally to enable a court to pronounce on legal questions, it must also be acquainted with, take into account and if necessary make findings as to the relevant factual issues. The limitation of the powers of the Court contended for by the Government of South Africa has no basis in the Charter or the Statute.[41]

It follows from these statements that a treaty interpretation question should be considered a legal one irrespective of the fact that the consequences which its determination produces may lie in the political field. A contrary position by the Court would definitely limit its role as a peace-maker and guardian of legal rights.

---

[39] Elias, *op. cit.*, p. 80.

[40] Advisory Opinion, *ICJ Reports*, (1947-48), p. 61.

[41] *ICJ Reports*, (1971), p. 27 para. 46.

Authorised Bodies to Request Advisory Opinions

A commendable innovation under the Charter of the UN of advisory practice of international courts is that contrary to what obtained during the League's period, a public international organisation can now fo, ward a matter straight to the Court and does not have to pass through the relevant member State. Under the League only the Assembly and the League's Council could request opinions. In any case only the Council made use of this facility.

By virtue of Article 96 of the Charter both the General Assembly and the Security Council have the widest power to make a request subject only to the limitation of its being a "legal opinion." In a converse situation in relation to the League, it is mainly the General Assembly of the UN and not the Council that has availed itself of the advisory competence of the Court. This we may posit is due to the emergence of many new States which are continually opposed to certain existing practices and customs of the United Nations especially as related to particular aspects of its work.

Apart from these principal organs of the UN, paragraph 2 of Article 96 provides that: "Other organs of the United Nations and specialized agencies which may at any time be so authorised by the General Assembly, may also request advisory opinons of the Court on legal questions arising within the scope of their activities."

The following UN organs and agencies are at present authorized to request advisory opinions:

General Assembly,

Security Council,

Economic and Social Council,

Trusteeship Council,

Interim Committee of the General Assembly,

Committee on Applications for Review cf Administrative Tribunal Judgements,

International Labour Organisation,

Food and Agriculture Organization of the United Nations,

United Nations Educational Scientific Cultural Organisation,

World Health Organisation,

International Bank for Reconstruction and Development,

International Finance Corporation,

International Development Association,
International Monetary Fund,
International Civil Aviation Organisation,
International Telecommunication Union,
International Fund for Agricultural Development,
World Meteorological Organisation,
International Maritime Organisation,
World Intellectual Property Organisation,
United Nations Industrial Development Organisation,
International Atomic Energy Agency.

Thus on the whole some twenty-two organs and agencies of the UN are entitled to request the Court for an opinion on a legal question. Although four organs of the UN have by resolution been authorised to request advisory opinions of the Court with respect to "legal questions arising within the scope of their activities" nevertheless only one has so far exercised this power. Out of the specialised agencies or entities which have been authorised to seek Advisory Opinions only four have so far done so; these are UNESCO, IMO (formerly IMCO), the WHO and the Committee on the Applications for Review of Administrative Tribunal Judgments (for judgments rendered before 1 January 1996). The constitutive instruments and the conventions or agreements concluded by these agencies or under their auspices, also confer advisory jurisdiction on the Court in relation to their interpretation or implementation or even to the interpretation of the Charter of the UN.

Requests Must be Written

A request for an opinion usually gives rise to written proceedings. This is the third element of Article 65 of the Charter. This then is followed by oral proceedings (Statute, Article 66; Rules, Articles 104 and 105). The position under the League Covenant was the same as that of the Charter of the UN except that under the latter the written statement need not be signed. The request is in practice normally embodied in a formal letter from the Secretary-General (as in the case of a letter originating from the Assembly) to the registrar of the Court, accompanied by a copy of the resolution of the organ or agency in English and French languages certified by the appropriate official of the Legal Department of the Secretariat. This comes usually in form of a special letter.

Other Conditions to Fulfill

The requirements remain same as under the League of Nations' Covenant. Two important prerequisites must be fulfilled. First, the Director or Secretary-General of the international organisation must forward either simultaneously with the request or as soon as possible thereafter, all documents that are likely to throw light upon the question asked. The second prerequisite is that in the case of the Security Council or the General Assembly, the Secretary-General may submit written and/or oral statements within the period fixed by the Court or by the Rules of Court. Heads of other bodies may be requested to supply supplementary documents or information but they might not respond. Thus the Director-General of UNESCO complied but not the Secretary-General of the IMCO.[42] Though it is categorically stated in Article 65(2) of the Statute that the requests for opinions must always contain an exact statement of the question, in practice the Court has always had to define the exact scope of the question as a necessary preliminary to carrying out the judicial function of answering the request put before it.[43]

The reason that the Court begins with the attempt to define the exact scope of the question and the reason why Article 65(2) is so framed can be understood as measures that ensure that the real issues raised are understood and addressed.

The Advisory Procedure

The advisory proceedure is basically regulated by Articles 66-69 of the Statute of the Court. The Articles leave to the Court the power to appreciate the extent to which the provisions relating to the contentious proceedings are applicable in advisory cases. Article 68 which admits by analogy the application of rules of contentious procedure provides that "in exercise of its advisory functions the Court shall further be guided by the provisions of the Statute which

---

[42] *Ibid.*, p. 83
[43] *Ibid.*

apply in contentious cases to the extent to which it recognises them to be applicable."

Having said this, what then is the procedure on receipt of a request for an advisory opinion? On receipt of a request for an advisory opinion, the Court's Registry has to take the following measures in order to prepare the case for proceeding:

1. Notification of the Request is the first step. The registrar has to notify certain States and international organisations of its receipt of the request. This is usually done by circulating a certified copy of the request. The proceedure is the same as Article 73 of the PCIJ. The requirement of notice is to accord opportunity to States and organisations to present their views to the Court on the question so requested and also enables the Court to obtain all relevant information. Article 66(2) in particular states:

   > The Registrar shall also by means of a special and direct communication, notify any state entitled to appear before the court or international organisation considered by the Court, or, as likely to be able to furnish information on the question, that the court will be prepared to receive, within a time limit to be fixed by the President, written statements, or to hear, at a public sitting to be held for the purpose, oral statement relating to the question.

   The determination of the States and organisation for notification by special and direct communication according to this Article is done by the President without any consultations by an order which also fixes the time limits within which written statements may be filed or oral arguments presented.

   The Request is entered into the General list. This is done at the same time as the sending of notice by the Registrar. A folio is opened in the General List and is given a title.

3. Priority of Hearing: The purpose of a General List is to prevent unjustified preference being given to one case over another in regard to hearing. The order of hearing is however subject to certain priorities. Prataap noted rightly that generally speaking advisory proceedings are given priority over contentious proceedings because they are shorter, not controlled by "parties" as in contentious proceedings and are less susceptible to delays. Sometimes the resolution may ask the Court to treat the request "as a matter of urgency" or give the opinion in time to enable the

requesting body to take a decision on the matter at a particular session, or to examine the questions submitted if possible in an extraordinary session.[44]

There are strictly speaking no Parties in advisory proceedings as in contentious proceedings. Access to the Court by private persons in advisory proceedings refers to the capacity to furnish information and not request advisory opinions. Thus, States and organisations have that capacity. Where the advisory opinion is with respect to a dispute between two or more States, the States will not only be interested in submitting information but will be concerned with the opinion as it will directly affect their rights and interests. In this regard we opine that States may be considered as Parties in a sense.

The same rule applies to international organisations. In addition to organisations which have been authorised to request advisory opinions, other organisations may also present information on questions raised by a request. For instance, the Organisation of American States was invited by the Court to present information in the Reservations case. However, although they may submit information, international organisations can never be "Parties" in advisory proceedings in the sense in which States can be when a question is recognised by the Court to be actually pending between them.

The expression "international organisation" has never been defined anywhere in the Charter or Statute; the practice of the Court has been inconclusive. In *the Southwest Africa (Status) Case*, the Court allowed the International League for the Rights of Man to submit a written statement. But later, in the *UN Administrative Tribunal Case*, the same Court refused the same permission to the Federation of International Civil Servants' Association on the grounds that the Court was not authorised to receive statements from a body such as the Federation. One may wonder why the Court displays this inconsistency. (However, this is not to prejudice the competence of the Court to determine its own competence.)

Individuals have no access to the Court in an advisory proceeding as is the case in contentious proceedings. They cannot

[44] Prataap, *op. cit.*, p. 173.

give information and their representatives cannot hold a watching brief or receive copies of pleadings. Their position is likened to that of non-governmental international organisations.[45]

Even in the *UN Administrative Tribunal Case*, following the Court's refusal to allow the Federation of International Civil Servants' Association to place before the Court its views on the question in the request, a firm of conveyers sought permission from the Court to submit a written memorandum and to participate in the oral arguments since its clients were directly affected by the judgment of the Tribunal which assesses their conduct and awards them compensation for breach of contract and it was the finality of these judgments which was the subject of the proceedings before the Court.

But the Registrar's reply stated that the Court would be bound by the limitations set forth in Article 66(2) of the Statute and "would therefore not be authorised to request or receive written or oral statements either from your clients or on their behalf from the counsel who represented them before the Administrative Tribunal."[46] On the whole, we submit that Article 66(2) of the Statute is too narrow and is a flagrant violation of the principle of *audiatur et altera pars* as it is tantamount to preventing individuals and certain organisations from having a say on matters which affect them directly.[47] The Article should be reframed to accommodate at least counsel for individuals and organisations that appear to have sufficient interest in the matter before it.

The Secretary-General is also not a party in advisory proceedings even though he has certain functions to perform. On the

---

[45] On this issue it might be pertinent to mention briefly Prataap's view on the relationship between the contentious and advisory procedures: "However, although the advisory is largely assimilated to contentious procedure, the former maintains a flexibility not obtaining under the latter. Otherwise it would scarcely have been possible in the ILO Administrative Tribunal Case for the Court to adopt a procedure which allowed the contentions of the staff members of UNESCO to be brought before it without compromising the judicial character of the proceedings," See Prataap, *Ibid.*, p. 174.

[46] *Ibid.*

[47] *Ibid.*

other hand, representatives of States are allowed to appear as Agents.[48]

Composition of the Court for Advisory Proceedings

As in contentious cases, advisory proceedings take place before the full Court. This proceedure is buttressed by Article 25 of the Statute of the Court which thus provides:

> 1. "The full court shall sit except when it is expressly provided otherwise in the present Statute.
>
> 2. Subject to the condition that the number of judges available to constitute the Court is not thereby reduced below eleven, the rules of the Court may provide for allowing one or more judges, according to circumstances and in relation, to be dispensed from sitting.
>
> 3. A quorum of nine judges shall suffice to constitute the court."

The Statute does not specify what constitutes "full Court."[49] Where the question before the Court relates to a dispute, parties are at liberty to appoint a judge *ad hoc* where they do not have a regular judges of their own nationality. When the Court is sitting, in accordance with Article 25 of the Statute of the Court as in contentious Cases, it proceeds with the conduct of advisory proceedings. Generally speaking, there is no fundamental difference between the conduct of advisory proceedings and that of contentious matters. The Court proceeds with an examination of the written statements already submitted to it by the organisations and States concerned. The Court may then follow with an oral hearing or statements whose purpose is to have supplementary verbal explanations on essential points in the written statements and matters which may appear superfluous to the decision of the Court. The Court may decide to dispense with oral proceedings as it did in the *ILO Administrative Tribunal Case*. But if it decides to hear oral evidence, it becomes incumbent on the registrar to fix and communicate the date of the hearing to the States and organisations that may be interested. In fixing the hearing date, consideration is

---

[48] *Ibid.*
[49] *Ibid.*

given to convenience and interests of the organisations concerned. Sitting of the Court is public.[50]

In the course of oral hearings, the Court may put questions to agents, counsel and experts or representatives of organisations. Documents could be tendered if they had not been submitted earlier in the course of the hearing. In some cases interested States could seek the production of documents or evidence from the opposing State. For instance, in the *Polish War Vessels in Danzig Case*, the documents cited by the Polish Government during oral proceedings were communicated to the Agent for Danzig on his request. On the other hand, in the *Danube Commission Case* the Court refused permission to the Rumanian representative to read from a document because it had not "been placed before the court by, or with the consent of, the competent authority."[51] Incidently, the British representative had objected to its citation on the ground of it being a confidential document.

The closure of the proceedings is regulated by Article 54(1) of the Statute of Court which provides: "When, subject to the control of the Court, the Agents, counsel and advocate have completed their representation of the case, the President shall declare the hearing closed."

This provision is applicable by analogy to the advisory proceedings and normally terminates the proceedings after the oral hearing has been heard, subject to the right of the Court to call upon the parties to furnish any additional information which might subsequently be required.[52]

The Reception of the Opinion

As has been pointed out earlier, there is no legal obligation either on the part of the organisation requesting the opinion or of the States which may be concerned to accept and give effect to the opinion in practice. Opinions may be favourably received or may be disregarded. In considering the reception of the opinion, regard must be given to opinions directly requested by the Assembly or Council

[50] *Ibid.*, p. 115.
[51] Hudson, *Permanent Court of International Justice, 1920-42, op. cit.*, pp. 355-6.
[52] For a fuller account of the proceedings, see Chapter 5 of this work.

to “take note” of the opinion and to direct the Secretary-General to communicate it to the administrative head of the body which has solicited it, or simply to direct the Secretary-General to communicate it to the organisation concerned.

As regards the opinions of the ICJ, we note with satisfaction that they have been accepted by the body which requested them, namely by General Assembly and other specialised agencies such as ILO, UNESCO and IMCO. The acceptance of the opinion can be seen in the resolutions of these bodies. For instance, in accepting the opinion in the *Admissions Case*, the General Assembly in its resolution recommended that each member of the Security Council and General Assembly should act in accordance with the opinion. Further in the same resolution, the General Assembly "noted" the opinion and asked the Security Council to reconsider the previous applications for membership. In its resolution at the completion of the *Reparation Case*, the Assembly, "having regard to" the opinion, authorised the Secretary-General to bring international proceedings against any State with a view to receiving reparation for damage to the United Nations or to the individual in the service of the organisation. Thus, we agree with Renouff when he concludes that these resolutions are cases of implied acceptance of the Advisory Opinions.[53]

In the *ILÒ Administrative Tribunal Case*, the Executive Board of UNESCO took note of the opinion and authorised the Director-General to pay the sum awarded by the tribunal.

The view of the member States concerning the authority of the opinions has not been one of uncritical acceptance. The erstwhile Soviet Union and other Communist countries have at various times, for instance, not only objected to requests for advisory opinions, but after the opinions, have been given, have asserted either that the Court was not competent to give the opinion or that the opinion should be ignored, or that it was contrary to the Charter. On the other hand, for instance, delegates of other countries in the *Competence of the General Assembly Case for the Admission of a State to the United Nations*, stated after the opinion was rendered that they would accept "unreservedly" the advisory opinions of the Court. Sir

---

[53] Renouff, "Reception of Advisory Opinions by the General Assembly of the United Nations," *Canadian Bar Review*, 28 (1950) pp. 424-5.

G. Fitzmaurice, the United Kingdom delegate, stated that it could not be argued that the opinion of the Court was wrong from the legal standpoint or that the Assembly did not argue with the Court in its finding, because the Assembly could only accept or reject the opinion. In reality the opinions have been criticised and their adoption by the General Assembly has been opposed not only by representatives of communist countries, but sometimes also by other States when these opinions have not been in tune with States' own views on the question.

With regard to the action of the State concerned, there have been some opinions of the ICJ in respect of which States concerned were expected to take action individually. In five such cases they have opposed the resolutions requesting the opinion, consequently, they have refused to implement them. In the *Peace Treaties Case* the three States -- Bulgaria, Hungary, and Rumania -- which were mainly concerned, declared in advance that they would not be bound by the opinion, and continued to maintain the same attitude even after its delivery.[54] Rumania contended that the Court in assuming jurisdiction in the case had acted in violation of international law because it had taken upon itself the right to express an opinion on the question, without the Romanian Government's consent. A similar view was expressed by Bulgaria and Hungary.[55]

Also on the South Africa question, the South African government had refused to accept the opinions and had consistently maintained the position that the mandate over the territory had lapsed; that the United Nations had no Jurisdiction over the former mandated territory; that South Africa was under no obligation to submit information under Article 73(e) of the Charter; and that since the mandate for the territory had been created by the Allied and Associated Powers of the first World War, South Africa would therefore only negotiate a settlement with the remaining principal Allied and Associated Powers.[56]

---

[54] Prataap, *op. cit.*, p. 245.

[55] Hudson, "The Twenty-ninth year of the World Court," *op. cit.*, p. 10.

[56] Prataap, *loc. cit.*

The Effect of Advisory Opinions

We agree with Prataap in noting that the primary and immediate effect of an advisory opinion lies in the resolution of the difficulty that leads to the request for it. It is true that there are also other long-range effects which necessarily flow from its authoritative character. The opinions produce effects upon the Court as a means of developing international law.[57]

We disagree, however, with Prataap, in his observation that the effect of the opinions given by the present Court on the solution of political issues has been small. For instance, he wrote that the first opinions on the *Admissions Case* had no influence on the final solution of the problem. Since it involved disapproval of the attitude of the Soviet Union which denied that the Court was entitled to subordinate the admission of certain States to the condition of the simultaneous admission of certain other States it did not have the slightest chance of being adopted and put into effect by the Security Council.[58] Initially, the opinion was intended to obtain a ruling on the conditions under provisions of the Charter regarding admission of new members to the organisation. But in the end a "package deal" was negotiated, and by a resolution of December 14, 1953, sixteen new numbers were admitted. The Court said the provisions in Article 4 were exhaustive, and if a member State made its consent to the admission of a new State dependent on the admission of others, it would be introducing extraneous conditions in violation of the Charter provision. For these reasons, some text writers believe the opinion contributed little towards resolving the political problem of the admission of new members because the problem "did not originate in the explanations given for the negative vote, but in the underlying political situation in which these votes were merely an expression."[59] In our view, no matter how inadequate the Court's advisory work may seem, it has helped to discipline the activities of the political organs of the UN.

In a second opinion rendered by the Court, i.e the *Reparations Case,* the Court's work was clearly effective because the Secretary-

[57] Prataap, *op. cit.*, p. 246.
[58] *Ibid.*, p. 250.
[59] *Ibid.*, p. 250.

General was successful in recovering the United Nations claim for pecuniary reparation from the Government of Israel. Although It has been argued that Israel at that time was in a difficult position, and that it paid the reparation because it could not have afforded to be recalcitrant to resolutions of the organisation to which it owed its existence. Other States concerned did not pay, contesting the basis for the calculation for damages.[60]

The third opinion, on the competence of the General Assembly, could not be expected to produce any positive effect because it confined itself to the negative statement that the Assembly cannot admit a member without a positive recommendation by the Security Council. But it was effective in stopping extravagant claims which were being put forward in the General Assembly before the ICJ delivered its opinion and which did not find any support therein.[61]

Other effects of advisory opinions lie in their use as precedents. However, the Court has complete discretion not to so use them. The Court in several instances has demonstrated that it follows the law it laid down in earlier judgments. It cites them as precedent in subsequent cases, both advisory and contentious, making no difference for this purpose between advisory opinions and judgments. Another aspect of the Court's opinions can be found in their acceptance as "law making," which is clearly not an intention of the Court. As Prataap rightly notes, "...in applying general rules of law to the particular cases, it was inevitable that the Court should perform a law making function."[62]

It is interesting to observe the positive effects which the Court's opinion in the recent case of *Legality of the Threat or Use of Nuclear Weapons* is generating in the field of nuclear disarmament. Since the begining of the 1990s, there has been a lot of movement without motion on the nuclear disarmament front. By July 1996 the epoch making opinion was delivered to the effect that nuclear powers had an obligation to achieve nuclear disarmament under the provisions of Article VI of the Nuclear Proliferation Treaty (NPT). In the light of this by September of the same year it became possible for the UN to

---

[60] *Ibid.*, p. 251.
[61] *Ibid.*
[62] *Ibid.*

adopt the Comprehensive Test Ban Treaty. By January 1997 a total of 140 States had signed it. The immediate effect of these development is a widening gap between majority of the non-nuclear States, particularly the developing States, and the nuclear powers (except China) and their allies.

The "divergencies" were clearly brought to the fore in the sharp reactions generated by a new resolution offered by Malaysia and co-sponsored by 45 other States. The resolution was rooted in the World Court's unanimous advisory opinion that the "legal import" of Article VI of the NPT was that the nuclear powers had incurred "an obligation to achieve a precise result--nuclear disarmament in all its aspects--by adopting a particular course of conduct, namely the pursuit of negotiation on the matter in good faith."

After noting key provisions of Article VI of the NPT and language from the World Court opinion, the Malaysian resolution called "upon all States to fulfil that obligation immediately by commencing multilateral negotiations in 1997 leading to an early conclusion of a nuclear weapons convention prohibiting the development, production, testing, deployment, stockpiling, transfer, threat or use of nuclear weapons, and providing for their elimination."

Although the resolution avoided mentioning a time limit for the conclusion of the convention or for the elimination of the nuclear weapons (time limits are anathema to four of the declared nuclear powers -- the United States, Britain, France, and Russia) it nevertheless provoked what appeared to be carefully orchestrated criticism. In the end, the vote for the resolution was 94 in favour, 22 opposed, with 29 abstentions. Those who abstained or voted "no" asserted that the resolution quoted only parts of Article VI and portions of the Court's opinion. Whereas Article VI commits signatories to working toward "general and complete disarmament" as well as toward nuclear disarmament, the Malaysian resolution did not mention the former. That omission, said the United States, distorted the meaning of Article VI. The United States also said the resolution was "an attempt to turn the Court's advisory opinion into a legal edict that requires immediate negotiations and their rapid conclusion in a multilateral forum... A multilateral negotiating forum is simply not suited to the complexities of the measures to reduce nuclear weapons."

France insisted that the resolution gave a "tendentious and questionable interpretation of the advisory opinion and seeks to emphasise one specific aspect of an advisory opinion that has many facets that we believe cannot be separated and disassociated." Britain on its part deplored the "politicisation of the Court's opinion and thus of the Court itself. In a similar vein Russia's position was that the resolution was "an inaccurate and incomplete reflection" of the Court's opinion and it used "a selective and politicised approach." Of the declared nuclear powers, only China supported the Malaysian resolution, saying that its "thrust is basically consistent with China's position on nuclear disarmament."

On the other hand non-nuclear nations (including several "Western" States) that supported the Malaysian resolution took the position that its language was consistent with the intent of Article VI. The Chilean response was:

> It is difficult to understand, how or why the reference to undertake and conclude in good faith negotiations on all aspects of nuclear disarmament can be considered selective. This is in obvious agreement with the note sent by Malaysia to all member States in an effort to rebut negative comments about the resolution after the vote in the First Committee but before consideration of the resolution by the General Assembly, stating: The resolution is intended to be focused and straightforward, reflecting the thrust of the unanimous conclusion rendered by the World Court...[63]

The General Assembly voted on the resolution: 115 in favour, 22 against, with 32 abstentions. It therefore becomes evident that irrespective of the Court's opinion the attitude of the nuclear powers might remain what it has been for years. While China supports, at least rhetorically, multilateral negotiations leading to total nuclear

[63] This note further stated "Bilateral negotiations relate only to the reduction of numbers of nuclear weapons to a certain ceiling and not on their elimination or on changing existing policies to threaten or use them. The Court's conclusion that there is an obligation to negotiate nuclear disarmament made no link between such an obligation and general and complete disarmament. Nor does the NPT make a direct link; it merely states that there is an obligation to do both. See William Epstein, "Nuclear Powers Take a Hard Line," *Bulletin of Atomic Scientists,* Vol. 53, Issue [illegible], March-April 1997, p.13-14.

disarmament, the United States, Britain, France, and Russia have insisted that negotiations to rid the world of nuclear weapons should be left to the nuclear powers themselves.

In contrast, Article VI says that "Each of the parties to the Treaty" should pursue negotiations in good faith for nuclear disarmament. And the World Court opinion concluded that fulfilling the Article VI obligation was "an objective of vital importance to the whole of the international community today."

We need only say that though the position of the United States, Britain, France, and Russia may have hardened, the debate over the Malaysian resolution clearly suggests that the effects of the ICJ opinion on the important nuclear question is one of general acceptance. It also forms the basis upon which much positive legal development in this field will be based.

In sum, the import of an ICJ opinion on international relations is awesome. Its effects transcend the immediate needs for clarification by the bodies that make the requests and have legal, political, social and even cultural value on our ever more interrelated international community.

Binding Effects of the Opinion

A very pertinent point to ponder as regards the advisory role of the ICJ is the binding effects of the opinions rendered. Since that is the case, the practice of giving advisory opinions should be examined in relation to certain provisions of the Charter and Statute in a form of contrastive analysis. For instance, Article 94, paragraph I states as follows: "Each Member of the United Nations undertakes to comply with the decision of the International Court of Justice in any case to which it is a party." Article 59 of the Statute also states: "The decision of the Court has no binding force except between the parties and in respect of that particular case."

The important thing to remember here is that judgments awarded by the Court to Parties are binding at least in respect of that case. But then that is true only as per "judgments" passed on "Parties" -- how about "opinions" given to "authorised bodies?" Advisory opinions are devoid of any binding force. The Court itself has explicitly stated this in the *Peace Treaties Case*[64] in the *South West Africa Cases*[65]

[64] *Peace Treaties Case (Advisory Opinion)* ICJ Reports (1949), p. 109.

[65] *South West Africa Cases (Preliminary Objections)* ICJ Reports (1962), p. 337.

and others.[66] In the *Peace Treaties Case* it pronounced: "The Court's reply is only of an advisory character; as such it has no binding force." A lot of writers would seem to have agreed on this point.[67]

In fact there is no obligation on the body requesting the opinions to give effect to them. Still less are those States likely to be affected legally bound to implement them in action. The opinions are not binding upon the States individually even if accepted by the requesting body. This would seem clear from the reception of the opinions in the *South West Africa Cases* by the General Assembly and by the Union of South West Africa.[68]

Opinions of the Court are not binding in the sense of *res judicata* (that is following the principle that an issue decided by a Court should not be reopened); neither are they binding *stare decisis* (that is, following the principle that a tribunal should follow its own previous decisions and those of other tribunals of equal or greater authority). However, the argument has been convincigly advanced in various quarters that the Court's Opinions are binding in a negative sense. It is difficult not to agree with the writer who noted:

> ... Advisory Opinions may be negatively binding in the sense that if the Court were to indicate that a certain course of action would be definitely illegal or that, of various courses of actions proposed only one would be legal, it would be difficult in practice for the organ requesting the opinion not to follow the course advocated by the Court.[69]

It would appear that there is no prohibitory force attaching to the opinions, and that the requesting bodies and the States are under no obligation to refrain from adopting the prohibited course. However, it is very unlikely that the States and organisations would adopt such a course for two reasons, namely, the undisputable judicial and authoritative character of the opinions.[70]

Although the opinions are merely advisory they cannot be regarded as legal advice in the ordinary sense. They are not like views expressed by counsel for guidance of clients, but are judicial pronouncements. The Court has repeatedly stated that it is a judicial

---

[66] E.g., ILO Administrative Tribunal Case *ICJ Reports*, (1956), p. 47.
[67] On this issue, see the following; Prataap, *op. cit.*, p. 227; Rosenne, ICJ, *op. cit.*, p. 441; The World Court, *op. cit.*, p. 83; Kelson, *The Law of the United Nations*, p. 486; Gore-Booth, *op. cit.*, p. 367.
[68] Prataap, *op. cit.*, p. 367.
[69] Satow, *op. cit.*, p. 367.
[70] Prataap, *op. cit.*, p. 230.

body and that in rendering advisory opinions it performs a judicial function.[71] Underlying this assertion is the fact that the Court has "... assimilated its advisory procedure to its contentious procedure as closely as practicable.[72]

Again, one should note that though the advisory opinions are not binding, "their persuasive character and substantive authority is great."[73] This is because they are judicial pronouncements of the highest international tribunal and the statement of law contained in them is of the same high quality as of that contained in the judgments.[74] Their moral weight and influence therefore is great.[75] The 1978 Rules of Court also state: "The advisory opinion shall contain...a statement as to the text of the opinion which is authoritative."

The Court itself has always treated the opinions as being of equal authority with the judgments. For instance, the PCIJ recognised that answering the questions put to it in the *Eastern Carelia Case* would be "... substantially equivalent to deciding the dispute between the parties."[76] The way in which the Court repeatedly cites its opinions in subsequent decisions -- whether opinions or judgments -- clearly shows that it regards them as equally authoritative. It makes no distinction between the two in this connection.[77]

The bodies requesting opinions from the ICJ usually regard such opinions as authoritative expressions of law. Moreover, the opinions are "authoritative in the sense that their legal correctness cannot be officially or formally questioned by the organ to which they are rendered acting in its corporate capacity."[78] Such an organ could not be heard later on confessing a lack of guidiance relating to the issues covered in the Court's opinion.

Strong similarities do exist between Advisory Opinions and Declaratory Judgments. Prataap aptly captures this in the following statement:

---

[71] See Reuter *International Institutions*, p. 274.
[72] *Loc. cit.*
[73] *Ibid.*, p. 231. See also Fitzmaurice, *BYIL*, 29 (1952), p. 55.
[74] Rosenne (1961), *op. cit.*, p. 113.
[75] Prataap, *op. cit.*, p. 231.
[76] PCIJ Series B., No. 5, p. 29.
[77] *Ibid.*
[78] Fitzmaurice, *op. cit.*, p. 54.

The advisory opinions have been considered so authoritative by jurists as to be likened to declaratory judgments. The declaratory judgments on the other hand have been thought to be an indirect method of obtaining advisory opinions by States. In fact, there is hardly any distinction in substance and effect of the opinions and the judgments whether declaratory or otherwise. There are however formal differences between the two. The non-binding character of the opinions is an important difference, but too much emphasis must not be placed on the aspect. For although judgments are formally binding, their execution is not automatic and there is no certainty that they will be executed at all. There is no machinery in international law for enforcing them directly.[79]

Advisory Opinions with binding force or what we may term "compulsive opinions" do exist. This developed as a form of advisory arbitration under the League of Nations, where some organisations were authorised to request advisory opinions in case of disputes in which the organisation is one party and a State the other. In such instances the parties to the dispute are required to accept the opinion as binding. This type of provision may be contained in a convention, bilateral or multilateral treaty, or a constituent instrument drawn up to regulate relations between States and international bodies. Thus, section 30 of the General Convention on the Privileges and immunities of the United Nations provides as follows:

> If a difference arises between the United Nations on the one hand and a member on the other hand, a request shall be made for an advisory opinion on any legal question involved in accordance with Article 96 of the Charter and Article 65 of the Statute of the Court. The opinion given by the Court shall be accepted as decisive by the parties.

This system of advisory arbitration is seen in certain quarters as "... an attempt to overcome the procedural incapacity of international organisations to appear before the Court in disputes with States."[80] In conclusion, it is worthy of note that the procedure described above is a continuation of the practice initiated under the League's PCIJ. A radical and new development is the employment of the advisory procedure as part of the machinery for judicial review of the judgment of a Tribunal between an individual staff member and the organisation in a contentious case.

---

[79] Prataap, *op. cit.*, p. 232-233.

[80] See Rosenne (1961), *op. cit.*, p. 452; Kelson, *op. cit.*, p. 486; Prataap, *op. cit.*, pp. 47-48.

Chapter 7

Statistical Evaluation of the Court's Work in its First 50 years

Article 35, paragraph 1, of the Statute provides that the Court shall be open to the States which are Parties to the Statute, and Article 93,paragraph 1, of the Charter of the UN provides that all members of the UN are *ipso facto* Parties to the Statute. As at 31 July 1996, 185 States were Members of the UN. (See Table I).

TABLE I: Member States of the UN as at July 1996

State	Date of Admission
Afghanistan	19 November, 1946
Albania	14 December, 1955
Algeria	8 October, 1962
Andorra	28 July, 1993
Angola	1 December, 1976
Antigua and Barbuda	11 November, 1981
Argentina*	Original Member
Armenia	2 March, 1992
Australia*	Original Member
Austria	14 December, 1955
Azerbaijan	2 March, 1992
Bahamas	18 September, 1973
Bahrain	21 September, 1971
Bangladesh	17 September, 1974
Barbados	9 December, 1966
Belarus*	Original Member
Belgium*	Original Member
Belize	25 September, 1981
Benin	20 September, 1960

Bhutan	21 September, 1971
Bolivia*	Original Member
Bosnia and Herzegovina	22 May, 1992
Botswana	17 October, 1966
Brazil*	Original Member
Brunei Darussalam	21 September, 1984
Bulgaria	14 December, 1955
Burkina Faso	20 September, 1960
Burundi	18 September, 1962
Cambodia	14 December, 1955
Cameroon	20 September, 1960
Canada*	Original Member
Cape Verde	16 September, 1975
Central African Republic	20 September, 1960
Chad	20 September, 1960
Chile*	Original Member
China*	Original Member
Colombia*	Original Member
Comoros	12 November, 1975
Congo (Brazzaville), Republic of	20 September, 1960
Costa Rica*	Original Member
Cote d'Ivoire	20 September, 1960
Croatia	22 May, 1992
Cuba*	Original Member
Cyprus	20 September, 1960
Czech Republic	19 January, 1993
Democratic People's Republic of Korea	17 September, 1991
Denmark*	Original Member
Djibouti	20 September, 1977
Dominica	18 December, 1978
Dominican Republic*	Original Member
Ecuador*	Original Member
Egypt*	Original Member
El Salvador*	Original Member

Equatorial Guinea	12 November, 1968
Eritrea	28 May, 1993
Estonia	17 September, 1991
Ethiopia*	Original Member
Federated States of Micronesia	17 September, 1991
Fiji	13 October, 1970
Finland	14 December, 1955
France*	Original Member
Gabon	20 September, 1960
Gambia	21 September, 1965
Georgia	31 July, 1992
Germany	18 September, 1973
Ghana	8 March, 1957
Greece*	Original Member
Grenada	17 September, 1974
Guatemala*	Original Member
Guinea	12 December, 1958
Guinea-Bissau	17 September, 1974
Guyana	20 September, 1966
Haiti*	Original Member
Honduras*	Original Member
Hungary	14 December, 1955
Iceland	19 November, 1946
India*	Original Member
Indonesia	28 September, 1950
Iran (Islamic Republic of)*	Original Member
Iraq*	Original Member
Ireland	14 December, 1955
Israel	11 May, 1949
Italy	14 December, 1955
Jamaica	18 September, 1962
Japan	18 December, 1956
Jordan	14 December, 1955
Kazakhstan	2 March, 1992
Kenya	16 December, 1963

Kuwait	14 May, 1963
Kyrgyzstan	2 March, 1992
Lao People's Democratic Republic	14 December, 1955
Latvia	17 September, 1991
Lebanon*	Original Member
Lesotho	17 October, 1966
Liberia*	Original Member
Libyan Arab Jamahiriya	14 December, 1955
Liechtenstein	18 September, 1990
Lithuania	17 September, 1991
Luxembourg*	Original Member
Madagascar	20 September, 1960
Malawi	1 December, 1964
Malaysia	17 September, 1957
Maldives	21 September, 1965
Mali	28 September, 1960
Malta	1 December, 1964
Marshall Islands	17 September, 1991
Mauritania	27 October, 1961
Mauritius	24 April, 1968
Mexico*	Original Member
Moldova	2 March, 1992
Monaco	28 May, 1993
Mongolia	27 October, 1961
Morocco	12 November, 1956
Mozambique	16 September, 1975
Myanmar	19 April, 1948
Namibia	23 April, 1990
Nepal	14 December, 1955
Netherlands*	Original Member
New Zealand*	Original Member
Nicaragua*	Original Member
Niger	20 September, 1960
Nigeria	7 October, 1960
Norway*	Original Member

Oman	7 October, 1971
Pakistan	30 September, 1947
Palau	15 December, 1994
Panama*	Original Member
Papua New Guinea	10 October, 1975
Paraguay*	Original Member
Peru*	Original Member
Philippines*	Original Member
Poland*	Original Member
Portugal	14 December, 1955
Qatar	21 September, 1971
Republic of Korea	17 September, 1991
Romania	14 December, 1955
Russian Federation*	Original Member
Rwanda	18 September, 1962
St. Kitts and Nevis	23 September, 1983
St. Lucia	18 September, 1962
St. Vincent and the Grenadines	16 September, 1980
Samoa	15 December, 1976
San Marino	2 March, 1992
Sao Tome and Principe	16 September, 1975
Saudi Arabia*	Original Member
Senegal	28 September, 1960
Seychelles	21 September, 1976
Sierra Leone	27 September, 1961
Singapore	21 September, 1965
Slovakia	19 January, 1993
Slovenia	22 May, 1992
Solomon Islands	19 September, 1978
Somalia	20 September, 1960
South Africa*	Original Member
Spain	14 December, 1955
Sri Lanka	14 December, 1955
Sudan	12 November, 1956
Suriname	4 December, 1975

Swaziland	24 September, 1968
Sweden	19 November, 1946
Syrian Arab Republic*	Original Member
Tajikistan	2 March, 1992
Thailand	16 December, 1946
The former Yugoslav Republic of Macedonia	8 April, 1993
Togo	20 September, 1960
Trinidad and Tobago	18 September, 1962
Tunisia	12 November, 1956
Turkey*	Original Member
Turkmenistan	2 March, 1992
Uganda	25 October, 1962
Ukraine*	Original Member
United Arab Emirates	9 December, 1971
United Kingdom of Great Britain and Northern Ireland*	Original Member
United Republic of Tanzania	14 December, 1961
United States of America*	Original Member
Uruguay*	Original Member
Uzbekistan	2 March, 1992
Vanuatu	15 September, 1981
Venezuela*	Original Member
Viet Nam	20 September, 1977
Yemen	30 September, 1947
Yugoslavia*	Original Member
Zaire (Congo (Kinshasha), Democratic Republic of)	20 September, 1960
Zambia	1 December, 1964
Zimbabwe	25 August, 1980

* Original Member States. There were 51 of these in 1945 including the erstwhile Soviet Socialist Republics: Bylorussian Soviet Republic and Ukranian Soviet Socialist Republic.

It is noteworthy that Nauru and Switzerland not being members of the UN are nevertheless at present parties to the Statute. Thus 187 States are potentially subject to the Court's jurisdiction. *Prima facie* this proves that the ICJ is probably the most popular organ of the UN. In other words rather than question the popularity of the Court or its usefulness what may be questioned is the level of commitment to the Court's ideals and the actual performance of the Court itself. The universal acceptance of the Court's Statute obviously places the Court in a better position than any other institution in the history of mankind to administer justice and guard the international rule of law. Furthermore, the future of judicial settlement of international disputes would appear to be assured.

The Charter of the United Nations and the Statute of the Court entered into force on 24th October, 1945. After the election of its members on 6th February 1946, the Court met for the first time in The Hague on 1st April of the same year. The first case entered in the General List of the Court was *Corfu Channel (United Kingdom v. Albania)* submitted on 22nd May, 1947. Between that date and 31st July 1996 (i.e. in about fifty years of existence) the Court dealt with a total of 75 contentious cases and 22 advisory opinions. For a listing in a chronological manner see Table II. In those cases it gave 61 judgements of which 39 were on the merits, and a total of 23 advisory opinions. Of the 295 orders made in this period 224 related solely to the fixing or extending of time limits, while 263 orders related to contentious cases and 32 to advisory cases.[1]

Table II: Chronological List of Contentious Cases	
TITLE	**DATES**
Corfu Channel (United Kingdom v. Albania)	1947-1949
Fisheries (United Kingdom v. Norway)	1949-1951
Protection of French Nationals and Protected Persons in Egypt (France v. Egypt)	1949-1950
Asylum (Colombia v. Peru)	1949-1950

[1] See *ICJ Year Book*, 1995-96.

Rights of Nationals of the United States of America in Morocco (France v. United States)	1950-1952
Request to Interpretation of the Judgement of 20 November 1950 in the Asylum Case (Colombia v. Peru)	1950
Haya de la Torre (Colombia v. Peru)	1950-1951
Ambatielos (Greece v. United Kingdom)	1951-1953
Anglo-Iranian Oil Co. (United Kingdom v. Iran)	1951-1952
Minquiers and Ecrehos (France v. United Kingdom)	1951-1953
Nottebohm (Liechtenstein v Guatemala)	1951-1955
Monetary Gold Removed from Rome in 1951 (Italy v. France, United Kingdom and United States)	1953-1964
Treatment in Hungary of Aircraft and Crew of United Sates of America (United States v. Hungary)	1954
Treatment in Hungary of Aircraft and Crew of United Sates of America (United States v. USSR)	1954
Aerial Incident of 10 March 1953 (United States v. Czecheslovakia)	1955-1956
Antarctica (United Kingdom v. Argentina)	1955-1956
Antarctica (United Kingdom v. Chile)	1955-1956
Aerial Incident of 7 October 1952 (United States v. USSR)	1955-1956
Certain Norwegian Loans (France v. Norway)	1955-1957
Right of Passage over Indian Territory (Portugal v. India)	1955-60
Application of the Convention of 1902 Governing the Guardianship of Infants (Netherlands v. Sweden)	1957-1958
Interhandel (Switzerland v. United States)	1957-1959
Aerial Incident of 27 July 1955 (Israel v. Bulgaria)	1957-1959
Aerial Incident of 27 July 1955 (United States v. Bulgaria)	1957-1960
Aerial Incident of 27 July 1955 (United Kingdom v. Bulgaria)	1957-1959
Sovereignty over Certain Frontier Land (Belgium v. Netherlands)	1957-1959
Arbitral Award Made by the King of Spain on 23 December 1906 (Honduras v. Nicaragua)	1958-1960
Aerial Incident of 4 September 1954 (United States v. USSR)	1958
Bercelona Traction, Light and Power Company, Limited	1958-1961

(Belgium v. Spain)	
Compaignie du Port, de Quais et des Enterpots de Beyrouth and Societe Radio-Orient (France v. Lebanon	1959-1960
Aerial Incident of 7 November 1954 (United States v. USSR)	1959
Temple of Preah Vihear (Cambodia v. Thailand)	1959-1962
South West Africa (Ethiopia v. South Africa; Liberia v. South Africa)	1960-1966
Northern Cameroons (Cameroon v. United Kingdom)	1961-1963
Barcelona Traction, Light and power Company, Limited (New Application: 1962) (Belgium v. Spain)	1962-1970
North Sea Continental Shelf (Federal Republic of Germany v. Denmark; Federal Republic of Germany v. Netherlands)	1967-1969
Appeal Relating to the jurisdiction of the ICAO Council (India v. Pakistan)	1971-1972
Fisheries Jurisdiction (United Kingdom v. Iceland)	1972-1974
Nuclear Tests (Australia v. France)	1973-1974
Nuclear Tests (New Zealand v. France)	1973-1974
Trial of Pakistani Prisoners of War (Pakistan v. India)	1973
Aegean Sea Continental Shelf (Greece v. Turkey)	1976-1978
Continental Shelf (Tunisia v. Libyan Arab Jamahiriya)	1978-1982
United States Diplomatic and Consular Staff in Tehran (United States of America v. Iran)	1979-1981
Delimitation of the Maritime Boundary in the Gulf of Maine Area (Canada v. United Sates of America (Case referred to a Chamber)	1981-1984
Continental Shelf (Libyan Arab Jamahiriya v. Malta)	1982-1985
Frontier Dispute (Burkina Faso v. Republic of Mali) (Case referred to a Chamber)	1983-1986
Military and Paramilitary Activities in and against Nicaragua (Nicaragua v. United States of America)	1984-1991
Application for Revision and Interpretation of the Judgement of 24 February 1982 in the Case concerning the Continental Shelf (Tunisia v. Libyan Arab Jamahiriya)	1984-1985
Border and Transborder Armed Action (Nicaragua v. Costa Rica)	1986-1987

Border and Transborder Armed Action (Nicaragua v. Honduras)	1986-1992
Land, Island and Maritime Frontier Dispute (El Salvador v. Honduras; Nicaragua intervening) (Case referred to a Chamber)	1986-1992
Elettronica Sicula S.P.A. (ELSI) (United States of America v. Italy) (Case referred to Chamber)	1987-1989
Maritime Delimitation in the Area between Greenland and Jan Mayen (Denmark v. Norway)	1988-1993
Aerial Incident of 3 July 1988 (Islamic Republic of Iran v. United Stated States of America)	1989-1996
Certain Phosphate lands in Nauru (Nauru v. Australia)	1989-1993
Arbitral Award of 31 July 1989 (Guinea -Bissau v. Senegal)	1989-1991
Territorial Dispute (Libyan Arab Jamahiriya v. Chad)	1990-1994
East Timor (Portugal v. Australia)	1991-1995
Maritime Delimitation between Guinea-Bissau and Senegal (Guinea-Bissau v. Senegal)	1991-1995
Passage through the Great Belt (Finland v. Denmark)	1991-1992
Maritime Delimitation and Territorial Questions between Qatar and Bahrain (Qatar v. Bahrain)	1991-
Case Concerning Questions of Interpretation and Application of the 1971 Montreal Convention Arising from the Aerial Incident at Lockerbie (Libyan Arab Jamahiriya v. United Kingdom)	1992-
Case Concerning Questions of Interpretation and Application of the 1991 Montreal Convention Arising from the Aerial Incident at Lockerbie (Libyan Arab Jamahiriya v. United States of America)	1992-
Case Concerning Oil platforms (Islamic Republic of Iran v. United States of America)	1992-
Case Concerning Application of the Convention on the Prevention of the Crime of Genocide (Bosnia and Herzegovina v. Yugoslavia)	1993-
Gabcikovo-Nagymaros Project (Hungary v. Slovakia)	1993-1997
Land and Maritime Boundary (Cameroon v. Nigeria)	1994-

Fisheries Jurisdictions (Spain v. Canada)	1995-
Request for an Examination of Situation in Accordance with paragraph 63 of the Court's Judgement of 20 December 1974 in the Nuclear Tests (New Zealand v. France) case	1995
Kasikili Sedudu Island (Botswana v. Namibia)	1996-

It may prove useful to our analysis to show exactly how many times each of the States listed in Table II have appeared before the Court so far, as parties to a dispute. Table III lists by country the cases in which each was a participant. This may help in determining those particular States or group of States that demonstrate more willingness and by implication greater confidence in the Court's work.

Table III: Actual use by States of the Court's Contentious Jrisdiction

State	Number of Appearances
United Kingdom	1947-49; 1949-51; 1951-53; 1951-52; 1951-53; 1953-54; 1955-56; 1957-59; 1961-63; 1972-74; 1992-
Albania	1947-49
France	1949-50; 1950-52; 1951-53; 1953-54; 1953-54; 1955-57; 1959-60; 1973-74; 1973-74; 1995-
Egypt	1949-50
Colombia	1949-50; 1950; 1950-51
Peru	1949-50; 1950; 1950-51
United States	1950-52; 1953-54; 1954; 1955-56; 1957-59; 1957-60; 1958; 1959; 1979-81; 1981-84; 1984-91; 1987-89; 1989-96; 1992-;

	1992-
Iran	1951-52; 1979-81; 1989-96; 1992
Liechtenstein	1951-55
Guatemala	1951-55
Italy	1953-54; 1987-89
Lebanon	1953-54; 1959-60
Hungary	1954; 1993- 97
USSR	1954; 1955-56; 1958; 1959
Czechoslovakia	1955-56
Argentina	1955-56
Chile	1955-56
Norway	1955-56; 1988-93
Portugal	1955-1960; 1991-95
India	1955-56; 1971-72; 1973
Netherlands	1957-58; 1957-59; 1967-69
Sweden	1957-59
Switzerland	1957-59
Israel	1957-59
Bulgaria	1957-59; 1957-59-; 1957-59
Belgium	1957-59; 1958-61; 1962-70
Honduras	1958-60; 1986; 1986
Nicaragua	1958-60; 1984-90; 1986-87; 1986

Spain	1958-61; 1962-70; 1995
Cambodia	1959-62
Thailand	1959-62
Ethiopia	1960-66
Liberia	1960-66
South Africa	1960-66
Cameroon	1961-63; 1994-
Germany	1967-69; 1972-74
Denmark	1967-69; 1988-93; 1991-92
Pakistan	1971-72; 1973
Iceland	1972-74; 1972-74
New Zealand	1973-74; 1995
Greece	1976-78
Turkey	1976-78
Tunisia	1978-82; 1984-85
Libya	1978-82; 1982-85; 1984-85; 1990-94; 1992-;1992-
Canada	1981-84; 1995-
Malta	1982-85
Burkina Faso	1983-86
Mali	1983-86
Costa Rica	1986-87
El Salvador	1986-92

Nauru	1989-93
Australia	1989-96; 1991-95
Guinea-Bissau	1989-91; 1991-95
Senegal	1989-91; 1991-95
Chad	1990-94
Inland	1991-92
Qatar	1991-
Bahrain	1991-
Yugoslavia	1993-
Bosnia And Herzegovina	1993
Slovakia	1993-97
Nigeria	1994-
Botswana	1996-
Namibia	1996-

These tables (i.e., Table I, II and III) show that 64 nations have so far made use of the ICJ's contentious jurisdiction. It is worthy of note that during the first twenty five years of the existence of the Court 46 contentious cases were referred to the Court whereas at the end of the first half century the Court had been seized of only a total of 74 contentious cases. It is thus obvious that the record of the Court's work in numerical terms has not exactly been of linear progression. Indeed there have been fallow periods of inactivity. To bring the figures within a comparative context we may consider how the PCIJ performed within similar time frame. In 25 years, that is between 1921 and 1945, the PCIJ rendered some 31 judgments, 25 substantive orders, and 27 advisory opinions. In fact the high water mark for the PCIJ came in the 1920's. Specifically, 50 out of 66 cases were brought during the first decade representing over two thirds of the PCIJ's work and roughly an average of three or four decisions were rendered annually.

In the case of the ICJ there was surely a much less pronounced initial enthusiasm. However, three phases are noticeable. The Court also had a short burst of initial activity between 1947 to 1960 in which hopes were high for the utility and value of the Court. It has been suggested that the first crisis of confidence in the Court leading to a noticeable phase of falling off in the Court's work arose out of the Court's sterile judgment of 1966 in the South West Africa case. The highly political nature of that case leading to an unconvincing judgment arrived at via the President of the Court's casting vote, may well have had a delayed shock effect on the community of States, for by the late seventies there was a worrisome lack of use of the Court. It may well have been in an attempt to save the situation that the Court made a revision of its Resolution on the Internal Practice of the Court (1976) and of its Rules (1978).

The third phase in the Court's 50 years experience represents a steady if not surprising increase in its caseload from the late 80's up to the mid 90's. This may well be as a result of the Court's efforts to re-engage the attention of Developing States and wash itself clean of stain left by its judgment of 1966. By the year 1995 the Court's docket had become uncharacteristically full. A total of 13 cases appeared on the general list. In 1996, this dropped to eleven cases. The Court had begun deliberating on three cases simultaneously in contrast with its earlier proceedure of taking one case at a time.

This situation however does not mean that all is now well with the Court. Indeed the reality is far from ideal. Lest we are confused by the increase in the case load of the Court we may take a look back at our list of Parties to the Court's statute. As at 31 July 1996 no less than 185 States (members of the UN) together with Switzerland and Nauru were parties to the statute. In 1945 there were only 51 original member States. Thus there has been more than 300% increase in the number of prospective clients of the court. With this in mind there really ought to be more cases. It would not have been any surprise if the number of cases before the Court presently were double its number. The fact that this is not so gives cause for concern. Moreover, it is worthy of note that of the 64 states which have appeared before the court so far, 30 of them are among the 51 original member states of the UN. Confidence in the use of the Court by the new Parties to the statute has not been exactly infectious.

It is clear also from Table III that though many States have resorted to the use of the Court in resolving disputes, some countries have demonstrated greater confidence in the Court by appearing before it several times more than others. The top three users of the Court are Western super-powers, who are also permanent members of the Security Council. The US has appeared before the Court 15 times, the UK 11 times and France 10 times. The former Union Soviet Socialist Republics appeared in a total of four cases and the Federal Republic of Germany appeared twice. These five countries were and probably still are (of course with the exception of the USSR whose enviable position could be said to be somewhat taken over by present day Russia) the top ranking industrialised military and economic super powers of the world. Between them they have put up 42 appearances in 35 cases out of the total of 69 contentious disputes adjudicated by the Court. That means that over half of the Court's work since its inception has involved settling disputes in which the super-powers were parties.

The developing country with the highest number of appearances is Libya which has appeared before the Court six times. The next two developing States which have recorded a relatively high number of appearances before the Court are Iran and Nicaragua, both appearing four times each. These facts surely prove something, especially if one considers that there are three to four times more developing countries than there are developed ones.

It is also interesting to note that the communist States of China and Cuba have never appeared before the Court in a contentious dispute. These are States which were very active in the cold war and have since the period of the existence of the Court been involved in many serious disputes and situations that indeed threaten world peace. Yet not once were they parties in a contentious dispute before the Court. Considering this in conjunction with the fact that even the former Soviet Union put up only four appearances--much fewer than the capitalist super-powers of France, Britain and the US--the impression we have is that the erstwhile communist States, especially those not on the European continent, do not display any measure of confidence in the use of the Court. We are strengthened in this view by the fact that not on one occasion has a communist country instituted proceedings against any of the Western nations. However, to get a clearer picture of the lopsided display of confidence in the use of the Court's jurisdiction, we may make an examination of how particular regions in the world have responded to the availability of the Court's contentious jurisdiction (see Table IV).

Table IV: Geographic Distribution of Countries which have Appeared before the International Court of Justice

Europe	Asia	North and South America	Africa	Australia
UK	Iran	Canada	Cameroon	Australia
Albania	Lebanon	USA	Libya	New Zealand
France	India	Colombia	Egypt	
Liechtenstein	Israel	Peru	Ethiopia	
Italy	Cambodia	Guatemala	Liberia	
Hungary	Thailand	Argentina	South Africa	
*USSR	Pakistan	Chile	Burkina Faso	
Czechoslovakia	Turkey	Honduras	Tunisia	
Norway	Nauru	Nicaragua	Mali	
Portugal	Qatar	Costa Rica	Guinea Bissau	
Netherlands	Bahrain	El Salvador	Senegal	
Sweden			Chad	
Switzerland			Nigeria	
Bulgaria			Botswana	
Belgium			Namibia	
Spain				
Germany				
Denmark				

Yugoslavia				
Iceland				
Finland				
**Bosnia and Herzegovina				
Slovakia				
Greece				
Turkey				
Malta				
* The former USSR spans Europe and Asia geographically but for the purposes of our analysis the USSR is treated as an European country alone. * The Court regards Bosnia and Herzegovina as a Republic (See Application of The Crime of Genocide, Order of 16 April 1993, ICJ Reports 1993, p. 29.				

We must note from a cursory glance at this table that for some reasons, the other continents apart from Europe (in which the Court is situated) have under-utilised the judicial settlement procedures of the ICJ in the settlement of their disputes. For instance, whereas 26 States out of the States in Europe have appeared as parties in cases before the Court, only 15 have done so out of the 50 States in Africa, within the period of our analysis.

In order to bring the whole situation into better perspective we have--using various subjective criteria such as economic indices, relative military capacity and even historical linkage--divided the 64 States that have appeared so far before the Court into two groups: the developed or older generation of States (i.e., the European States, USA, Canada, Australia, New Zealand, South Africa and Israel) and the developing or/and newer generation of States (African, Asian and Latin American States). Thirty-one States of the first group have appeared before the Court a total of 87 times and 33 developing nations have made a total of only 58 appearances. We may further note that there is a difference in frequency of appearance as shown in Table III. Whereas 18 of the 31 developed States have appeared before the Court more than once, only 13 of the larger group of developing nations have appeared more than once. Note must be taken of the fact that there are always more developing States who are party to the Statute of the Court than developed ones.

It is also true that the developed nations have litigated more among themselves. This is shown in Table V.

Table V: Cases Between Nations of Europe, Australia and North America		
1	UK v. Norway	Fisheries: 1949-51
2	France v. USA	Rights of Nationals of the USA in Morocco: 1950-52
3	Greece v. UK	Ambatielos: 1951-53
4	France v. UK	Minquiers & Ecrehos: 1951-53
5	Italy v. France, UK & USA	Monetary Gold Removed from Rome in 1943: 1953-54
6	US v. Hungary	Treatment in Hungary of Aircraft and Crew of USA: 1954
7	USA v. USSR	Treatment in Hungary of Aircraft and Crew of USA: 1954
8	France v. Norway	Certain Norwegian Loans: 1955-57
9	Netherlands v. Sweden	Application of the Convention of 1902: 1957-58
10	Switzerland v. US	Interhandel: 1957-59
11	Israel v. Bulgaria	Aerial Incident of 27 July 1955: 1957-60
12	USA.v. Bulgaria	Aerial Incident of July 1955: 1957-60
13	UK v. Bulgaria	Aerial Incident of July 1955: 1957-59
14	Belgium v. Netherlands	Certain Frontier Land: 1957-59
15	Belgium v. Spain	Barcelona Traction Light and Power Company, Ltd. 1958-61
16	USA v. USSR	Aerial Incident of 7 November 1954: 1959
17	Belgium v. Spain	Barcelona Traction Light and Power Co. Ltd. (New Application 1962): 1962-70
18	Fed. Rep. Germany v. Netherlands	North-sea Continental Shelf: 1967-69
19	UK v. Iceland	Fisheries Jurisdiction: 1972-74

20	FRGermany v. Iceland	Fisheries Jurisdiction: 1972-74
21	Australia v. France	Nuclear Tests: 1973-74
22	New Zealand v. France	Nuclear Tests: 1973-74
23	Canada v. USA	Delimitation of the Maritime Boundary in the Gulf of Maine Area: 1981-84
24	USA v. Italy	Electronica Sicula SPA (ELSI) Case referred to a special Chamber: 1987-89
25	Portugal v. Australia	East Timor: 1991-1995
26	Finland v. Denmark	Passage through the Great Belt: 1991-92
27	Bosnia and Herzegovina v. Yugoslavia	Case concerning Application of the Convention on the Prevention of the Crime of Genocide: 1993-
28	Hungary v. Slovakia	Gabcikovo Nagymaros Project: 1993-97
29	Spain v. Canada	Fisheries Jurisdiction: 1995-
30	New Zealand v. France	Request for an examination of the situation in accordance with paragraph 63 of the Court's Judgement of 20 December 1974 in the Nuclear Test (New Zealand v. France) Case: 1995

The developed and older nations have also displayed a readiness to drag developing countries to the ICJ. This is clear from our Table VI.

Table VI: Cases Instituted by Developed Nations Against Third World Countries		
1	France v. Egypt	Protection of French National and Protected Persons in Egypt: 1949-50
2	UK v. Iran	Anglo-Iranian Oil Co.: 1951-52
3	Liechtenstein v.	Nottebohm: 1951-55

	Guatemala	
4	France v. Lebanon	Electricite de Beyrouth Company: 1953-54
5	UK v. Argentina	Antarctica: 1955-56
6	UK v. Chile	Antarctica: 1955-56
7	Portugal v. India	Right of Passage Over Indian Territory: 1955-6
8	France v. Lebanon	Compagnies du Port, des Quais et des Entrepots de Beyrouth and Societe Radio-Orient: 1959-60
9	Greece v. Turkey	Aegean Sea Continental Shelf: 1976-78
10	USA v. Iran	United States Diplomatic and Consular Staff in Tehran: 1979-81

Apparently in the early stages of the Court's existence the developed States found it very useful to press legal action against the developing States. In the first fifteen years alone nine of such cases were instituted. Since that time, however, there has been a recognisable drop in this pattern with only two other such cases; the last of which was instituted in 1979. It would prove quite instructive to compare Table VI with those cases instituted by third world nations against more Developed Nations. That brings us to our Table VII.

Table VII: Cases Instituted by Developing States Against Developed Nations	
1	Ethiopia v. South Africa; Liberia v. South Africa (South West Africa): 1960-1966
2	Cameroon v. United Kingdom (Northern Cameroon): 1961-63
3	Libya v. Malta (Continental Shelf):1982-84
4	Nicaragua v. USA (Military and Paramilitary Activities in and against Nicaragua): 1984-90
5	Iran v. USA (Aerial Incident of 3 July 1988): 1989-1996
6	Nauru v. Australia (Certain Phosphate Lands in Nauru): 1989-1993
7	Libya v. U.K. (Case Concerning Questions of Interpretation and Application of the 1971 Montreal Convention Arising from the Aerial Incident at Lockerbie): 1992-
8	Libya v. US (Case Concerning Questions of Interpretation and

	Application of the 1971 Montreal Convention Arising From the Aerial Incident at Lockerbie): 1992-
9	Iran v. USA (Case Concerning Oil Platforms): 1992-

The fact that third world States have also on at least nine occasions (compared to the ten instances delineated in Table VI) instituted proceedings against the developed nations is quite noteworthy. This in our view shows that though these under-developed States have made relatively less use of the Court; they still have some commendable measure of confidence in judicial settlement via the ICJ to the extent of initiating proceedings against stronger and wealthier nations in what could be regarded as "their court". We also must note that it was 14 years after the Court's establishment that the first developing countries took a more developed State and an ally of the West (i.e., South Africa) to the Court. This is the exact contrary of the pattern of developed States litigation against developing States. As we noted above there was a rash of cases against developing nations in the beginning. It is also encouraging to note that in the last 15 years before the Court's 50th anniversary, developing States have initiated quite a few proceedings against developed States; although it must be admitted that most of these cases were instituted by countries (notably Iran and Libya) which already had a history of submitting their international disputes to the Court for adjudication.

As expected, it is of interest to our analysis to find out the number of occasions when developing States have litigated against each other. This in our view can help confirm or disprove the school of thought which says that third world countries have no confidence whatsoever in the ICJ.

Table VIII: Case Between Developing States of Africa, Asia and South America	
1	Colombia v. Peru: (Request for interpretation of the Judgement of 20 November 1950 in the Asylum Case) 1950
2	Colombia v. Peru: (Haya de la Torre) 1950-51
3	Honduras v. Nicaragua: (Arbitral Award Made by the King of Spain on 23 December 1906) 1958-60
4	Cambodia v. Thailand: (Temple of Preah Vihear) 1959-62

5	India v. Pakistan: (Appeal Relating to Jurisdiction of the I.C.A.O. Council) 1971-72
6	Pakistan v. India: (Trial of Pakistani Prisoners of War) 1973
7	Tunisia v. Libya: (Continental Shelf) 1978-82
8	Libya v. Malta: (Continental Shelf) 1982-85
9	Burkina Faso v. Republic of Mali: (Frontier Dispute) (Case referred to a Chamber) 1983-86
10	Tunisia v. Libya: (Application for Revisions and Interpretation of the Judgement of 24 February 1982 in the Case concerning the Continental Shelf) 1984-85
11	Nicaragua v. Costa Rica: (Border and Transborder Armed Actions) 1986-87
12	Nicaragua v. Honduras: (Border and Transborder Armed Actions) 1986-92
13	El Salvador v. Honduras: (Land, Island and Maritime Frontier Dispute) (Case referred to a Chamber) 1986-92
14	Guinea-Bissau v. Senegal: (Arbitral Award of 31 July 1989)
15	Libya Arab Jamahiriya v. Chad: (Territorial Dispute) 1990-94
16	`Guinea-Bissau v. Senegal: (Maritime Delimitation between Guinea Bissau and Senegal) 1991-95
17	Qatar v. Bahrain: (Maritime Delimitation and Territorial Questions between Qatar and Bahrain) 1991-
18	Cameroon v. Nigeria: (Land and Maritime Boundary between Cameroon and Nigeria:1994-
19	Botswana v. Namibia: (Kasikili/Sedudu Island) 1996-

There are at least 19 contentious cases between developing nations that have been submitted to the Court. This is much less than the 30 contentious cases between the developed nations delineated in Table V. However, we wish to state that the picture is not too gloomy. The important thing to note about Table VIII is that there is a growing trend in recent times among the developing nations to solve their intra-continental disputes through judicial settlement. However, there has been no inter-continental contentious case between developing States, whereas on 14 occasions cases involving developed States from different continents have been submitted before the Court (See Table V). Nonetheless it suffice to say here that there is a ray of hope on the horizon for the practice of judicial settlement of disputes among the entire members of the UN if the right steps are taken now to address the inhibiting factors facing developing States in the use of the contentious jurisdiction of the ICJ. It may also be noticed that in the cases between African States, the francophone States have litigated more among themselves; the case between Cameroon and Nigeria represents the first case before the Court between a francophone and an anglophone African state.

It may also be highlighted that among the developing States (just as occurs generally) a history of litigation before the Court seems to spur on repeat performances. In this category we may put countries like Libya, Honduras, Nicaragua, India, Pakistan and Cameroon. It may well be that it is because Cameroon has been before the Court before that it saw it fit to refer the long lasting dispute over the Bakassi area to the Court. Thus it may be said that some States have developed a culture of international litigation. Some of these States at certain periods are parties to two or more cases contemporaneously before the Court. This litigious attitude is not necessarily negative. In fact it is hoped that more and more States will adopt this proceedure.

The existence of the Court has been dogged by a clear reluctance of respondent States to submit to its jurisdiction. Even those States which have appeared before the Court before either as plaintiffs or respondents still display much reluctance in submitting themselves to the jurisdiction of the Court when newer disputes crop up. Generous use has been made of the practice of preliminary objections to challenge and block the Court's ability to adjudicate on the merits or the admissibility of most cases or of particular claims made in them. Preliminary objections were made in 26 cases within the first 50 years of the Court (see Table IX).

Table IX: Cases Involving Preliminary Objections
Corfu Channel (United Kingdom v. Albania)
Rights of Nationals of the United States of America in Morocco (France v. United States of America)
Ambatielos (Greece v. United Kingdom)
Anglo-Iranian Oil Co. (United Kingdom v. Iran)
Nottebohm (Liechtenstein v. Guatemala)
Monetary Gold Removed from Rome in 1943 (Italy v. France, United

Kingdom and United States of America)
Certain Norwegian Loans (France v. Norway)
Right of Passage over Indian Territory (Portugal v. India)
Interhandel (Switzerland v. United States of America)
Aerial Incident of 27 July 1955 (Israel v. Bulgaria)
Aerial Incident of 27 July 1955 (United States of America v. Bulgaria)
Barcelona Traction, Light and Power Company, Limited (Belgium v. Spain)
Compagnie du Port, des Quais et des Entrepots de Beyrouth and Societe Radio-Orient (France v. Lebanon)
Temple of Preah Vihear (Cambodia v. Thailand)
South West Africa (Ethiopia v. South Africa; Liberia v. South Africa)
Northern Cameroons (Cameroons v. United Kingdom)
Barcelona Traction, Light and Power Company, Limited (New Application; 1962) (Belgium v. Spain)
Eletronica Sicula S.P.A (ELSI) (United States of America v. Italy)
Aerial Incident of 3 July 1988 (Islamic Republic of Iran v. United States of America)
Certain Phosphate Lands in Nauru (Nauru v. Australia)
Oil Platforms (Islamic Republic of Iran v. United States of America)
Questions of Interpretation and Application of the 1971 Montreal Convention arising out of the Aerial Incident at Lockerbie (Libyan Arab Jamahiriya v. United Kingdom)
Questions of Interpretation and Application of the 1971 Montreal Convention arising out of the Aerial Incident at Lockerbie (Libyan Arab Jamahiriya v. United States of America)
Application of the Convention on the Prevention and Punishment of the Crime of Genocide (Bosnia and Herzegovina v. Yugoslavia)
Land and Maritime Boundary between Cameroon and Nigeria (Cameroon v. Nigeria).

Table X: Cases Involving Other Questions of Jurisdiction or Admissibility
Appeal Relating to the Jurisdiction of the ICAO Council (India v. Pakistan)
Fisheries Jurisdiction (United Kingdom v. Iceland Fisheries Jurisdiction (Federal Republic of Germany v. Iceland)
Nuclear Tests (Australia v. France) Nuclear Tests (New Zealand v. France)
Trial of Pakistani Prisoners of War (Pakistan v. India)

Aegean Sea Continental Shelf (Greece v. Turkey)
United States Diplomatic and Consular Staff in Tehran (United States of America v. Iran)
Military and Paramilitary Activities in and against Nicaragua (Nicaragua v. United States of America)
Border and Transborder Armed Actions (Nicaragua v. Honduras)
Maritime Delimitation and Territorial Questions between Qatar and Bahrain (Qatar v. Bahrain)
East Timor (Portugal v. Australia)
Fisheries Jurisdiction (Spain v. Canada)

In the eight cases in Table XI, the Court found that it could take no further steps upon an Application in which it was admitted that the opposing party did not accept its jurisdiction. Nowhere else has the case of the contentious objector to the Court's jurisdiction been more strongly conveyed than in those cases arising out of cold war tensions involving the USA and its erstwhile superpower rival the USSR and its satellite States. As it can be seen only in the Antarctic case was such a result reached in relation to a non-cold war related case. Evidently, the Court has through the years liberally construed the basis of its jurisdiction in many cases; otherwise, as shown by Tables IX and X there could have been many more cases where a finding of no jurisdiction would have been reached.

Table XI: Cases Where Respondent Successfully Denied Jurisdiction

Cases	Date
Treatment in Hungary of Aircraft and Crew of United States of America (United States of America v. Hungary)	1954
Treatment in Hungary of Aircraft and Crew of United States of America (United States of America v. USSR);	1954
Aerial Incident of 10 March 1953 (United States of America v. Czechoslovakia);	1955-1956
Antarctica (United Kingdom v. Argentina)	1955-1956
Antarctica (United Kingdom v. Chile)	1955-1956
Aerial Incident of 7 October 1952 (United States of America v. USSR)	1955-1956

Aerial Incident of 4 September 1954 (United States of America v. USSR)	1955
Aerial Incident of 7 November 1954 (United States of America v. USSR)	1958

It is noteworthy that in the following 13 cases (see Table XII) the dispute was submitted to the Court by means of special agreements:[2]

Table XII: Cases Submitted by Special Agreements	
Title	Date
Asylum (Colombia/Peru)	*1949-50*
Minquiers and Ecrehos (France/United Kingdom)	*1951-53*
Sovereignty over Certain Frontier Land (Belgium/Netherlands)	*1957-59*
North Sea Continental Shelf (Federal Republic of Germany/Denmark, Federal Republic of Germany/Netherlands)	*1967-69*
Continental Shelf (Tunisia/Libyan Arab Jamahiriya)	*1978-82*
Delimitation of the Maritime Boundary in the Gulf of Maine Area (Canada/United States of America) (case referred to a Chamber)	*1981-84*
Continental Shelf (Libyan Arab Jamahiriya/Malta)	*1982-85*
Frontier Dispute (Burkina Faso/Republic of Mali) (case referred to a Chamber)	*1983-86*
Land, Island and Maritime Frontier Dispute (El Salvador/Honduras) (case referred to a Chamber)	*1986-92*
Territorial Dispute (Libyan Arab Jamahiriya/Chad)	*1990-94*
Gabcikovo-Nagymaros Project (Hungary/Slovakia)	*1993-97*
Kasikili/Sedudu Island (Botswana/Namibia)	*1996-*

[2] In the Corfu Channel Case (United Kingdom v. Albania) the Parties made a special agreement after delivery of the Judgment on the Preliminary Objection. The case concerning the Arbitral Award Made by the King of Spain on 23 December 1906 (Honduras v. Nicaragua) was submitted by means of an application, but the Parties had previously concluded an agreement on the procedure to be followed in submitting the dispute to the Court.

During the 50 years of the Court the following 25 cases (see Table XIII) were submitted for adjudication based upon the provisions of the optional clause (though sometimes this is not the only basis relied on). This dismal rating of the compulsory jurisdiction method under the ICJ is even more glaring when one considers that during the 18 years of the PCIJ's existence 11 cases based on the optional clause in its Statute (Article 36(2)) were brought before the Court.

Table XIII: Case Submitted based on Compulsory Jurisdiction Clause	
Title	**Date**
Fisheries (United Kingdom v. Norway)	1949-51
Rights of Nationals of the United States of America in Morocco (France v. United States)	1950-52
Application of the Convention of 1902 governing the Guardianship of Infants (Netherlands v. Sweden)	1957-58
Anglo-Iranian Oil Company (United Kingdom v. Iran)	1952-2
Certain Norwegian Loans (France v. Norway)	1955-7
Interhandel (Switzerland v. United States)	1957-9
Aerial Incident of 27 July 1955 (Israel v. Bulgaria; United States v. Bulgaria; United Kingdom v. Bulgaria)	1957-60
Nottebohm (Liechtenstein v. Guatemala)	1951-5
Right of Passage over Indian Territory (Portugal v. India)	1955-60
Arbitral Award made by the King of Spain on 23 December 1906 (Honduras v. Nicaragua)	1958-60
Temple of Preah Vihear (Cambodia v. Thailand)	1959-62
Nuclear Tests (Australia v. France; New Zealand v. France)	1973-4
Military and Paramilitary Activities in and against Nicaragua (Nicaragua v. United States of America)	1984-91
Border and Transborder Armed Actions (Nicaragua v. Costa Rica)	1986-87
Border and Transborder Armed Actions (Nicaragua v. Honduras)	1986-92
Maritime Delimitation in the Area between Greenland and Jan Mayen (Denmark v. Norway)	1988-93

Certain Phosphate Lands in Nauru (Nauru v. Australia)	1989-93
Arbitral Award of 31 July 1989 (Guinea-Bissau v. Senegal)	1989-91
East Timor (Portugal v. Australia)	1991-95
Maritime Delimitation (Guinea-Bissau v. Senegal)	1991-95
Passage through the Great Belt (Finland v. Denmark)	1991-92
Land and Maritime Boundary between Cameroon and Nigeria (Cameroon v. Nigeria)	1994-

If we compare the number of declarations to the optional clause which have been made under both courts we will also find out that the PCIJ has fared better. In 1925 more than half (20 states out of 35) of the States which were Parties to the statute of the PCIJ had made a declaration under this clause. In 1934 these declarations reached maximum of 42 declarations from 49 States (i.e. 85 per cent), though the proportion reduced slightly before the onset of the Second World War when there were 40 declarations from 50 States.

The history of compulsory jurisdiction by the ICJ has, at least in statistical terms, been less encouraging. In 1947, 25 out of the 55 States Parties to the statute had accepted the compulsory jurisdiction of the Court. This represented a proportion of 45 per cent. Unfortunately even that proportion has declined steadily since that time. By 1967 it fell to 42 declarations from 125 states (i.e., 33 per cent). By 1977 it fell further to 45 declarations from 150 States (i.e., 30 per cent). From an all time low in 1987 of 46 declarations out of 162 States (i.e., 28 per cent) there has been a somewhat encouraging increase of 59 declarations from the 187 States parties to the Statute (i.e., 32 per cent) in 1996.

Nevertheless 25 cases brought under the optional clause in 50 years is low, especially when compared with the declarations in force. Furthermore, it can be seen from Tables IX and X that in at least 16 of the cases submitted under the optional clause, preliminary objections or other challenges to the Court's jurisdiction were raised. Whereas, it has been noted that not once in the 11 cases submitted under the optional clause during the life of the PCIJ was the authority of the Court exposed to mockery.[3] These facts raise the

[3] See Szafarz, *op. cit.*, p. 90

presumption that most States still view with suspicion the system of compulsory jurisdiction under the present Court. The system therefore is, to say the least, in dire need of rejuvenation.

One area which must not be left out of any such analysis of the Court's record of contentious cases is those cases arising out of Cold War politics and tensions. The Cold War refers to the ensuing tense relations between the Capitalist world and the Communist world between the end of World War II and the early 1960s. Fear and suspicion dominated the relations between the two groups led respectively by the United States and the Soviet Union who accused each other of expansionist policies. It is a truism that the ideological conflict and the severe tensions generated in this period lasted until the beginnings of the doctrines of Perestroika and Glasnost initiated by the USSR towards the end of the 1980s.The end of the Cold War could probably be pinned down to the break-up of the USSR and the political emancipation of its many satellite States. Much of international relations in the UN era has been dictated by the realities of Cold War politics. Indeed some aspects of international law and the Court's jurisprudence have been influenced by it. No less than 10 disputes out of the entire 60 contentious cases between 1946 and 1989 were born out of super power rivalry (see Table XIV).

Table XIV: Contentious Cases Related to the Cold War

1	Corfu Channel (United Kingdom v. Albania) 1947-1949
2	Treatment in Hungary of Aircraft and Crew of United States of America (USA v. Hungary) 1954
3	Treatment in Hungary of Aircraft and Crew of United States of America (USA v. USSR) 1954
4	Aerial Incident of 10 March 1953 (US v. Czechoslovakia) 1955 - 56
5	Aerial Incident of 7 October 1952, (US v. USSR) 1955 - 56
6	Aerial incident of 27 July 1955 (Israel v. Bulgaria)1957 - 59
7	Aerial Incident of 27 July 1955 (US v. Bulgaria)1957 - 60
8	Aerial Incident of 27 July 1955 (UK v. Bulgaria) 1957 - 59
9	Aerial Incident of 4 September 1954 (US v. USSR)
10	Military and Paramilitary Activities in and against Nicaragua (Nicaragua v. US) 1984

The Cases listed in Table XIV reveal a ratio of about 1:6 as regards the number of contentious cases related to the Cold War. Thus the Court undoubtedly has been of immense use in curtailing and containing potentially explosive situations in the Cold War. The Court's existence and *modus operandi* literally worked wonders in ensuring a cooling off mechanism for tensions that threatened to escalate into all out military--and perhaps nuclear--warfare. This is particularly true in relation to the rash of contentious cases which arose out of aerial incidents occurring whenever the iron curtain of the USSR and its allies was overflown.

Table XV: Chronological List of Advisory Cases

Title	Dates
Conditions of Admission of a State to Membership in the United Nations	1947-1948
Reparation for Injuries Suffered in the Service of the United Nations	1948-1949
Interpretation of Peace Treaties with Bulgaria, Hungary and Romania	1949-1950
Competence of the General Assembly for the Admission of a State to the United Nations	1949-1950
International Status of South West Africa	1949-1950
Reservations to the Convention on the Prevention of the Crime of Genocide	1950-1951
Effects of Awards of Compensation Made by the United Nations Administrative Tribunal	1953-1954
Voting Procedure on Questions relating to Reports and Petitions concerning the Territory of South West Africa	1954-1955
Judgements of the Administrative Tribunal of the ILO upon Complaints Made against UNESCO	1955-1956
Admissibility of Hearings of Petitioners by the Committee on South West Africa	1955-1956
Constitution of the Maritime Safety Committee of the Inter-Governmental Maritime Consultative Organisation	1959-1960
Certain Expenses of the United Nations (Article 17,	1961-1962

paragraph 2, of the Charter)	
Legal Consequences for States of the Continued Presence of South Africa in Namibia (South West Africa) notwithstanding Security Council Resolution 276 (1970)	1970-1971
Application for Review of Judgment No. 158 of the United Nations Administrative Tribunal	1972-1973
Western Sahara	1974-1975
Interpretation of the Agreement of 25 March 1951 between WHO and Egypt	1980
Application for Review of Judgment No. 273 of the United Nations Administrative Tribunal	1981-1982
Application for Review of Judgment No. 333 of the United Nations Administrative Tribunal	1984-1987
Applicability of the Obligation to Arbitrate under Section 21 of the United Nations Headquarters Agreement of 26 June 1947	1988
Applicability of Article VI, Section 22 of the Convention on the Privileges and Immunities of the United Nations	1989
Legality of the Use by a State of Nuclear Weapons in Armed Conflict	1993- 1996
Legality of the Threat or Use of Nuclear Weapons	1994-1996

It needs only be said that if there is any aspect of the Court's work in which there is an obvious falling off in activity it is in relation to its advisory practice. In the first decade of the Court's work there were 10 advisory cases. Response has since been on the wane--so much so that in the 1970s only three requests were made to the Court. There was a slight increase in the 1980s with five advisory cases dealt with by the Court. With the 1990s fast coming to a close there have been only two advisory requests made upon the Court. The question may then be asked whether the authorised bodies within the UN are so well guided in their affairs by their legal departments that there is no real need for the Court's authoritative guidance. A positive answer to this query may appear unduly optimistic whereas to insist that there really should have been much more resort to the Court's advisory opinion by the requisite UN bodies is to underestimate the calibre and quality of the Staff and the decision making capacity of these bodies. What appears to be clear, however, is that the more politically charged the nature of the function performed by a UN organ the more likely it is to submit requests to the Court.

Table XVI: Pattern of Requests for Advisory Cases	
REQUESTING BODY	CASES
General Assembly	(1) Conditions of Admission of a State to Membership in the United Nations (Article 4 of Charter)); (2) Reparation for Injuries Suffered in the Service of the United Nations; (3) Interpretation of Peace Treaties with Bulgaria, Hungary and Romania, First Phase; id., Second Phase; (4) Competence of the General Assembly for the Admission of a State to the United Nations; (5) International Status of South West Africa; (6) Reservations to the Convention on the Prevention and Punishment of the Crime of Genocide; (7) Effects of Awards of Compensation Made by the United Nations Administrative Tribunal; (8) Voting procedure on Questions Relating to Reports and Petitions concerning the Territory of South West Africa; (9) Admissibility of Hearings of Petitioners by the Committee on South West Africa; (10) Certain Expenses of the United Nations (Article 17, Paragraph 2, of the Charter); (11) Western Sahara; (12) Applicability of the Obligation to Arbitrate under Section 21 of the United Nations Headquarters Agreement of 26 June 1947; (13) Legality of the Threat or Use of Nuclear Weapons.
Security Council	(1) Legal consequences for States of the Continued Presence of South Africa in Namibia (South West Africa) notwithstanding Security Council Resolution 276 (1970).

Economic and Social Council	(1) Case concerning the Applicability of Article VI, Section 22, of the Convention on the Privileges and Immunities of the United Nations.
Committee on Applications for Review of Administrative Tribunal Judgement	(1) Application for Review of Judgement No. 158 of the United Nations Administrative Tribunal; (2) Application for Review of Judgement No. 273 of the United Nations Administrative Tribunal; (3) Application for Review of Judgement No. 333 of the United Nations Administrative Tribunal.
United Nations Education and Scientific Organisation	1) Judgements of the Administrative Tribunal of the ILO upon Complaints made against UNESCO.
World Health Organisation	(1) Interpretation of the Agreement of 25 March 1951 between WHO and Egypt; (2) Legality of the Use by a State of Nuclear Weapons in Armed Conflict.
International Maritime Organisation	(1) Constitution of the Maritime Safety Committee of the Inter-Governmental Maritime Consultative Organisation.

From the above it can be seen that the General Assembly in particular has made generous use of the Court's advisory jurisdiction. Whatever inadequacies developing countries have in individually instituting proceedings against the developed States would seem to have been favourably supplemented with the frequent demands for advisory opinions which put to stringent legal scrutiny the actions and activities of the superpowers in relation to the UN. Thus, there have been at least four advisory requests related to the struggle to end colonial rule in territories in Southern Africa. Other opinions were, in effect, either directed against the interests of the erstwhile communist powers, or against the perceived interests of the Western Powers. In short the use of the advisory jurisdiction has reflected the interests of the dominant forces shaping international relations in recent times and may be considered a continuation of politics by other means. At least 12 of the 22 advisory cases would appear to have been clearly instigated against positions maintained by the superpowers (see Table XVII).

Table XVII: Advisory Cases Instigated by Developing Nations Against the Superpowers

Title	Date
Conditions of Admission of a State to Membership in the United Nations	1947-1948
Competence of the General Assembly for the Admission of a State to the United Nations	1949-1950
International Status of South West Africa	1949-1950
Voting Procedure on Questions relating to Reports and Petitions concerning the Territory of South West Africa	1954-1955
Admissibility of Hearings of Petitioners by the Committee on South West Africa	1955-1956
Certain Expenses of the United Nations (Article 17, paragraph 2, of the Charter)	1961-1962
Legal Consequences for States of the Continued Presence of South Africa in Namibia (South West Africa) notwithstanding Security Council Resolution 276 (1970)	1970-1971
Western Sahara	1974-1975
Applicability of the Obligation to Arbitrate under Section 21 of the United Nations Headquarters Agreement of 26 June 1947	1988
Applicability of Article VI, Section 22 of the Convention on the Privileges and Immunities of the United Nations	1989
Legality of the Use by a State of Nuclear Weapons in Armed Conflict	1993- 1996
Legality of the Threat or Use of Nuclear Weapons	1994-1996

It must be understood that the decision to instigate these advisory requests particularly by the General Assembly, is more often than not influenced by the members of the Non-Aligned Movement, which was the dominant group in numerical terms during the crucial period of superpower rivalries. It may indeed be predicted that in the future economic interests such as the transfer of technology and redistribution of wealth would determine the types of advisory requests that developed countries may find it necessary to instigate.

Chapter 8

Overview Of The Court's Jurisprudence

It would amount to unforgivable negligence if in such a work on the ICJ as this we failed to include, even if only very briefly, a report of some decided cases. Thus in the next few pages we shall highlight some major judgements and opinions reached. This would be done in order to reveal some of the successes as well as the failures of the Court.

Cases submitted to the Court have come in all imaginable variations. They have ranged from one to a combination of the following classifications: questions involving territorial rights; questions involving the law of the sea; questions relating to treaty interpretation; questions concerning the Mandated Territories; questions on international criminal law; questions relating to environmental issues; questions involving extra-territorial rights and disputes involving the interests of natural persons, etc. We shall briefly examine a few of these in the following sections.

Question Involving Territorial Rights

In the rank of questions involving territorial rights, the Court has done tremendous work in the legal resolution of conflict. In a case between the United Kingdom and France the Court found that certain Channel Islets were under British sovereignty. In another case in 1959, the Court up-held the claims of Belgium to an enclave situated near its frontier with the Netherlands. In a case decided in 1960, the Court decided that it could not find that India had acted contrary to the obligations imposed on it by the existence of Portugal's right of passage between enclaves. It was in 1975 that the Court found in respect of the Western Sahara that there had been legal ties of allegiance between the Sultan of Morocco and some tribes living in Western Sahara, as well as legal ties between the Mauritania entity and the territory. The Court considered, however, that those legal ties were not of such a nature as might preclude application of the principle of self-determination through the free and genuine expression of the will of the peoples of the "Territory" of Western Sahara. Mali and Upper Volta (now Burkina Faso) submitted to the Court a question concerning the delimitation of a part of the land frontier between the two States. The judgement delivered on the 22nd of December 1986 confirmed the existing line of the frontier.

However, in the resolution of disputes involving territorial rights the Court has in some cases been insensitive to the peculiar demands of developing States. A good example of the alienation the Court has brought upon itself in this manner is the Temple of Preah Vihear case (Cambodia v. Thailand). The parties in this case (both ex-colonies) did not restrict their arguments within traditional narrow limits; other considerations, maybe even more important for them, were raised but the Court ignored them.

The Temple of Preah Vihear case concerned a boundary conflict between Cambodia and Thailand (formerly known as Siam). The disputed area contained an old temple of great archaeological significance. It had been built by the Khmer Peoples, the ancestors of the present Cambodian population, at the high point of their power; since then the Khmer Peoples have been forced back into smaller areas. The Siamese (from Thailand) had become stronger; they had moved into many areas of the older Cambodian empire. The temple Preah Vihear was situated high in the Dangrek mountains, which the Siamese had in their possession until the beginning of the French colonial period in Cambodia, and which were clearly separated from the Cambodian plain beneath. Both parties relied on an old agreement between France and Siam; While Cambodia relied on the annexed plan, Thailand relied on the text.

The considerations the parties wished the Court to pronounce upon included: To which of the two countries' history is the temple more related? Was the temple really under Thai control when the treaty was signed? Who had the strongest cultural relationship to the temple? Unfortunately, the important parts of these questions were, with the exception of one or two separate opinions, not dealt with by the judges at all.[1] In fact the majority rejected these arguments in a single sentence: "The parties have also relied on other arguments of a physical, historical, religious and archaeological nature, but the

[1] Prott, *op. cit.*, p. 158; see also Casteneda J., "The underdeveloped Nations and the Development of Int. Law," *International Organisation* 15 (1961) p. 38

Court is unable to regard them as decisive... The present proceedings are burdened with a great volume of evidence, a considerable amount of which is quite irrelevant.[2]

What the Court really should have examined in its majority judgements was the question of the colonial pressure of France on Siam. Consideration of the possibilities of undue influence, duress and pressure might have helped the Court reach a different, conclusion in that case. Siam's silence and lack of protest at the appropriate time was probably due to apprehension of the aspirations of France in that region at the time. It appears that the Court expected Siam of that time to conform to standards comparable to those of an independent State of developed European standards. Thus Asian scholars have looked suspiciously at this judgement. For as Judge Wellington-Koo rightly noted in his dissenting judgement, where he cited the eyewitness account of one of the Siam royalties: "It was generally known at the time that we would only give the French an excuse to seize more territory by protesting. Things had been like that ever since they came into the River Chao Phya with their gunboats and their seizure of Chantaburi."[3] Kelly's submission that as a precedent, the Temple case may be dangerously narrow in declining to look beyond immediate questions of treaty law into the broad and equivocal sphere of historical justice, is therefore correct.[4] It is probably for such reasons that African countries have been quite reluctant to send their boundary disputes arising out of their colonial experience to the ICJ.

Indeed the Court continues even in very recent cases to adopt this unsupportable stance on territorial matters arising from the colonial past, thus prompting Judge Bola Ajibola to attest in his separate opinion in the Chadian case that it appeared that territorial issues relating to Africa are constantly being judged from Eurocentric eyes.

In the Territorial Dispute between Libya and Chad, the Court was requested to determine the course of the frontier between the

---

[2] Kelly, G.M. "The Temple Case in "Historical Perspective" *BYIL.* 39 (1993) p. 462..

[3] Temple Case, *Diss. Op.* 15 and 101

[4] *Basic Facts About the United Nations*, (New York: UN Department of Public Information, 1991). pp. 132-133.

two countries in accordance with the principles and rules of international law applicable in the matter. Libya proceeded on the basis that there was no existing boundary and asked the Court to determine one. Chad, on the other hand, proceeded upon the basis that there was an existing boundary, and asked the Court to declare where that boundary was; Libya's claim was on the basis of a coalescence of rights and titles of the indigenous inhabitants (before colonial conquests) the Senoussi Order, the Ottoman Empire, Italy and Libya itself. Chad, however, pinned its claim on a Treaty of Friendship and Good Neighbourliness concluded by France and Libya on 10 August 1955, or alternatively, on French effectivites either in relation to, or independently of, other provisions in the earlier treaty.

In its judgement of 3 February 1994 the Court found in favour of the Chadian claims that the boundary between the Great Socialist Peoples Libyan Arab Jamahiriya and the Republic of Chad is defined by the Treaty of Friendship and Good Neighbourliness concluded on 10 August 1955 between the French Republic and the United Kingdom of Libya.[5] Importantly, the Court was of the view that in order not to vitiate the rule of stability of boundaries, a boundary established by treaty achieves a permanence which the treaty itself does not enjoy. Thus, the continued existence of a boundary is not dependent upon the continued life of the treaty under which the boundary had been agreed. In this manner the judgement is sound. But again it ignores the important question of the legality of colonial disposition of territories previously held by indigenous societies.

Disputes Involving Questions on the Law of the Sea

On cases relating to questions on the Law of the Sea, the ICJ has not failed to live up to its duties. In 1949, the Court found Albania responsible for the damage caused by mines in its territorial waters to British warships. The Court upheld the right of straits in time of

---

[5] Thus, the Court found the course of the boundary as follows: "From the point of intersection of the 24th Meridian East with the parallel 19°3° of Latitude north, a straight line to the point of intersection of the Tropic of Cancer with the 16th Meridian East; and from that point a straight line to the intersection of the 15th Meridian East and parallel of 23° of Latitude North." See *ICJ Reports,* 1994, p. 39.

peace. However, the Court found the United Kingdom guilty of violating Albanian sovereignty by attempting to sweep the area clear of mines, (without the permission of Albania), after the initial damage had been done. In the fisheries dispute between the United Kingdom and Norway, the Court held in 1951 that the method employed by Norway in delimiting its territorial waters was not contrary to international law. Also in 1969 there was a request emanating from Denmark, the Netherlands and the Federal Republic of Germany which led the Court to indicate the principles and rules of international law applicable to the delimitation of the areas of the North Sea Continental Shelf appertaining to each of them. The Court found in 1974 that Iceland was not entitled unilaterally to exclude the fishing vessels of the United Kingdom and the Federal Republic of Germany from areas between fishery limits earlier agreed upon in 1961 and the 50 nautical mile limit proclaimed by Iceland in 1972. In 1982, at the request of Tunisia and Libya, and in 1985, in a case referred to it by means of a special agreement between Libya and Malta, the Court indicated clearly principles and rules of international law applicable to the delimitation of the areas of the Mediterranean continental shelf appertaining to each of them. In 1981 Canada and the United States submitted as well a question as to the course of the maritime boundary dividing the continental shelf of the two countries in the Gulf of Maine area.[6] Disputes relating to the Law of the Sea are usually very contentious and evoke serious economic and political implications. However, we hold the opinion that judicial settlement via the International Court of Justice has created order in what otherwise would have been an avenue for war mongering and test of naval power among countries. The UN as a body deserves great credit for work done on the Law of the Sea. Through the Conference by the International Law Commission (a body under its control) it makes the laws while the ICJ Interprets and adjudicates them.

---

[6] See generally ICJ, *Background Note VI Collected Unofficial Summaries of Decisions Concerning the Law of the Sea 1976-1986*, 1987.

Disputes Involving Questions of Treaty Interpretation and International Economic Law

Cases involving questions of treaty interpretation have as expected arisen on several occasions. Columbia and Peru were the first to take themselves before the Court in a case involving questions of treaty interpretation: the rights of asylum in Latin America. The decision of the Court has been greatly debated in various quarters. Many scholars, especially Latin American ones, disagree entirely with the Court's judgement. It would suffice to mention Nascimento Da Silva's words here:

> The sentence passed in (sic) 20 November 1950 was most unsatisfactory and avoided taking a clear stand on the various points raised. From a Latin American point of view it contains certain affirmations which simply went to prove that the Court was not qualified to pass judgement since it had examined a typical Latin American juridical institution exclusively from an European and biased point of view.[7]

For these reasons some scholars believe that the arguments put forward by the Court... are completely unacceptable. The Court argued, however, that:

> The facts brought to the knowledge of the Court disclose so much uncertainty and contradiction, so much fluctuation and discrepancy in the exercise of diplomatic asylum and in the official views expressed on various occasions; there had been so much inconsistency on the rapid succession of conventions on asylum, ratified by some states and rejected by others, and the practice has been so much influenced by considerations of political expediency in the various cases, that it is not possible to discern in all this any constant and uniform usage accepted as law, with regard to the alleged rule of unilateral and definitive qualification of the offence. The Court cannot therefore find that the Colombian Government has proved the existence of such a custom. But even if the could be supposed that such a custom existed between certain Latin American States only, it could not be invoked against Peru which, far from having by its attitude adhered to it, has on the contrary repudiated it by refraining from ratifying the Montevideo Conventions of 1933 which were the first to include a rule concerning the qualification of the offence in matters of diplomatic asylum... For these reasons the Court has arrived at the conclusion that Columbia, as the

[7] Nascimento Da Silva, *op. cit.*, p. 105.

state granting asylum, is not competent to qualify the offence by a unilateral and definitive decision binding on Peru.[8]

While we do not want to and probably must not attempt to prove the Court completely erroneous in its judgements, we must also not fail to underscore the fact that just as the sentences of the ICJ on the question of the international status of South-West Africa made most African and Asian States distrust the Court, the Haya de la Torre Case alienated most Latin-American states, thus contributing to the atmosphere of ill-will which characterises the relations between most developing States and the principal judicial organ of the United Nations.

Tension between Iran and the UK over the affairs of the Anglo-Iranian Oil Company which have persisted throughout the present century took a dramatic turn in March 1951. The Iranian Parliament enacted a law which by imperial assent nationalised the oil company. The British Government instituted proceedings in the Anglo-Iranian Oil Company Case on 26 May. In its judgement of 22 July 1952, the Court found that it had no jurisdiction on a number of technical grounds. However, it dwelt upon an important facet of the dispute which was quite relevant for the complicated legal relations between developing States of that time and the multinational Western interests. As stated, the concession agreement of 1933 which had been negotiated between the Iranian Government and the Company through the good offices of the Rapporteur appointed by the Council of the League of Nations was held not to be an international convention.[9]

The British Government had also applied to the President of the Court to appoint an umpire for the arbitration tribunal between the Company and the Iranian Government. This was in accordance with a provision in the 1933 concession conferring such powers on the President of the PCIJ. In the absence of the Iranian Government's consent, the Court found that it was not authorised to make the appointment.

At the turn of the century, Norway floated loans on various foreign markets including that of Paris. A "gold clause" was inserted

[8] *Ibid.*

[9] *ICJ Reports,* 1952, p. 93.

in the bonds. As a result of the turbulent financial crisis arising after the first World War and the market crash of 1931, the convertibility of the notes was suspended indefinitely. Diplomatic attempts were made to require that Norway fulfill the gold clause. Norway rejected all proposals to arbitrate or to face adjudication. France eventually instituted proceedings on 6 July 1955 under the compulsory jurisdiction of the Court. The French declaration under Art. 36 of the Statute had however employed the "subjective domestic jurisdiction clause" reservation, saying it exempts from the Court's jurisdiction disputes relating to matters essentially within the national jurisdiction as understood by the French Government. This was cleverly invoked by Norway. On the basis of the principle of reciprocity, it claimed in one of its objections that the matter was within its domestic jurisdiction because the loan contracts were governed by domestic law and not by international law. The Court found that it was without jurisdiction.[10] But for the disingenuous use of the self-judging reservation employed at that time by France (it has been subsequently revoked) the legal validity of gold clauses would have received full elaboration before the ICJ on that occasion.

In 1942, the US invoked the Trading with the Enemy Act and vested in itself all the shares of the General Aniline and Film Company. The company was incorporated in the US but in reality was under the control of a German concern based in Frankfurt. The German owners controlled Aniline through a company incorporated in Switzerland later known as Interhandel. Switzerland asserted that links with the German Company had been severed by Interhandel in 1940 and therefore General Aniline was in fact Swiss and neutral when it was seized. Switzerland on that basis, refused to block Interhandel's assets along with other war property of Germans. An agreement of 1946 allowed for unlocking Swiss assets in the US. The time charter of Interhandel was in dispute up to 1948 when the US Courts were asked by Interhandel to release the assets of General Aniline. A major obstacle to the proceedings was the refusal of Interhandel to produce certain documents in court on the grounds that their production would be contrary to Swiss law. In the course of diplomatic correspondence, the US prematurely informed

---

[10] *ICJ Reports,* 1957, p. 9.

Switzerland that Interhandel's suit had been unsuccessful. Switzerland subsequently on 2 October 1957, instituted proceedings before the ICJ relying on the compulsory jurisdiction. It sought interim measures of protection to bar any sales of shares along with its claim of restoration of Interhandel's property. The US invoked its subjective domestic jurisdiction clause along with the argument that Interhandel had not exhausted local remedies. The request for interim measures was rendered unnecessary by the US undertaking not to sell shares pending the legal suit in Court. The Court ultimately decided that since legal proceedings continued in the US local remedies had not been exhausted thus upholding the US argument.[11]

In the Affairs of The Barcelona Traction Light and Power Company case, Belgium claimed reparation and compensation from Spain to the tune of $78,000,000 plus cost and interests (equivalent of 80% of assets of the company) for damage allegedly sustained by Belgian nationals who were shareholders in the Barcelona Traction Co. Extensive written and oral pleadings ensued and no less than 64 public hearings were held between April and July 1969. In its judgement of 5 February 1970, the Court found that the Belgian Government had no *locus standi* in this case. Therefore, the Belgian claims were rejected.[12]

On 6 February 1987, the US instituted proceedings against Italy in respect of a dispute arising out of the requisition of an Italian company stated to have been owned by United States' corporations. The Court constituted a special chamber to deal with the case.[13]

The work of the Court in resolving cases involving private economic interests of corporate nationals could obviously have been made more complete and relevant if States had not placed so many obstacles in the way of the Court on these matters. Probably due to dire economic considerations there is hardly any instance where

---

[11] *ICJ Reports*, 1959, p. 6. The protracted domestic litigation ended in 1965 after proceedings in the US Court of Appeals and Supreme Court. Agreement in principle was reached between the principal parties for the settlement of the litigation. the intervention of the Courts, however, was still needed on matters of detail. see Rosenne (1973), p. 150.

[12] *ICJ Reports*, 1970, p. 3.

[13] *Basic Facts about the UN*, *op.cit*., p. 134.

strenuous preliminary objections have not been made to impede the Court's jurisdiction. The result mostly has been that the merits of the cases were hardly convincingly treated if reached at all. Whereas in the Barcelona Traction the question of *locus standi* was joined to the merit, it appears that the particular issue was in fact a question of law as raised in an earlier objection in the first phase. Thus the litigants were put through unnecessary expense. Nonetheless, much has been gained in the experience of litigating International Economic law disputes before the Court. For instance, novel procedures for securing satisfaction of judgement debt previously awarded to a party was attempted in the Monetary Gold case. The prolixity of pleading in the Barcelona Traction also led to the revisions of the Rules of Court of 1972.

Case Involving the Interests of Natural Persons

In October 1949, France brought an application against Egypt, based upon the Montreal Convention of 1937. France brought the abrogation of the Capitulation's asking for compensation for the damage suffered by a number of French nationals and protected persons, to their persons, property rights and interests, as a result of certain measures taken by the Egyptian Government in May 1948 in connection with hostilities which broke out upon the termination of the Mandate for Palestine. After protracted negotiations before and after the suit the oppressive measures were repealed in February 1950 and the proceedings were subsequently discontinued.[14]

The right of US Nationals in (French) Morocco was the subject of dispute before the Court in 1950. The dispute originated from measures of currency control and control of imports introduced in 1948. Questions were raised concerning the extent of rights of exterritoriality enjoyed by US citizens under the system of capitulation and the method of evaluating imports for customs purposes under the so-called Act of Algeciras of 1906. In a long and complicated judgement of 27 July 1952 the Court decided on the various issues presented to it.[15]

[14] French Nationals in Egypt *ICJ Reports*, 1950, 59.

[15] *ICJ Reports* 1951 109; 1952, 176 Questions relating to the Act of Algeciras were earlier raised in the PCIJ case of Phosphates in Morocco (1938).

In 1919, Greek ship-owner Nicholas Ambatielos contracted with the British Government for the purchase of a number of ships still under construction. The ships were not delivered as soon as anticipated and Mr. Ambatielos became heavily indebted to the British Government. Part of the money was secured by a mortgage on the ships. Legal proceedings ensued in London in 1920 and certain official minutes were not produced by the British Government. This fact gave rise to a claim by Ambatielos for denial of "Justice." Ambatielos lost his case in the Court of Appeal in London, and made no attempt to appeal to the House of Lords. Diplomatic correspondence ensued and Britain claimed there was no international dispute. On April 1951, Greece instituted proceedings against the UK The Court was asked to declare that based upon certain agreements between the parties, the UK was obliged to determine the merits of the dispute. On 19 May 1953 the Court found that the UK was under the obligation to submit the dispute to arbitration.[16]

The rights of a German national claiming restoration of his sequestered property arose in the Nottebohm case (Liechtenstein v. Guatemala). Herr Friedrich Nottebohm was born at Hamburg in September 1881 of German nationality. In 1905 he migrated and settled in Guatemala. Following the unfortunate events of the World War, Guatemala declared war on Germany in 1943 and Nottebohm was arrested, deported to the United States and subsequently interned. His substantial property was immediately sequestered under laws similar to the UK "Trading with the Enemy" legislation. Prior to that time shortly after the outbreak of the war he visited Liechtenstein and obtained the nationality of that State, undertaking to pay annually a naturalisation tax. It was on the basis of his new nationality that he applied for a visa to return to Guatemala to resume his business activities. After the war Liechtenstein moved to recover Nottebohm's sequestered property. Upon the failure of negotiations Liechtenstein was not entitled to pursue its diplomatic protection over a national so as to transform enemy (German)

---

[16] The final award before the arbitration commission containing three neutral members was in the favour of the UK.

property into neutral property. This view was upheld by the ICJ in its judgement of 6 April 1955.

The question of who shall appoint a guardian over an infant surfaced in a legal dispute between Netherlands and Sweden. The marriage between a Dutchman and a Swedish woman produced an infant born in May 1945. The child lived all her life in Sweden. When the mother died in 1953 the father automatically became guardian under Dutch law but later a female guardian was appointed by a Dutch court handling such matters. Simultaneously a Swedish court instituted measures of protective upbringing based on a Swedish law for the protection of infants. Consequently, Swedish authorities refused the transfer of the child to the Netherlands. Diplomatic negotiations failed. On 9 July 1957 Netherlands instituted proceedings at The Hague. The legal questions at issue involved interpretation of certain provision in the Hague Convention of 1902 on the Guardianships of Infants. In its judgement of 28 November 1958 the ICJ rejected Netherlands's claims and decided to leave existing arrangements unchanged.[17]

We must note that cases involving the pursuance of the interests of specific persons are quite scanty. This probably raises the presumption that diplomatic negotiations are a preferred means of settlement of these matters. It may, however, appear that the interest of an individual is weighed against prevailing political interests in such cases. Thus the refusal of the prayers of a German by blood (albeit through his new State) to free his sequestered assets in the Nottebohm judgement. The after effects of Germany's erstwhile status as an "enemy state" surely made the judges, most of whom were from the allied States, less than enthusiastic about upholding Nottebohm's case.

There is also the undeserved inclination to view proceedings brought in the interest of individuals as bordering on trivia. Whereas, in reality what are at stake are difficult issues based on interpretation of existing international treaties, just as in the last category discussed, i.e. questions relating to international economic law. There is therefore no reason why the Court should not more often be called to adjudicate on them. In some cases, by the time the

[17] *ICJ Reports*, 1958, p. 55.

case comes before the Court, conflicting judgements would have emanated from different municipal courts making international legal proceedings particularly appropriate for overcoming such difficulty.

Cases Relating To Mandate Territories

In the cases bordering on the discharge of duties of the mandatory powers over the Mandate Territories, the ICJ's work has been more significant in its advisory jurisdiction than in its contentious jurisdiction. Four advisory opinions concerning Namibia were rendered by the Court, of whom the General Assembly requested three and the Security Council one. In the first opinion, the Court in 1950 declared that South Africa continued to have international obligations under the Mandate despite the dissolution of the League of Nations. In 1955, the Court stated over South African objections that the Assembly was correct in treating decisions concerning South Africa as "important questions" requiring a two-thirds majority vote. In 1956 also the Court declared the oral hearing of petitioners by the Committee on South West Africa as admissible and as a necessary means to enable the United Nations to perform its supervisory duties effectively. In the opinion requested by the Security Council, the Court stated categorically and unequivocally that the continued presence of South Africa in Namibia was illegal and that South Africa was under an obligation to withdraw its administration and put an end to its occupation of the territory.[18]

With respect to the colonial cases under the contentious jurisdiction of the Court however the Court seems in retrospect to have been unduly conservative and unimaginative. The South West Africa judgement for instance was a landmark decision in the history of the Court. It still stands as a veritable source of suspicion of the Court by developing States. The case was in two phases. The first phase was in the South West Africa Preliminary Objections.[19] The second phase was South West Africa (Ethiopia v. South Africa;

[18] J.B. Syatauw, *Decisions of the International Court of Justice: a Digest*, Leyden: A. W. Sijthoff Dobbs Ferry, NY: Oceana Publications, 1962, p. 342-345.
[19] *ICJ Reports* 1966, p. 319.

Liberia v. South Africa).[20] For convenience both phases of the case are treated in this work together.

On 4 November 1960 Ethiopia and Liberia -- the oldest sovereign States on the African continent--instituted separate proceedings against South Africa in a case concerning the continued existence of the mandate for South-West Africa and the duties and performance of South Africa as mandatory power. The Court was requested to make declarations to the effect that South West Africa remained a Territory under a mandate; that South Africa had been in breach of its obligations under that mandate, and that the mandate--and hence the mandatory authority were subject to the supervision of the--United Nations. On 20 May 1961 the Court made an Order finding Ethiopia and Liberia to be in the same interest and joining the proceedings each had instituted.[21]

Their common demands were that: (i) The Court should declare that South West Africa had remained a Mandated Territory as laid down by the Court itself in its advisory opinion of 1950; (ii) South Africa had continued to be in breach of the obligations imposed upon it under that mandate in accordance with Article 22 of the League's Convenient; (iii) The mandate and hence the mandatory power continued to be under the international supervision of the United Nations, which had replaced the League of Nations in this respect.

South Africa in its own response filed four preliminary objections to the Court's jurisdiction: (i) That the mandate for South-West Africa had never been or at any rate now is since the dissolution of the League of Nations no longer a "treaty or convention in force" within the meaning of Article 37 of the Statute of the Court, this submission being advanced, (a) with respect to the mandate as a whole, including Article 7 thereof and (b) in any event with respect to Article 7 itself; (ii) That neither the Government of Ethiopia nor the Government of Liberia is "another member of the League of Nations" as required for *locus standi* by Article 7 of the Mandate for South West Africa; (iii) The conflict or disagreement alleged by the Governments of Ethiopia and Liberia to exist between them and the Government of the Republic of South Africa is by reason of its nature and content not a "dispute" as envisaged in Article 7 of the Mandate for South West Africa, more particularly in

[20] *ICJ Reports* 1966. p.6.

[21] See The ICJ: *The International Court of Justice* 3rd Ed. (Hague,: 1986) p.7.

that no material interests of Ethiopia or Liberia are involved therein or affected thereby; (iv) The alleged conflict or disagreement is as regards its state of development not a "dispute which cannot be settled by negotiations" within the meaning of Article 7 of the Mandate for South West Africa.[22]

For six years, not only the parties but also the rest of the world waited expectantly for the final judgement of the World Court in this case. On July 18 1966, the Court handed down a decision which Bin Cheng characterised thus: "The decision took almost everyone by surprise; for after all the time, energy and money that had been spent on these cases the Court held that the applicants were not entitled to a judgement on their submissions because they had not established any legal right or interest in the subject matter of their claim."[23]

The Algerian government declared that the ICJ having being conceived in 1945 to direct international law by the standards of a period now gone is no longer able to meet the present requirements of international relations.[24] A representative of Brazil in the UN General Assembly called the verdict a triumph of formalism and warned on the dangers of formalism in international law.[25] It is gratifying to note today that the law has eventually had its due course (Namibia received its independence in 1990) and it has done so in favour of the right of the Namibian people to self-determination and independence. The ICJ, however, missed its opportunity to pronounce, within its contentious jurisdiction, on the illegalities perpetuated by the erstwhile apartheid machinery and by so doing help to bring it to a quicker end.

Cases bordering on International Criminal Law and Extra-Territorial Rights

The USA brought a case in 1979 against Iran concerning the seizure of its embassy in Tehran and the illegal detention of its diplomatic

---

[22] T. O. Elias, International Court of Justice Contemporary Problems: Essays on International Law (The Hague: Martinus Nijhoff Publishers, 1983) p. 342.

[23] Binn Cheng "The 1966 South-West Africa judgement of the World Court," *Current Legal Problems*, vol. 20 (1967) p. 181.

[24] UNGA Official Records, 21st Session, item 66 Provisional Agenda, 1429.

[25] *Ibid.*

and consular staff. The Court first indicated interim measures of protection (in December 1979), ordering that the Embassy should be immediately given back and the detained staff released. Subsequently in May 1980 the Court, after examining the merits of the case, found that Iran had violated its international obligations to the United States and therefore must release all hostages, hand back the embassy and make reparations. However, before the Court had occasion to fix the amount to be paid in reparation, the case was withdrawn as a result of agreement reached by both parties to the dispute.[26]

In April 1984, the Nicaraguan Government filed an application instituting proceedings against the United States on the grounds that the United States was using military force against Nicaragua and intervening in its internal affairs in flagrant violation of its sovereignty. The United States' initial reaction was in the form of an objection to the Court's jurisdiction. On May 10, of the same year, the request of the US that the case be removed from the Court's list was rejected. The Court then called on the US to refrain from action against Nicaraguan ports and in particular, the laying of mines. On 26 November 1984, the Court found that it had jurisdiction to entertain the case and that Nicaragua's application was admissible. On 27 June 1986, the Court ruled, having determined that the United States' actions towards Nicaragua were in direct breach of its obligations under international law and that it was under an obligation to desist from these actions and to make reparations to Nicaragua.[27]

We cannot fail but mention here that the conduct of the United States before the case was submitted to the Court, during the trials, and after the judgement, leaves so much to be desired. Though it is true that:

> ... United States' action against Nicaragua under international law remains illegal. The Court has by this series of decisions, established a high standard of proof and held itself unable to conclude that the United States had exercised control and sufficient discretion over the Contras

---

[26] *Ibid*, p. 135.
[27] *Ibid.*

to make their actions generally imputable to the United States of America...[28]

It remains to say that the United States of America withdrew from the merit stage of the case and refused in advance to accept the judgement of the International Court of Justice. Curiously enough both Congress and Senate by August 1986 approved 70 million dollars in military aid and 30 million dollars in so-called "humanitarian assistance" for the Contras in spite of the fact that this would strengthen the United States of America's defiance of the Court's decision of 27 June 1986.[29] On 31 July 1986 the Security Council approved a resolution calling for full compliance with the Court's decision. Elias, a former president of the ICJ stated categorically that "... the defiance of the United States of America on 27 June constitutes a clear violation of Article 94 paragraph 1, of the UN Charter.[30] The United States of America recorded a vote at the Security Council, though the "no" votes were eleven to one, with Britain, France and Thailand abstaining.[31]

In an apparent attempt to criminalize the use of nuclear weapons, the General Assembly posed the question before the Court: Is the threat or use of nuclear weapons in any circumstance permitted under international law? The Court found unanimously that there was in neither customary nor conventional international law any specific authorisation of the threat or use of nuclear weapons and, by 11 votes to 3 that neither was there "any comprehensive and universal prohibition in that regard."

The ICJ was also unanimous in concluding that threat or use of force by means of nuclear weapons which was contrary to Article 2, paragraph 4, of the United Nations Charter and failed to meet all requirements of Article 51 was "unlawful"; that a threat or use of nuclear weapons should also be "compatible with the requirements of the international law applicable in armed conflict," particularly those of international humanitarian law, as well as with specific

---

28 T.O. Elias, *United Nations Charter and the World Court*, Law Series No. 1; Institute of Advanced Legal Studies Law Series (Ibadan, 1989) p. 79.

29 *Ibid.*

30 *Ibid.*

31 *Ibid.*

obligations under treaties and other undertakings expressly dealing with nuclear weapons; and there existed an "obligation to pursue in good faith and bring to a conclusion negotiations leading to nuclear disarmament all its aspects under strict and effective international control."

However, the World Court was divided, by a vote of 7 to 7, on whether the threat or use of nuclear weapons would "generally be contrary to the rules of international law applicable in armed conflict, and in particular the principles and rules of humanitarian law," and whether "in view of the current state of international law, and of the elements of the facts at its disposal," the Court could conclude "definitively whether the threat or use of nuclear weapons would be lawful or unlawful in an extreme circumstance of self defence, in which the very survival of a State would be at stake."

Case Bordering on Environmental Issues

In 1973 the Australian and New Zealand Governments each instituted a case against France, concerning the deposit of radioactive fallout from nuclear tests conducted by France in the atmosphere above the pacific atoll of Mururoa. The Court first indicated that pending a final decision France should refrain from conducting further tests in the area. Later in 1974, judgement was delivered on the basis of statements made by French authorities that France had undertaken to refrain from atmospheric nuclear testing after 1974, so that the claims of the applicant States no longer had any object and the Court was no longer called on to render decisions on the issue.[32]

The rehabilitation of certain phosphate lands mined under Australian administration before Nauran independence became subject of a dispute in 1989.[33] Nauru claimed that Australia had breached the trusteeship obligations it accepted over Nauru under Article 76 of the Charter of the UN and under Articles 3 and 5 of the Trusteeship Agreement for Nauru of 1 November 1947. Nauru further claimed "that Australia has incurred an international legal responsibility and is bound to make restitution or other appropriate

---

[32] *Ibid.*

[33] Certain Phosphate Lands in Nauru (Nauru v. Australia).

reparation to Nauru for the damage and prejudice suffered... that the nature and amount of such restitution or reparation should, in the absence of agreement between the Parties, be assessed and determined by the Court, if necessary in a separate phase of the proceedings."

On 26 June, 1992 at a public sitting, the Court delivered its Judgement on the Preliminary Objections and found jurisdiction to entertain the dispute. However, by a joint notification filed in the Registry on 9 September 1993 the Parties informed the Court that they had, in consequence of having reached a settlement agreed to discontinue the proceedings. By an Order made on 13 September 1993 the Court placed on record the discontinuance and directed that the case be removed from the list.[34]

21 years later after the Nuclear Tests Case on August 21, 1995 New Zealand again instituted proceedings against France basing it's action on the Court judgement of December 20 1974 in the Nuclear Tests Case (New Zealand .v. France). New Zealand asked that the Court declare French underground nuclear tests on the territory of French Polynesia a violation of New Zealand's rights under international law, and further or in the alternative, that such testing was illegal unless France embarked upon an enviromental impact assessment according to accepted international standards.[35]

In a disappointing decision expressed in its order of September 22,1995,the Court dismissed New Zealand 's action holding that it was not authorised by the Judgement of 1974 because that decision only dealt with atmospheric testing. The 1995 Request by New Zealand was triggered by France's announcement on June 13, 1995, that it would conduct a final series of eight underground nuclear weapons tests at the atolls of Mururoa and Fangataufu starting September 1995 .

Though the Court stated that "the present order is without prejudice to the obligations of States to respect and protect the natural environment, obligations to which both New Zealand and

[34] *ICJ Reports,* 1993, p. 322.

[35] New Zealand introduced its claim by way of a request for an examination of the situation (Request)under paragraph 63 of the Court's judgement of 1974.

France have in the present instance affirmed their commitment"[36] it would appear that better reasoning about the lost opportunity was captured in the dissenting opinions of Judge Weeramantry and Judge (ad hoc) Palmer who both expressed their regret that the Court had not met the challenge presented by this unusual case to define and develop international environmental law.[37] This again points to fundamental differences within the Court as to its role and function in the international legal system.[38]

Recently again in Gabcikovo-Nagymaros (Hungary v. Slovakia) the Court treated another case involving complicated issues of treaty law, international economic law, State succession and the law of international water courses. This case also presents probably the first opportunity for the Court to clarify the legal obligation of a State to protect the environment in its development and in the exploitation of shared natural resources.

The case concerns the Gabciko-Nagymaros dam project. This is a large hydropower facility being constructed by the Slovakian Government on the Danube River on the basis of a 1977 bilateral treaty between the former communist States of Hungary and Czechoslovakia. The completed project will cause the diversion of over 85 per cent of the Danube's flow. There are perceived threats of contaminated drinking water, the drying up of wells, damage to farmlands, deprivation of minority rights, and danger of extinction of certain biological species. There are also fears that the largest major inland delta in Europe which contains the continent's last remaining flood - plain forest may suffer severe ecological damage. The dam is situated on a geoseismic fault and is not designed to withstand a major earthquake. In the event of the Dam ever collapsing the repercussions would be catastrophic for lives and properties in downstream villages.

---

[36] *ICJ Report* 1995, p. 306 para. 64.

[37] See the explanation offered by Judge *ad hoc* Palmer of the inclusion of paragraph 63 in the judgement of 1974, it is perhaps true of paragraph 64 of the order of 1995.

[38] see Peter H.F. Bekker "New Zealand challenge to underground nuclear testing by France in Sahara Pacific - ICJ judgement in 1974 nuclear testing case (New Zealand v. France)" *AJIL,* April 1996.

As a result of widespread public protests and increasing awareness of the adverse environmental impact of the project, the new democratic government of Hungary suspended construction. On March 24, 1992, the Hungarian parliament moved to approve the termination of the treaty and a diplomatic note to this effect was delivered to the Czech and Slovak Federal Republic on May 19, 1992. Slovakia announced its readiness to continue unilaterally the construction and diversion of the river in spite of Hungary's request to negotiate a solution to the problem. On October 23, 1992 Slovakia began unilateral diversion of the Danube. The two parties signed a special agreement on April 7, 1993, to refer the dispute to the ICJ. The case was duly filed July 2, 1993. Hopes were high that the judgement in this case would enunciate environmental law principles which would become *erga omnes* for the next century.

In an inconclusive ruling the Court simply held that Hungary was wrong to suspend and then in 1989 to abandon its obligations to the dam project as spelled out in its treaty obligations to the dam project. But the Court also said Czechoslovakia had proceeded illegally when it diverted the river through the dam in 1992. The countries were then ordered to proceed to negotiate in good faith to ensure the achievement of the objectives of the 1977 treaty. It is clear that this judgement ignores the crucial environmental considerations upon which the entire case rests. The real loser in this judgement is nature particularly the River Danube. Farmers in the region had testified that they saw magnificent wetlands dry up before their eyes. Such evidence if ignored can only be to the detriment of mankind.[39]

Also on 8 July, the ICJ decided, by 11 votes to 3, that it was not able to give the advisory opinion requested by the World Health Organisation (WHO) in May 1993 on the question: "In view of the health and environment effects, would the use of nuclear weapons by the State in war or armed conflict be a breach of its obligations under international law including the WHO constitution?" The Court established that although WHO was "authorised to deal with the effects on health of the use of nuclear weapons, or of any hazardous

---

[39] Cf. James Perlez, "World Court Leaves Fight over Danube Unresolved," *New York Times*, Sep.26, 1997,.p.12.

such activities engaged in, the question put to the Court in the present case relates not to the effects of the use of nuclear weapons on health, but to the legality of the use of such weapons in view of their health and environmental effects." The view was taken that whatever those effects might be, WHO competence to deal with them was not dependent on the legality of the acts that caused them, and there was no doubt that questions concerning the use of force, the regulation of armaments and disarmament are within the competence of the United Nations and lie outside that of the specialised agencies.

It is needless to say that this decision is little more than a triumph of formalism. The Court's discretion should have been exercised in favour of rendering the opinion requested since the issues raised go to the very root of the continued existence of the human race. Obviously the attitude of the Court to adjudication of environmental problems is very conservative and the Court seems to avoid dealing directly with the environmental issues raised probably in an attempt to avoid rocking the boat and radically raising environmental standards. In this light the jurisprudence of the erstwhile PCIJ is more impressive. For instance a land-mark decision of the PCIJ in the *Chorzow Factory case*[40] stated without equivocation that it was wrong for a State to allow the conduct of activities within its territory in such a way that environmental damage is caused to the interests of other States.

In any event the least that the Court should have done with respect to those contentious cases bordering on environmental issues would have been to give declaratory judgement. Such a declaration by the Court as to the illegality of the act of the defendant State would constitute both a measure of satisfaction to the wronged State as well as a rebuke to the *tortfeasor* State. By so doing States would be discouraged from further harming the environment. It can only be hoped that with the advent of the Standing Environmental Chamber of the ICJ the record of the Court with regards to environmental disputes will improve.

---

[40] PCIJ (1928), Series A, no. 9

Nigeria Before the Court

The history of the involvement of Nigeria with the ICJ is a long and noble one. Of the ten judges who have served on the Court's Bench between 1946 and 1997, three were of Nigerian nationality. One of these -- Judge Taslim Elias--served as Vice-President and President of the Court between 1979 and 1985. The other two judges are C.D. Onyeama (1967-1976) and Prince Bola Ajibola (1991-1994).Through these jurists of distinction and international repute Nigeria has surely contributed its "widow's mite" to the development and success of the Court.

A host of international treaties to which Nigeria is party provide for the jurisdiction of the Court. The acceptance of the Court's compulsory jurisdiction is now over 30 years old. having been signed in 1965 by the then Minister of State for External Affairs, Nuhu Bamali. Nigeria thus became among the first African countries to embrace this remarkable tool for pacific settlement of dispute. By so doing it expressed great confidence in the work of the Court and its ultimate utility in the preservation of world peace. Nigeria's early acceptance of the optional clause may most likely have served as encouragement to other African and developing countries to accept the jurisdiction of the Court in this manner. Thus for instance, just before Cameroon dragged Nigeria before the Court recently, it hurriedly accepted the optional clause in order to take advantage of Nigerian declaration.

Eminent jurists have also noted that the Nigerian Government's acceptance of the optional clause in its declaration signed by Nuhu Bamali, Minister of State for External Affairs, is less complicated than most other declarations. It does not harbour any of the abominable *Connally* type reservations or some of the less audacious but equally obtrusive reservations known to exist. Transparent and genuine intent to accept the Court's jurisdiction in all legal disputes is demonstrated. The text of the declaration Acceptance of Compulsory Jurisdiction by Nigeria dated 14 August 1960 reads as follows:

> Whereas under Article 93 of the United Nations Charter all Member States are *ipso facto* parties to the Statute of the International Court of Justice;

> And, whereas the Government of the Federal Republic of Nigeria has decided to accept the Compulsory Jurisdiction of the International Court of Justice and it is necessary to make a declaration in terms of Article 36 (2) of the Statute of the Court; Now therefore I, Nuhu Bamali, Minister of State for External Affairs, hereby declare that the Government of the Federal Republic of Nigeria recognises as compulsory *ipso facto* and without special agreement, in relation to any other State accepting the same obligation that is to say, on the sole condition of reciprocity, the jurisdiction of the International Court of Justice in conformity with Article 36, paragraph 2, of the Statute of the Court.

On 29 March 1994 the Republic of Cameroon filed in the Registry of the Court an Application instituting proceedings against the Federal Republic of Nigeria in a dispute concerning the question of sovereignty over the Peninsula of Bakassi, and requesting the Court to determine the course of the maritime frontier between the two States in so far as that frontier had not already been established in 1975.

As a basis of the jurisdiction of the Court in this case, *The Land and Maritime Boundary between Cameroon and Nigeria*, the Application refers to the declarations made by Cameroon and Nigeria under Article 36, paragraph 2, of the Statute of the Court, by which they accept that jurisdiction as compulsory.

In the Application Cameroon refers to "an aggression by the Federal Republic of Nigeria whose troops are occupying several Cameroonian localities on the Bakassi Peninsula," resulting in great prejudice to the Republic of Cameroon," and requests the Court to adjudge and declare:

> (a) that sovereignty over the Peninsula of Bakassi is Cameroonian, by virtue of international law, and that that Peninsula is an integral part of the territory of Cameroon;
>
> (b) that the Federal Republic of Nigeria has violated and is violating the fundamental principle of respect for frontiers inherited from colonisation (uti possidetis juris);
>
> (c) that by using force against the Republic of Cameroon, the Federal Republic of Nigeria has violated and is violating its obligations under international treaty law and customary law;
>
> (d) that the Federal Republic of Nigeria, by militarily occupying the Cameroonian Peninsula of Bakassi, has violated and is violating the

obligations incumbent upon it by virtue of treaty law and customary law;

(e) that in view of these breaches of legal obligations, mentioned above, the Federal Republic of Nigeria has the express duty of putting an end to its military presence in Cameroonian territory, and effecting an immediate and unconditional withdrawal of its troops from the Cameroonian Peninsula of Bakassi;

(f) that the internationally unlawful acts referred to under (a), (b), (c), (d), (e) above involve the responsibility of the Federal Republic of Nigeria;

(g) that, consequently, and on account of the material and non-material damage inflicted upon the Republic of Cameroon, reparation in an amount to be determined by the Court is due from the Federal Republic of Nigeria to the Republic of Cameroon, which reserves the introduction before the Court of (proceedings for) a precise assessment of the damage done by the Federal Republic of Nigeria;

(h) in order to prevent any dispute arising between the two States concerning their maritime boundary, the Republic of Cameroon requests the Court to proceed to prolong the course of its maritime boundary with the Federal Republic of Nigeria up to the limit of the maritime zones which international law places under their respective jurisdictions.

Again on 6 June 1994 Cameroon filed in the Registry of the Court an Additional application "for the purpose of extending the subject of the dispute to a further dispute" described as relating essentially to the question of sovereignty over a part of the territory of Cameroon in the area of Lake Chad," while also asking the Court to specify definitively the frontier between Cameroon and Nigeria from Lake Chad to the sea. Cameroon requested the Court to adjudge and declare:

(a) that sovereignty over the disputed parcel in the area of Lake Chad is Cameroonian, by virtue of international law, and that that parcel is an integral part of the territory of Cameroon;

(b) that the Federal Republic of Nigeria has violated and is violating the fundamental principle of respect for frontiers inherited from colonisation (uti possidetis juris), and its recent legal commitments concerning the demarcation of frontiers in Lake Chad;

(c) that the Federal Republic of Nigeria, by occupying, with the support of its security forces , parcels of Cameroonian territory in the area of

Lake Chad, has violated and is violating its obligations under treaty law and customary law;

(d) that in view of these legal obligations, mentioned above , the Federal Republic of Nigeria has the express duty of effecting an immediate and unconditional withdrawal of its troops from Cameroonian territory in the area of Lake Chad;

(e) that the internationally unlawful acts referred to under (a), (b), (c) and (d) above involve the responsibility of the Federal Republic of Nigeria;

(f) that consequently, and on account of the material and non-material damage inflicted upon the Republic of Cameroon, reparation in an amount to be determined by the Court is due from the Republic of Nigeria to the Republic of Cameroon, which reserves the introduction before the Court of (proceedings for) a precise assessment of the damage caused by the Federal Republic of Nigeria;

(g) that in view of the repeated incursions of Nigerian groups and armed forces into the Cameroonian territory, all along the frontier between the two countries, the consequent grave and repeated incidents, and the vacillating and contradictory attitude of the Federal Republic of Nigeria in regard to the legal instruments defining the frontier between the two countries and the exact course of that frontier, the Republic of Cameroon respectfully asks the Court to specify definitely the frontier between Cameroon and the Federal Republic of Nigeria from Lake Chad to the sea.

Cameroon further requested the Court to join the two Applications "and to examine the whole in a single case."

At a meeting between the President of the Court and the representatives of the Parties held on 14 June 1994, the Agent of Nigeria indicated that his Government had no objection to the Additional Application being treated as an amendment to the initial Application, so that the Court could deal with the whole as one case. Cameroon chose Mr. Keba Mbaye and Nigeria Prince Bola A. Ajibola to sit as judges *ad hoc*.

By an order of 16 June 1994,[41] the Court seeing no objection to the procedure suggested, fixed 16 March 1995 as the time limit for filing the Memorial of Cameroon, and 18 December 1995 as the time limit for filing the Counter Memorial of Nigeria. The Memorial was filed within the prescribed time limit. On 13 December 1995, within

[41] *ICJ. Reports* 1994,p.105.

the time limit for the filing of its Counter Memorial, Nigeria filed certain preliminary objections to the jurisdiction of the Court and to the admissibility of the claims of Cameroon.[42]

According to the provisions of Article 79, paragraph 3, of the Rules of the Court, proceedings on the merits are suspended when preliminary objections are filed. The proceedings have then to be organised for the consideration of those preliminary objections in accordance with the provisions of that Article.

By an order of 10 January 1996,[43] the President of the Court, taking into account the views expressed by the Parties at a meeting between the President and the Agents of the Parties held on 10 January 1996, fixed 15 May 1996 as the time limit within which Cameroon might present a written statement of its observations and submissions on the preliminary objections raised by Nigeria. Cameroon thereafter filed such a statement within the prescribed time limit.

On 12 February 1996, the Court Registry received from Cameroon a request for the indication of provisional measures, with reference to serious armed incidents which had taken place between Cameroonian and Nigerian forces in the Bakassi Peninsula beginning on 3 February 1996. In this request Cameroon made reference to submissions made in its Application of 29 May 1994, further supplemented by an Additional Application of 6 June of that year, as also summed up in its Memorial of 16 March 1995, and requested the Court to indicate the following provisional measures:

(i) the armed forces of the Parties shall withdraw to the position they were occupying before the Nigerian armed attack of 3 February 1996;

(2) the parties shall abstain from all military activity along the entire boundary until the judgement of the Court has taken place;

(3) the parties shall abstain from any act or action which might hamper the gathering of evidence in the present case.

The Court held Public sittings to hear the oral observations of the Parties on the request for the indication of provisional measures between 5 and 8 March 1996. At another public sitting on 15 March 1996, the President of the Court read the Order on the request for

42 *ICJ Yearbook* (1995-96) p.190-193.
43 *ICJ. Reports* 1996, p. 3.

provisional measures made by Cameroon.[44] In its Order the Court first recited the history of the proceedings. The Court then began by considering that the two Parties had each made a declaration neither of which included any reservation recognising the compulsory jurisdiction of the Court in accordance with Article 36, paragraph 2, of the Statute and that those declarations constituted a *prima facie* basis upon which the Court's jurisdiction in the present case might be founded. The Court further considered that the consolidated Application of Cameroon does not appear *prima facie* to be inadmissible in light of the preliminary objections raised by Nigeria.

The Court went on to observe that the power conferred upon it by Articles 41 of the Statute of the Court and 73 of the Rules of the Court to indicate provisional measures had as its object to preserve the respective rights of the Parties, pending a decision of the Court, and presupposed that irreparable prejudice should not be caused to rights which were the subject of dispute in judicial proceedings. Thus it followed that the Court should be concerned to preserve by such measures the rights which might subsequently be adjudged by the Court to belong either to the Applicant or to the Respondent; such measures being only justified if there was urgency.[45]

The Court came to the conclusion that the mediation conducted by the President of the Republic of Togo and the ensuing communique announcing the cessation of all hostilities published on 17 February 1996 did not deprive the Court of the rights and duties pertaining to it in the case brought before it. It was clear from the submissions of both Parties to the Court that there were indeed military incidents and that they caused much suffering, occasioned fatalities -- of both military and civilian population--causing many to be wounded or unaccounted for, in addition to causing major material damage. The rights at issue in the proceedings were sovereign rights which both parties claimed over territory, and these rights also concerned persons; and armed actions had regrettably occurred on territory which was the subject of proceedings before the Court.

Independently of the requests for the indication of provisional measures submitted by the Parties to preserve specific rights, the Court possessed by virtue of Article 41 of the Statute the power to

[44] *ICJ Reports* 1996, p.13.
[45] See further our discussion of Interim Measures above.

indicate provisional measures with a view to preventing the aggravation or extension of the dispute whenever it considered that circumstances so required.

The Court found that the events that had given rise to the request, and more especially the killing of persons, had caused irreparable damage to the rights that the Parties might have over the Peninsula; that persons in the disputed area and, as a consequence, the rights of the Parties within that area were exposed to serious risk of further irreparable damage; and that armed actions within the territory in dispute could jeopardise the existence of evidence relevant to the present case. From the elements of information available to it, the Court took the view that there was a risk that events likely to aggravate or extend the dispute might occur again, thus rendering any settlement of that dispute more difficult.[46]

The Court here observed that, in the context of proceedings concerning the indications of provisional measures, it could make definitive findings of fact or of imputability, and that the right of each Party to dispute the facts alleged against it, or challenge the attribution to it of responsibility for those facts, and to submit arguments, if appropriate, in respect of the merits, should remain unaffected by the Court's decision. The Court then drew attention to the important fact that the decision given in the current proceedings in no way prejudged the question of the jurisdiction of the Court to deal with the merits of the case, or any questions relating to the admissibility of the Application, or relating to the merits themselves and also left unaffected the right of the Governments of Cameroon and Nigeria to submit arguments in respect of those questions.[47]

The Court took judicial notice of letters of the President of the Security Council, dated 29 February 1996, which called upon the two Parties to respect the cease-fire they agreed to on 17 February in Kara, Togo; to refrain from further violence, and to take necessary steps to return their forces to the positions they occupied before the dispute was referred to the International Court (of Justice); and also the proposal of the Secretary-General of the United Nations to despatch a fact-finding mission into the area in dispute (Bakassi Peninsula), the Court indicated the following interim measures of control:

---

[46] *ICJ Yearbook*, 1995-96, *op.cit.* pp.194-5.
[47] *Ibid.*

(1) Both Parties should ensure that no action of any kind, and particularly no action by their armed forces, is taken which might prejudice the rights of the other in respect of whatever judgement the Court may render in the case, or which aggravate or extend the dispute before it;[48]

(2) Both Parties should observe the agreement reached between the Ministers for Foreign Affairs in Kara, Togo, on 17 February 1996, for the cessation of all hostilities in the Bakassi Peninsula;[49]

(3) Both Parties should ensure that the presence of any armed forces in the Bakassi Peninsula does not extend beyond the positions which they were situated prior to 3 February 1996.[50]

(4) Both Parties should take necessary steps to conserve evidence relevant to the present case within the disputed area.[51]

(5) Both Parties should lend every assistance to the fact-finding mission which the Secretary-General of the United Nations has proposed to send to the Bakassi peninsula.[52]

There is no doubt that the interim measures indicated by the Court are in this case both necessary and adequate. Any one familiar with the history of the Bakassi dispute will attest to the severity of the positions adopted by both parties since the dispute started at the time of Nigerian Independence. There have been in this period numerous military skirmishes involving both armies and most times leading to the loss of civilian lives. It is in fact nearly impossible to put an actual figure on the number of alleged attacks since in most cases both countries deny each others allegations and counter allegations.

What might appear curious is the position adopted by Nigeria's *ad hoc* Judge Ajibola. He was against four of the five measures indicated by the Court; in three of these he found himself in the minority of one. A cursory look at the measures indicated will however, reveal that there is nothing inherently against the interest

[48] This was held unanimously.

[49] This was held by sixteen votes to one with Judge ad hoc Ajibola against.

[50] This was held by twelve votes to five with Judge Ajibola being among the minority.

[51] Held by sixteen vote to one with Judge *ad hoc* Ajibola against.

[52] Held by sixteen votes to one with Judge Ajibola against.

of Nigeria contained in them. All that the measures seek to achieve is to retain the *status quo* so that whatever eventual judgement reached by the Court will not have been prejudiced by illegal acts of the parties. Resort to the force of arms is clearly one of such possible illegal acts. Since the parties are already before the Court further armed incidents no matter by which side initiated should not arise. With due respect to the learned Judge, it must be said that there appears to be nothing to be gained where a national judge whether titular or *ad hoc* adopts a dissenting stance against such clearly just measures deliberated upon by the Court in favour of his country. In fact, the only thing achieved by this stance is to heighten the probable suspicion that Nigeria may have initiated fresh aggression leading to the situation where Cameroon had to approach the Court for measures of protection; a conception very damaging to the overall image (if not the case) of Nigeria.

Such instances lend credence to critics of the institution of *ad hoc* judges in international litigation before the Court. The experience that has been gained since 1947 of the participation of judges *ad hoc* is that it appears more difficult for *ad hoc*, Judges to reach decisions unfavourable to the position of their States. Apologetics of the system of *ad hoc* judges think that this is not necessarily a manifestation of bias, and may be explained by a similarity of outlook and legal tradition."[53] At least in this instance this cannot be said to be so since Judge Ajibola was himself a one time titular judge of the ICJ with good knowledge of what influences the Court's reasoning in such matters.

It is hoped that the learned Judge will continue to serve even in his new role in the enviable tradition he displayed as an ICJ Judge. The aim of Judges of the Court whether titular or *ad hoc* should be resolution of contentious disputes based upon true sense of justice. Instances occur of members of the Court being included in the majority decision against the contentions of their States. There are at least two remarkable instances where national Judges stated in their individual opinions positions which in some respect go beyond the judgement itself in dismissing the case of their respective States.

---

[53] See Rosenne (1957).

Chapter 9

Problems of the Court

Reluctance of Developing States to Submit Disputes to the Court

On the issue of reluctance of developing States to submit disputes to the World Court there have been various theories posited. For scholars like Anand; apart from the general international climate since the Second World War--the political and ideological division of the World society, tension between communist and non-communist nations--one of the most important reasons for the present crisis of confidence in the Court is the vast expansion of the international society from the old "Hague community."[1] So far we agree with this school of thought. We, however, disagree with the analysis given as to why the new States are not enthusiastic about employing the existing International Court. First, we disagree with the claim that Western States have a monopoly in the belief in the so called Hague Tradition which implicitly possesses "...a deep faith in the rule of law, in the primacy and superiority of the important role of International Courts in the establishment and maintenance of international peace and security." Secondly, one greets indignantly the proclaimation that the ".. new nations which had so far no voice and no status" and were "... no more than objects of international law ...neither European or Western, but represent former colonies or vassals of the Western world"[2] have their own completely different religions, social and cultural background with little or no legal culture. This it is believed "..partly explains their intransigent

[1] Anand, *The Future of the International Court of Justice*: (Dobbs Ferry, NY: Oceana, 1986)

[2] *Ibid.*

behaviour and their attitude towards judicial settlement of their international disputes."[3]

It is our considered opinion that these views are a misrepresentation of history and falsification of facts. Though it is true that developed countries have utilised the Court a lot (as shown in our statistical survey), we would like to state here that it is only so when compared to the number of times the third world countries have refered their disputes to the Court. If we are really to compare the number of times judicial settlements is used by developed countries to the number of times they actually engaged in international conflicts one would wonder wherein lies the so-called "Hague tradition." It would be clear from such an exercise that developed nations have more often than not, refused to resort to judicial settlement. This view is given a backing by the fact that developed countries of the World have fought more international wars than all new-developing States put together. For instance, one may ask where the Hague tradition was during the two world wars. It is also not true that developing States do not believe or are averse to, legal procedures and judicial settlement. It is our view that African cultures, for example, have their own long standing concepts of judicial practice based on justice and fair play. In this light we tend to believe Anand when he writes that:

> The history of the International Court since the Second World War does not show that the reasons for their reluctance to go before the Court more often are related to their different religious or cultural backgrounds. In fact, during the last decade they have shown a somewhat greater tendency to resort to the Court than any other group. The new countries have, of course, been extremely cautious and have not been prepared to accept any far- reaching obligations in regard to compulsory jurisdiction.

Another view as to why newer States in the international system reject the existing International Courts and the International law they profess is that, the UN through its International Court perpetuates an "Old Law of Domination."[4] The newer States reject the Court not just because of differences between it and their indigenous cultural

[3] *Ibid.*

[4] This term was borrowed from R.P Anand" Role of International Adjudication " in *The Future of the International Court of Justice*. v.1 (1986)p.3.

traditions (except that they are not prepared to accept any more the view that their civilisations or cultural traditions are inferior to any other), but because of their resentment of their past history of subjugation. While we will not subscribe to the view that the Court applies only "an old law of domination," we cannot but accept that: "Much of western law, including international law, has developed in response to requirements of the western business and civilisation."[5] Gross also wrote that: "No one can of course deny that the traditional international law, inherited today by the world-wide community of States, is a product of the Western Christian civilisation."[6] Thus it would be true that the jurisprudence of the Court is biased in the favour of the old colonials. This law according to Anand not only permitted discrimination against the non-western peoples, but sanctified their exploitation and subjugation. It recognised the use of force and war as legal and cared little about intervention in the internal affairs of other States. It sanctified colonialism and accepted the unequal treaties forced upon weaker States as valid and legal.[7] Thus it seems that the law relating to responsibility of States did no more than to have "served to cloak and protect the imperialistic interests of the international oligarchy."[8] In our view then what the Third World States resent and react to in regards to judicial settlement is their incorporation into an international judicial system designed without them and in effect against them.

The new States, eager to annul the former law of domination as expressed in the criminal system and unequal treaties, were and still are obsessed with nailing the coffin shut on colonialism and racism by making use of every means at their disposal. They even seem to have used the International Court to achieve this goal. As Anand notes:

> They view colonialism as a form of 'permanent aggression' against their territories and want it to be accepted as such. It is important to note that they were happy with various advisory opinions of the International

[5] O. J. Lissitzyn, "International Law in a Divided World" *International Conciliation*, No. 542 (March 1963) p. 37.

[6] Cross, *Ibid.*, p. 39.

[7] Jorge Castaneda, "The Underdeveloped Nations and the Development of International Law," *International Organisation*, (1961) p. 39.

[8] *Ibid.*, p. 39.

Court of Justice in the South-West Africa cases because the Court on the whole supported their views. but when the Court rejected in 1966 the demand of Ethiopia and Liberia to declare the colonial rule of South Africa over South-West Africa as illegal and dropped the case on a preliminary ground, the new countries in a mood of frustration and anger attacked the Court and its members[9]

Thus, as of now, no party can be blamed for the situation. The Court can not be blamed since it must enforce established legal rights; and the under-developed states must not be blamed either for hesitating to take their disputes to a Court where they are most likely to lose. This situation accounts for objections to the jurisdiction of the Court in such cases as the *Anglo-Iranian Oil Company Case*; the Nationalisation of the Suez Canal; the Incorporation of Dutch properties in Indonesia and the Right of Passage of the Portuguese territories over independent Indian territory[10]

It is, therefore, suggested that international law can only win the respect of the new States if it reflects attitudes toward justice that correspond with the attitudes held by the majority of States in the international system. We agree with scholars like Professor Northrop who believe that the creation of an effective world law requires a new conceptual synthesis grounded on the basic fact of ideological and cultural pluralism. He wrote: "No nation will ever accept, nor should it ever accept, any positive legal decision by any legal body that relates its own indigenous living law norms." To him international law must contain, not only the legal thinking of the West, but must also include the living law norms of Confucian, Buddhist, Hindu and Muslim countries of Asia and Africa.[11] This is very desirable. We agree with C.W. Jenks[12] when he explains that if we wish the law of nations to retain an authority in a period when the political texture of world affairs has completely changed we must seek a wider basis of authority for the fundamentals of existing law.

---

[9] Anand, *op.cit.*, p. 7-8.

[10] More cynical scholars like Guha Roy believe that the reaction is very normal. He believes that, "... to the extent of which the law favours such rights and interests, it protects an unjustified statues quo." So therefore the Law should be ignored. See S.N. Guha Roy, "Is the Law of Responsibility of States for Injuries to Aliens a part of Universal International Law? *AJIL*:55 (1961) p.866.

[11] Northrop, *The Training of the Nations* (1952) p. 269.

[12] C.W. Jenks, *Prospects of International Adjudication* (1964)

He wrote: "An international law which is but Roman law writ large, with a dash of empiricism derived from the common law tradition, lacks sufficiently broad and deep foundations to impose itself upon the seething world of today." The world, he pointed out, needs an intellectual revolution which will give us a legal system with sufficiently broad and deep foundations to command the allegiance of the world community with a fundamentally changed composition and distribution of influence. He reasonably concludes that: "Only a multicultural and multi-legal system will enable us to master the task."

Developing States on their part must also realise that submission to international law and international jurisdiction can not be excluded from the determining boundaries and contemporary considerations of State sovereignty. It is clear that the old concept of absolute and exclusive sovereignty has been jettisoned. It will therefore not serve a State any useful purpose to cling tenaciously to outmoded theories in order to avoid international jurisdiction in all instances. The new States must therefore not attempt to use sovereignty granted them by international law in a manner subversive of international law and justice itself.

Need to Accept Judicial Settlement

There have been varying and divergent views by learned authors as to whether the ICJ has performed well in judicial settlement of international disputes. As a matter of fact the efficacy of judicial settlement of international disputes has been put to question by States and individuals alike. There are those who believe that the ICJ has been a total failure and there are those who regard the achievements of the Court as a complete success. It is our opinion that one must be wary of falling into these extremes.

For instance, Weisberg's observation in his study on the role of the ICJ in the United Nations System has

> ... revealed that the International Court of Justice, the principal organ of the United Nations, has failed to meet the expectations of its founders. It has not played a significant part in the peaceful settlement of disputes and has not resolved the major or even most of the minor issues of the

> last decades. Perhaps the expectations envisaged for it were unfounded, conceivably they were misplaced.[13]

Anand also sounded a pessimistic note on judicial settlement when he wrote that:

> the judicial approach was limited by the fact that given the nature of major disputes in international relations and the clashes of political and economic interests *a judgement might not always constitute a settlement* (*emphasis mine*). There was little doubt that a much disputed line between legal and political disputes was purely a subjective phenomenon born in the minds and will of the disputants. But many issues would be as far from settlement after the judge had said all that a judge could properly say as they were before any such pronouncement. It is difficult to circumscribe world history in unemotional legal procedures (emphasis mine). Similarly, when states demanded a change in the law, a decision according to law could hardly help to resolve the dispute. Indeed, authoritative statements of legal rights could even impede settlement by encouraging rigidity on one side in a controversy which might have been settled by a political compromise.[14]

As earlier mentioned these views can be regarded as unduly pessimistic and extreme. However, it is interesting to cite the optimistic views of Anand in another work where. he wrote as follows:

> It is almost universally recognised that the International Court is one of the noblest institutions we have achieved in modern times. It is, of course, possible to disagree with some of its decisions here and there, but generally speaking the quality and integrity of the Court's decisions are accepted by commentators as excellent. Judges being human are of course not infallible but no judge has ever been accused of being swayed by considerations of personal gain. In spite of all the criticism against the South West Africa case, there is no basis for any doubt about the independence of the Court as a whole. Indeed, it is entirely wrong and rash to denounce a legal institution on the basis of a single case. In any case the Court seems to have regained confidence in the Namibia opinion. The impartiality of its decisions and the integrity of its decisions and the integrity of its judges are unquestionable.[15]

Though we notice with concern some measure of vacillation on Anand's part, we tend to agree with his last view. It is true there is a problem of acceptability of the Court by all States in practice, but

---

[13] Guenter Weisberg, "The Place of the International Court of Justice in the United Nations System" Leo Grass (ed.) *ibid.*, p. 186.

[14] Judicial Settlement of International Disputes *op. cit.*, p. 180.

[15] Anand in Leo Cross Ed., *op. cit.*, p. 16.

this does not make the Court a failure. It only points to the fact that the Court is not yet perfect and could still improve. The problem with judicial settlement of disputes in the international system, however, is not solely of the Court's making. As Rogers rightly notes

> The basic problem is the reluctance of States to refer international disputes to the Court. States have not been willing to accept the idea of going to the Court on a regular basis, expecting to win some cases and lose others. If the legal adviser of the Foreign Ministry is not confident of victory he recommends against litigation.[16]

Weisberg also noted this problem when he wrote that:

> A non-litigious attitude has been characteristic of many states whenever a conflict arises, and this position is entirely independent of any East-West confrontation. This is not to say that there are no differences between Communist and non-communist States or between Communist States.[17]

As though in reaction to the views of Rogers and Weisberg, Salmon said at a conference on Judicial Settlement of International Disputes that: "This negative view is not pessimistic merely realistic." He noted as well that:

> Even those states which championed compulsory adjudication most energetically made extremely little use of it... If our legal traditional placed so much emphasis on judicial settlement this was perhaps partly the result of projecting municipal models into the international system...[18]

Spectacular progress would have been made in this direction if the concerned States had heeded President Mikhail Gorbachev of the erstwhile Soviet Union in 1987 when he advised that all the five permanent members of the Security Council should set a good example by submitting themselves to the compulsory jurisdiction of the Court. The permanent members held a number of meetings at legal adviser level with a view to at least compiling a list of subjects which the Court would be likely to entertain in the event of a dispute. Eventually no agreement was reached. Only the UK among

---

[16] Rogers, "The Rule of Law and the Settlement of International Disputes" *AJIL*. Proc. 285 at 286 (1970).

[17] Weisberg *op. cit.*, p. 181.

[18] *Judicial Settlement of International Disputes, Symposium. op. cit.*, p. 165.

the veto-wielding permanent members currently subscribes in general terms to the compulsory jurisdiction of the Court. This fact is to say the least disturbing. If even the Super Power States shy away significantly from the Court's jurisdiction then it is hardly surprising that the Court remains underused.

The warning of Cecil Hurst (former legal Adviser to the British Foreign Office) to his country in 1929 on the eve of acceptance of obligatory jurisdiction of the PCIJ, is still relevant to all States which accept judicial settlement. He wrote:

> ... If this purpose materialises, the effect will touch the lives of all of us... the obligatory jurisdiction of an international tribunal means that within that field the Country imposes upon itself an authority to which we all must bow. It means the voluntary renunciation by the State of that non-subordination to any other authority which is the distinguishing feature of sovereignty... The day will come when the Court will give some decision which will be very unpopular. We shall not always be the victorious litigant in the disputes submitted to the Court. If the decision goes against us in some case which has evoked wide spread interest, and which is felt to touch the interests of the people at a vital spot, there may well be popular clamour, clamour which will become dangerous unless well-informed opinion knows enough about the Court to steady the opinion of the crowd, and to keep it from thinking that the Court was necessarily in the wrong because it decided against us.[19]

It is, unfortunate that this maturity of reasoning by Hurst is not widespread among States. The situation is that states loathe to submit their disputes for judicial settlement for the fear of losing.

Judge Jessup in a study he conducted, sampled nine situations which at one time or the other presented opportunities for judicial settlement. He found out that for the most part these disputes continued to linger or saw the application of a different technique. Given close scrutiny, some of the specified disputes listed by him reveal that, in each of the conflicts at least one party did not have the slightest interest in employing judicial procedure, and in some instances did not even acknowledged the existence of a dispute.[20]

There are many instances of this. The Philippines offer to Malaysia to refer the Sabah issue--the question of the Philippines'

---

[19] Cecil Hurst writing a preface to J. W. Wheeler-Bennett and Maurice Fanshawe; *Information on the World Court, 1918-1928* (London: George Allen and Unwin 1929), p. 5.

[20] Philip Jessup, *The Price of International Justice* (1971)p. 31-41.

claim of sovereignty from the Sultan of Sulu and Malaysia to Sabah (one of the constituent states of Malaysia)-- to the Court, led to a spirited debate. This was during the twenty-third session of the General-Assembly. To the Philippines: "[t]he conflict is of a legal nature." However, in the words of Malaysia's representative "pursuance of the claim as a justiciable matter adjudicable by the International Court is irrational" for it is considered as a mixture of "fantasy, fallacy and fiction." This assertion caused Ambassador Jiminez of the Philippines to inquire whether Malaysia agrees to fearing "fantastic, fallacious or fictional" action. To this, Malaysia's Ambassador in turn noted that he chooses to "disregard the *non-sequitor*" of the question. He added as follows:

> As a legal dispute it is incapable of precise description. It is incapable of proper formulation... for the reason that fiction is formless, features fathomless. its nature renders your grip of its essentials indecorously absurd. That is what the Philippine Government wants us to do.[21]

Such are the steamy arguments that take place before Nations agree or disagree to submit disputes to judicial settlement. Not always do plans to submit disputes to judicial settlement elicit such picturesque language but the results are mostly similar. According to Weisberg the list of such impasses is endless.[22]

The recommendation that the Court should be put to greater use by States is not one which rests upon the premise that it should be seised of all conceivable "small cases." This is a position that some suggested with the thinking that rapid settlement of small cases would enable the Court become part of the mechanics of international relations in the everyday life of peoples. Other jurists contend that it would rather be better if cases of medium importance are submitted before the Court, such as for instance, the limits and scope of territorial jurisdiction. Yet another group of jurists insist that the Court should ideally be only seised of vital issues such as the application of the Convention on the Prevention and Punishment of

---

[21] GAOR 23rd Sess., 1696th Plenary Mtg., Oct., 15, 1968, paragraphs 199, 200, pp. 22 and 1707th Plenary Mtg., Oct. 25, 1968, paras. 247-248, pp. 23-24, Quoted in Anand, *op. cit.*, p. 4.
[22] Weisberg, *op. cit.*, p. 177-8.

the Crime of Genocide or the lawfulness of the use of nuclear weapons.[23]

The fact is that in reality all these approaches in their strict sense are unrealistic, no matter how ingenious they may appear to be. It is difficult to know which case is vital or of medium or lesser importance . What is important is that States must be more willing to submit their disputes to Court more often than they do now particularly whenever there is a legal issue to be determined. It is probably necessary to consider the interesting proposal made by the Netherlands relating to General Assembly resolution 3232 (xxix) of 5 November, 1974. Here it was suggested that parties to a dispute could agree to submit certain legal questions to the Court, the political aspects of which would be settled separately.[24]

The reasoning has also been advanced that with the end of the cold war institutions such as the ICJ have lost their relevance and that what is needed now to resolve international disputes is mere diplomatic action. Such reasoning is impossible to defend against the background of the unique forms of tensions known to the world in recent times. The demise of the cold war and bi-polarity in the world has not led to an era of peace and stability. Rather fresh horrors are simply revealing themselves.[25] The Court on its part must therefore meet these new challenges.

Hopeful declarations in the early 1990s that the end of the Cold war would make possible a "new world order" have merely led to widespread disappointment and concern. While great power confrontations have eased, international stability has in fact eroded since the 1991 collapse of the Soviet Union. Not only have long-running regional conflicts persisted in Korea, Angola and Afghanistan, but substantial bloodshed and chaos have erupted in

[23] See the address of the President of the Court, Judge Mohammed Bediaoui at the 30th meeting of the fiftieth session of the General Assembly held on 12 October 1995, "The International Court of Justice: When will its future Be?" *ICJ Yearbook* 1995-96, pp. 268-270.

[24] See the Address of His Excellency Professor Diogo Freitas Do Amral, President of the UN General Assembly at the anniversary of the Court's fiftieth anniversary of its inaugural sitting held in April 1996 the text of which is reproduced in *ICJ Yearbook* 1995-96, p. 243.

[25] Micheal S. Lund, *Preventing Violent conflicts: a Strategy for Preventive Diplomacy*, (Washington, D. C.: United States Institute of Peace Press, 1997) p. ix.

such places as Somalia, Rwanda, Chechnya and the former Yugoslavia.

Recent quagmires point to the insufficiency of diplomacy. Experiences in places such as Angola, Liberia, Somalia and Bosnia have fostered a deep scepticism of the merits of peace- keeping and a widespread reluctance by States to become involved in other people's political and military quagmires. In the former Yugoslavia, for example, notwithstanding the eventual achievement of an uncertain Bosnia peace agreement, most of the time UN and European Union mediators had to demonstrate heroic perseverance and patience merely to arrange the occasional and short-lived cease-fires. International diplomacy unaccompanied by the credible threat of military force or powerful immediate sanctions has little effect in inducing combatants to desist from fighting. Even where UN economic sanctions have been imposed by the political organs they have not worked well nor have they been easy to implement, at least not until a great deal of harm has been caused to innocent civilians in the targeted countries as well as countries co-operating in the imposition of sanctions. Thus the limits of peace-keeping and diplomacy as international instruments have also been revealed. It may well be that what is required in most of these situations is judicial determination of existing rights and obligations. After this has been done sufficient guidance exists for collective action against erring States. Indeed many festering disputes are aided by the discordant reactions of the international community which is unsure as to where the legal fault lies in a particular set of relationships.

Now more than ever is the time to expand the use of the Court. If indeed it is true that we are living in a golden age of peace and high civilisation, it would appear to be true also that legal settlement is more widely supported, and even more sought after, when there is less tension in the international system. The proof of this may be found in the fact that it was during the periods of extreme international tension in the cold war that the Court was bereft of cases and could not perform its function. Although a query with some merit has been raised as to whether it would not be true to say that "tension" without any clearly defined object, generally prevented the emergence of specific legal disputes, which are the ones appropriate for submission to the Court?[26]

It is quite clear, as Weisberg also notes, that: "... States are more likely to prefer a process of negotiation, or the tactic of allowing the issues to linger in the hope that they may fade or that time may otherwise work to their advantage, than a system of adjudication."[27]This attitude in our view is deplorable as it can provide ground for unhealthy developments. If States refuse to resort to adjudication for no other reason than the furtherance of their selfish ends, the world is the worst for it. We agree totally with Weisberg when he postulate that:

> ... Such incidents were undoubtedly lost opportunities but the question arises--from whose view point? Surely from the standpoint of the international legal system; clearly from the standpoint of peaceful settlement; obviously from the standpoint of the international rule of law; unquestionably from the standpoint of the international community. However, they were not lost opportunities from the standpoint of one of the parties, or were they? Certainly the recalcitrant state did not think so, did not view the issue in this fashion and, therefore it may be asked if it placed the matter in a proper option in deciding not to litigate? In terms of this query there is no distinction between disputes and controversies involving members of the international community.[28]

If parties to a dispute seek the assistance of the ICJ and do not place unnecessary obstacles in its way, the Court will serve significantly in international conflict resolution. The heart of the problem of the Court is undoubtedly "... the policies and views of its potential clients, whether these be States in contentious cases or organisations in advisory opinion."[29] The refusal of states to submit their disputes to adjudication unless they are sure to win is very unfortunate. Such reluctance might have a short-term advantage from a national vantage point. However, what nations have refused to understand is that acceptance of judicial settlement has definite long term gain from an international vantage point. Settlement of international disputes via the ICJ on a frequent basis will help clarify, once and for all, legal rights and obligations pertaining to

---

[26] . Mohammed Bedjaoui, *ICJ Yearbook* 195-96, pp. 263, 276.
[27] Weisberg, *op. cit.*, p. 185.
[28] *Ibid.*, pp. 179-80.
[29] *Ibid.*, p. 176.

various countries. No one can seriously deny that justice is essential for world peace. Thus, Ferencz was very much in order when he stated categorically that there can be: "no peace without justice."[30] He reminds us that the first article of the UN Charter recognised that international security was linked to justice and law. Article 1 contains *inter alia* that one of the purposes of the United Nations is "... to maintain international peace and security adjustment of international disputes or situations which might lead to a breach of the peace... by peaceful means and in conformity with the principles of justice and international law." To conclude then there is no gainsaying that judicial settlement is prime among the most important means of ensuring peaceful co-existence among nations.

However, we agree totally with Ferencz when he points out that, for there to be lasting peace and security, not only the international judicial system and the International Court should be strengthened. We must break new grounds for peace in the judicial, economic and social spheres.[5] When former US Defence Secretary and World Bank President Robert McNamara described the plight of a billion humans living in poverty, he warned: "Unless there is visible progress toward a solution we shall not have a peaceful world."[32] In essence there is in reality, a symbiotic inter-relationship between the countries of the world. Therefore we posit that there is a link between international peace and international equity. Ferencz was quite correct when he expounded that:

> When it comes to international law enforcement, everything is linked. There can be no social justice without a peaceful method of settling irreconcilable disputes among states; no court with binding authority to resolve such disputes until states agree to give it the necessary power; no need for an international army if there is no international court; no consent to judicial determinations until there are common norms of international behaviour; no agreement on norms until nations with different values develop mutual confidence and a will to compromise in order to enhance the security and well-being of all peoples. Progress must be made in all areas if effective international law enforcement is to

---

[30] Benjamin B. Ferencz, *Enforcing International Law - A Way to World Peace: A Documentary History and Analysis*. Vol. 2 (Dobbs Ferry, NY: Oceana Publications 1983) p. 489.

[31] *Ibid.*

[32] *Ibid.*

become a reality. The ultimate challenge is whether human intellect will prevail over man's destructive capacity.[33]

These words of Ferencz mirror very adequately our position on the desirability of judicial settlement of international disputes. and also impressively covers our fears on why the full potentials of the Court may never be realised. However, there is a point of divergence between Ferencz's view and ours which is important to note. Ferencz believes that in accepting judicial authority; "if the parties failed to reconcile differences by such traditional methods as negotiation conciliation or arbitration compliance might be obtained by voluntarily turning to judicial settlement as prescribed in Art. 33 of the Charter."[34] It is our position that this view would not serve well in international dispute management. What is most disconcerting about this view is that it suggests that judicial settlement could always be totally removed from the picture of things, since States only "might ... voluntarily" settle judicially. This position is an inadequate interpretation of Article 33. This article does not discourage judicial settlement as a first stage. There is no reason why judicial settlement must play a second fiddle in the settlement of international disputes. Judicial settlement, in our view, should, and could adequately, come first. The idea that judicial settlement must only be resorted to when both parties expressly volunteer, has in our view become outmoded. This is clear from the number of states which are embracing the compulsory jurisdiction of the Court through the optional clause.[35]

We hereby recommend that judicial settlement be utilised more often than not by all State. It should no longer be viewed as an unfriendly act by States to take one and another to the International Court. The advantages of judicial settlement of international disputes far outweigh all probable disadvantages. For one, International judicial settlement-- following the dictates of natural justice--makes all parties to a dispute equal in its considerations. Thus a Superpower state expects and gets no special concessions in relation to a weaker state before the international tribunal. Secondly, judicial

---

[33] *Ibid.*, p. 493.
[34] *Ibid.*, pp. 481-2.
[35] *Supra* .

settlement by the International Court reduces political considerations to their barest minimum. Thirdly, though the cost of seeking judicial settlement via the ICJ. is by every means astronomical in monetary terms, it is eventually cheaper since it nullifies the possibility of war, -- a much more costly venture. Interim measures of protection rendered by the Court can also save States from further damages. Fourthly, judicial settlement via the International Court in our view renders the best third party settlement with the use of independent judges with tested and proven competence. Fifthly, the International Court makes use of established legal procedures which have proven to be very effective in dispute settlement even in the municipal setting.

Structure/Composition of the Court and the Law Applicable as Factors Militating Against the Acceptance of the Court

Judges are the one element which cannot be dispensed with if cases are to be submitted to a Court and decisions are to be given. Cases cannot be decided by a row of empty chairs. It is for this very reason that scholars agree that, "The Permanent Court of Arbitration was a Court only in name... the Conference could not agree as to how the men were to sit in the chairs"[36]. Fortunately, despite all the criticism that can be levied against the ICJ, it is clear that the law is settled as to whom can sit as a judge on the bench of the Court. How it has worked out in practice however is another thing.

The procedure for the appointment of judges is interesting. There is no doubt that it mixes both legal and political considerations while seeking to exclude as far as possible the influence of National States over the judges.[37] The members of the Court are elected by the General Assembly and Security Council (voting separately) from a list of qualified persons drawn up by the national groups of the Permanent Court of Arbitration, or by specially appointed national groups in the case of UN members not

---

[36] See Cecil Hurst, Legal Adviser to the Foregin Office In J. F. Wheeler-Bennet and Mourice Fanshawe, *Information on the World Court 1981 - 1928* (London: George Allen and Unwin , (1929) p. 6.

[37] Shaw, *op. cit.*, p. 658.

represented in the PCA (Article 4 and 5 of the Statute). The insertion of this provision was to restrict political pressures in the selection of judges, but in practice governments do exercise a major influence upon the nomination process of the national groups.[38] There is also a close co-ordination between the General Assembly and the Security Council in electing judges; so political considerations do obtrude.

There are fifteen judges on the bench of the ICJ. The members of the Court are elected for nine years, one third of the total number of judges being elected every three years; thus there is continuity in the Court's work. In the event of a vacancy, an election is held and the new judge holds office for the remainder of his predecessor's term (Statute Articles 14 and 15). The judges of the Court enjoy diplomatic privileges and immunities when on official business, and a judge's tenure is secured in that he cannot be dismissed except by unanimous decision of the other members of the Court that he has ceased to fulfil the required conditions (Statute, Article 18). These conditions include the requirement that no member may exercise any political or administrative function or engage in any other professional occupation. No member may act as agent, advocate, or counsel in any case and no member may participate in the decision of any case in which he has previously taken part as agent advocate, or counsel for one of the parties or as a member of an international or national court, or of a commission of inquiry, or in any other capacity (Statute, Article 16 and 17).

The requirement in Article 9 that persons to be elected should be representative of the main forms of civilisations as well as the principal legal systems of the world is undoubtedly based on lofty considerations, but it has engendered much bargaining at election time. It has also encouraged closer scrutiny of the political stances of individual candidates and has engendered much criticism.[39] However, what we find most disappointing is that in practice this lofty design has not been properly adhered to with the result that the

---

[38] *Ibid.*

[39] See for instance Rosenne, Law and Practice of the International Court, Vol. 1, 2nd ed., 1985 p. 184 et seq: Gros, The Future of the International Court of Justice, *op. cit.* pp. 373,381: Shaw, *op. cit.* p. 659.

law applied by the Court has been quite questionable for a long time now. Some problems invariably emanate from the composition of the Court in terms of the number, qualifications and nationality-spread of the judges. The newly independent countries of Asia and Africa have rightly been concerned that the composition of the Court has not kept pace with the increasingly universal composition of the international community. Like traditional International Law, it is still believed to be Eurocentric and biased in favour of European States.[40]

For instance, our study reveals that in the 50 year existence of the Court, only nine judges have been Africans. At most times there are no more than two judges from Africa on the Court's bench. Only three out of these have become vice-president of the Court out of which only one judge -- Taslim Elias from Nigeria-- has ever served as an elected President of the Court.

Whereas Table XVIII shows that only nine judges from five States out of the 50 states in Africa have served on the Court's bench, Table XIX shows us that 32 judges from 14 European States have sat on the Court's bench as full judges. The effect of this is that Europe always has an overwhelming majority of Judges at the Court.

TABLE XVIII: Judges from Africa who have served on the Court's Bench

	Name	**Period of office**	**Country**
1.	A.H .Badawi	1946-1965	Egypt
2.	El-Erian	1979-81	Egypt
3.	T.O. Elias	1979-81	Nigeria
4.	L. Ignatio-Pinto	1964-79	Benin
5.	I. Forster	1964-82	Senegal
6.	K. Mbaye	1982-91	Senegal

[40] Anand, "Role of International Adjudication," *op. cit.*, p. 7.

7.	C.D. Onyeama	1967-76	Nigeria
8	B.A. Ajibola	1994 (expired)	Nigeria
9.	M Bedjaoui	1997 (expired)	Alegeeria
10.	Koromah	2003 (expire)	Sierra Leone

TABLE XIX: Judges from Europe who have served on the Court's Branch

	Name	Period of Ofice	Country
1.	J. Basdevent	1946-94	France
2.	F. de Castro	1970-79	Spain
3.	Ch. De Visscher	1946-52	Beligium
4.	Sir G. Fitzmaurice	1960-73	U .K
5.	L. Ferrari Bravo	- 1997	Italy
6.	S. A. Colunsky	1960-53	USSR
7.	C. A. Fleischhauer	-2000	Germany
8.	A. Gros	1964-84	France
9.	G. Guillaume	-2000	France
10.	G. Herczegh	2003	France
11.	R. Higgins	-2000	UK
12.	H. Klaested	1946-61	Nonway
13.	V.M. Koretsky	1961-70	Norway
14.	S.B. Krylov	1946-52	USSR
15.	M. Lachs	1967-93	Poland
16.	G. Lactereitote Lacharriere	1982-87	France
17.	H. Lauterpacht	1955-60	UK
18.	Sir Arnold McNair	1946-55	UK
19.	G. Morrelli	1961-70	Italy

20.	P.D. Morozov	1970-85	UK
21.	H. Moster	1976-85	F.R.Germany
22.	S. Petren	1967-76	Sweden
23.	J. Spiropoulos	1958-67	Greece
24.	Sir H. Waldock	1973-81	UK
25.	B. Winarski	1946-67	Poland
26.	M. Zoricic	1946-58	Yogoslavia
27.	Sir Robert Jennings	1982-95	UK
28.	R. Ago	1979-95	Italy
29.	J. Evenson	1985-94	Norway
30.	N.K. Tarossov	1985-95	Russian Federation
31.	G. Guillaume	2000	France
32.	V.S. Vershchetin	2003	Russian Federation

The lopsidedness of representation of the continents before the Court is glaring. While more than half of the potential client States are based in Africa and Asia, their representation on the bench of the Court had hardly been commensurate with their number. From a dismal representation of only two judges from Africa and Asia in the Court's original composition in 1946 until fairly recently when the Court records an increase on its bench to three African judges and three Asian judges the effect has been that much of the law expounded by the Court in this century lacks the benefit of imput from African and Asian Countries.

An enquiry into the requirement that the "principal legal systems of the World should be assured" on the Court's bench also leaves much to be desired. This study examined the composition of the Court as at 1994 and picked out all the judges from the developing States. The discovery is that practically all these learned men were trained in European Laws and in the seats of Western legal education. Thus their legal view point has been conditioned to be Euro-centric and Western- oriented. One may then wonder what the `principal legal systems" requirement is worth.

Table XX: Academic Qualifications and Place of Legal Training of ICJ Judges From Developing Countires As at 1994		
Moh'd Shahabudden	Guyana	Bar final Inns of Court (1952); called Middle Temple, London (1954); Queens Council 1966; London University Degrees LL.B. B.Sc (Econ) LL.M, Ph.D
A. Aguilar Mawdsley	Venezuela	Master degree in Civil Law, McGill University Sunma cum Laude
R. 'Ranjeva	Madagascar	Diplome d'etudes superieures des sciences, University of Paris, called to the Bar Lincoln's Inn, 1962 (Barrister at Law) LL.B London University
B.A. Ajibola	Nigeria	Called to the Bar, Lincoln's Inn 1962 (Barrister at Law) LL.B London University
M. Bedjaoui	Algeria	Doctor of Law Diploma of the Institute of Political Studies University of Grenoble; Research Assistant at the Centre national de la recherche scientifique (CNRS) Fraance 1956-58.
C.G. Weeramantry	Sir Lanka	B.A., LL.B. LL.D., University of London honoris causa, University of Colombia. Sir Hayden Starke Professor of Law, Monash University, Melbourne, Australia.

If Prott's thesis that an ICJ judge's views on legal matters depends entirely on his training in a particular system of law is anything to go by then it is clear that the law applied by the ICJ so far is just European Law writ large. For fifty years none of the judges at the ICJ has had any special training in Islamic legal jurisprudence nor in say African traditional laws. Taslim Elias, who was once the Court's President admitted that nationality looms large in the selection of the members of the Court.[41] He noticed the apparent willingness with which the Western European judges of the Court and their associates adopted a teleological or even hyperteleological interpretation of the relevant provisions of the Charter in the Certain Expenses of the United Nations Case. They succeeded in establishing the liability of both the Soviet Union and

[41] Elias writing in Max Planck Institute, *op. cit.*, p. 24.

France to contribute their quotas to the cost of maintaining UN Peace- Keeping Forces in the Middle East and the Congo. This approach he notes might have appealed to the French judge had France's political attitude not dictated otherwise.[42]

It is true that the suggestion of a line of cleavage between developing and developed States' judicial philosophies can only be generally correct and is by no means true in every instance. For example, the French-trained judge Ignatio-Pinto of Benin has spoken out against a creative role of the Court.[43]

All the same the opinion in the Certain Expenses Case is curious since it has become recognised that it is the newer States and the judges therefrom that tend to see the law as a process. Syatauw regards it typical of many Asian countries to have less rigid rules open to more adjustments. On the other hand older States and the judges therefrom have a view of law as rules of attitude.[44]

Perhaps in no other place is this sharp divide so easily discernible as in the "colonial" cases such as the South-West Africa cases, Right of Passage Case and the Northern Cameroons Case. As we noted earlier on, varying opinions of the judicial role emerged clearly in the South West Africa cases of 1962 and 1966. In 1962 Judges Spender and Fitzmaurice wrote:[45]

> We are not unmindful of, nor are we insensible to, the various considerations of a non-judicial character, social humanitarian and others, which underlie this case; but these are matters for the political rather than the legal arena. They cannot be allowed to deflect us from our duty of reaching a conclusion strictly on the basis of what we believe to be a correct legal view..[46]

The majority of the Court adopted this view in 1966. Dismissing Ethiopia and Liberia's claims the Court readily pronounced that: "This is a court of law and can take account of moral principles only in so far as these are given a sufficient expression in Legal form."[47]

---

[42] *Ibid.*
[43] Ignatio-Pinto, Fisheries jurisdiction Case, Declaration 37-38.
[44] R. Higgins "Diverging Anglo-American Attitudes to International Law: Introductory Statement," J.J.C. Syattauw, *Some Newly Established Asian States and The Development of International Law.* 1981, p. 23.
[45] Spender and Fitzmaurice, South West Africa Case 1962, Joint Diss. *op. cit.*, 466.
[46] *Ibid.*
[47] South West Africa Case 1966, 34, para. 49.

The problem, however, is that what they believe and the "moral principles" of which they were willing to take account was what could be expected of a Court which had a majority of European nationals and European trained jurists on its bench. Shaw's note that the opinions of the individual judges can be crucial, particularly in sensitive cases, and that the alteration in the stance adopted by the Court with regard to the Namibia case between 1966 and 1971 can be attributed in large measure to changes in the composition of the Court that took place in the intervening period, is quite convincing.[48] Cheng's analysis of these changes in composition is also very instructive. In 1966 the judges that formed the majority were Gros (France), Fitzmaurice (U.K), Morrelli (Italy), Spender (Australia), Spiropoulos (Greece), Winiarski (Poland) and Van Wyk (South Africa) whereas in 1962 when the Court by eight votes to seven, affirmed its jurisdiction to adjudicate on the merits, the composition of the Court -- Alfaro (Panama), Badawi, (UAR), Bustamante Y. Rivero (Peru), Jessup (USA), Koo (China) Koretsku (USSR), Morreno Quiatana (Argentina),and Mbanefo (Judge *ad hoc* from Nigeria).-- was different and the majority included jurists from developing and communist states.

That the American judge voted along with those from the developing and communist worlds is curious but we shall able to explain this phenomenon shortly.

The philosophy behind the pronouncements of the majority, Prott warns, "can be identified with a significant theme of English jurisprudential writing, starting with Austin's determination to isolate norms of positive law from other ethical and moral considerations and still influential today in the work of Hart. Often related to this line of thought generally associated with a positivist view of law, is the influence of logic in legal theory.[49]

It may, however, be argued that European jurists do not possess a monopoly of logical reasoning. Indeed, Common Law (we are tempted to say) is not that common. There are indeed divisions of opinion on the common law among European and Western States which have left marks on the theory of international law.

---

[48] Shaw, *op. cit.*, p. 659.
[49] Prott, *op. cit.*, p. 205.

> The typical American International Lawyer regards his English counterpart as rigid, narrow and making little contribution to the needs of contemporary society; while the average English International Lawyer regards his American colleague as obsessed with politics and jargon and increasingly indifferent to the standards of meticulous scholarship.[50]

Thus while Prott protests that "it is simplistic to suggest as Elias has done that the stance of the Western European judges represented the national or group interests of States who elected them there,".his arguments that the agreement of the European judges in the South West Africa judgement... is probably better accounted for by the fundamental judicial philosophy which the old World judges shared and which was antipathetic to the views of the "New World" judges[51] only serves to underscore the need for a more balanced bench and change in the law applicable.

There is a clear and present need for a re-examination and reappraisal of the laws the ICJ applies and the way legal reasoning is carried on in the Court. There is the need for stability and there are demands for change. We make bold to say that it is how the Court handles these two antithetical features that determines its future. The newer States in the international system are wary of the international courts and the international law they profess. They perceive that the UN through its international court perpetuates an "Old Law of Domination"[52] as stated earlier in this chapter the newer States are wary of the ICJ not just because of differences between the Court and their indigenous cultural traditions (except that they are not prepared to accept any more the view that their civilisations or traditions are inferior to any other, but because of their resentment of their past history of subjugation.

Therefore (as another author noted) "the real dilemma of the Court is the dilemma of international law. The law created by a majority in another age under very different circumstances, it is felt, cannot guarantee the subjective rights of all states."[53] Developing

---

[50] Higgins, "Policy Considerations and the International Judicial Processs." ICLQ 17 (1968) p. 58.

[51] *Ibid.*

[52] Anand, "Role of International Adjudication" in Gross (1979) *op. cit.*, p. 3.

[53] *Ibid.*, p. 10.

countries have stressed many times that certain institutions of international law "... were the juridical expression of a few special political interests of a particular social structure and of a certain state of international relations." These institutions they view as having "...reflected the outlook and interests which had been established by economic and military might."[54] It has also been pointed out that certain customs of wide scope became incorporated into positive law when in fact they were the work of five or six powers.[55]

Such suspicions and disappointments are largely responsible for the reserved distance many developing States have kept from the Court especially in relation to its contentious jurisdiction. They have made good use of the Court's Advisory jurisdiction. There are many western scholars who would have none of this. Scholars like Professor Gross, Professor Schwarzenberger, Professors Kunz, Lauterpacht and Anand, deny the need for what we may call "international judicial activism."

Gross warns that "if the court should indulge in judicial law making and should make light of the consent of States to the law, it might abruptly find itself in the position of a leader without a following."[56] Kunz points out that "Courts are generally unfit except to give objective and impartial decisions.[57] Even more extremist views come from Lauterpacht and Schwarzenberger. Lauterpacht, for instance, believes that:

> However legitimate or unavoidable in some cases, judicial legislation cannot be the normal method of improving law, even when the application of existing law is felt to be unsatisfactory or distasteful as a matter of justice or common sense.[58]

This over-rigid position is also shared by Schwarzenberger who stated that:

---

[54] Martinez Morcillo (Spain) UNGAO 25th Sess. Sixth Committee: Provisional Summary Records, UN Doc. A/C6/SR 1211.

[55] *Ibid.*,

[56] *Ibid.*, p. 30.

[57] *Ibid.*, p. 12.

[58] H. Lauterpacht, *The Development of International Law by the International Court* (London: Oxford University Press, 198), p. 6.

> there are no gaps in international law which cannot be closed by resort to the sources of international law. The practice of the permanent Court of International Justice has shown that the problem of *non liquet* (i.e., that owing to the lack of relevant legal rules), a decision on the basis of law is not possible, is in international law merely imaginary.[59]

While we must agree that it is not the normal function of a court to engage in extensive legislation, we do not see any plausible reason why the Court should continue to apply rules which alienate it from most of the world. To claim that the present available rules are always adequate or that no grey areas exist, is to close one's eyes to reality. It is indisputable that international law is developing and in fact is bound to continue changing. The function of the Court to develop the law is attested to by its ability to decide *ex aequo et bono*. Schwazenberger himself writing on the jurisdiction to decide *ex aequo et bono* agrees that:

> Such authorisation does not include merely the application of equitable consideration within the limits of existing international law. It extends to the exercise of corrective equity, that is to say, to a legislative power granted ad *hoc* by the parties if the Court should find that within the limits of the existing law it cannot find an equitable solution.[60]

Therefore, we advocate greater flexibility by the Court. It is a fact that in international relations, the judicial function may be regarded as inapplicable to issues concerning the personality of parties to a dispute. However since a considerable proportion of crises and dispute which have occurred since 1945 have concerned secession and decolonisation wars, pitting the Western colonial masters against newer nationalities, the Court should have been more flexible in dealing with the issue of *locus standi*.

In terms of the law to be applied by the Court we agree with Schachter's advice that, in this as elsewhere, we can maintain our equilibrium by motion. The result may well be a less tidy, more uncertain, more confusing international law. But it will be surely responsive and relevant to what the people want. For the

---

[59] G. Schwarzenberger, *Manual of International Law*, 3rd ed. George W. Kelton (ed.) (London: Stevens and Sons, 192, p. 133.

[60] *Ibid.*, p. 14.

international lawyer, this should be more challenging and rewarding.[61]

Procedure of the Court and The Problem of Time and Costs

The length of time needed to prosecute a case at the ICJ is a problem. The time spent in the dispensation of justice by the Court is considered too long. Apart from the increases in cost accruable in a long lasting case, there is also great truth in the biblical saying that: "Hope deferred maketh the heart sick."[62] Unfortunately, again it is the developing States that are worst hit by this problem. Our analysis of Table II of this paper shows us that, not only do developing States have a poorer number of instances in which they submitted their disputes to the Court both individually and collectively (See also Tables VI, VII, VIII) but also that their cases tend to last longer at the ICJ. For instance, out of the 37 contentious cases that lasted for a period spanning between three to nine years; 19 of such long-lasting cases involved the developing countries. To paint the gloomy picture well, we must point that out of the eight longest lasting cases with duration spanning five to nine years (some of which are actually still pending), seven cases involve developing States.

The procedure in contentious cases starts with the institution of proceedings and appointment of Agents. As soon as proceedings are instituted the special agreement or the application filed is communicated to all concerned and to the States entitled to appear before the Court (Statute Article 40: Rules Article 38, paras 4 and 5; Artcle 39 para. 1 and Article 5: Artcle 39 para. 1 and Article 42) the Registrar arranges for the publication of a communiqué informing the general public and the press that proceedings have been instituted.

The party which files a document instituting proceedings informs the Court at the same time of the name of the Agent who will be its representative in the proceedings and take steps on its behalf; and the other party then appoints its agent as soon as possible

[61] Oscar Schachter, "The Generation Gap in International Law" Proceedingls of the American Society of International Law. Westview Press, 1969 p. 233.
[62] Good News Bible, *op. cit.*, Proverbs 13:12.

(Statute, Artcle. 42; Rules, Artcle 40). The President of the Court who is then required to ascertain the views of the parties on questions of procedure summons the agents to meet him as soon as possible after their appointment and whenever necessary thereafter (Rules, Art 31).

In the next few pages we shall be discussing some aspects of the *modus operandi* of the Court and the possible ways of rationalising it in order to be both effective and save time.

Rationalising the Procedure of the ICJ

It remains to consider how the proceedings of the Court can be speeded up. Various suggestions have been put forward. It has, for instance, been suggested that the Court should abandon oral hearings by adopting a procedure of dealing with certain categories of cases in Chambers, somewhat along the lines of the procedure followed by the United States, whereby cases are assigned to individual judges for summary judgements especially between court sessions. We have some reservation about this suggestion based on the fact that the ICJ normally sits as a Court of first instance. Nevertheless, a limited use of this procedure is recommended if only as an experiment.

Another suggestion equally relevant is that the practice of exchanging memorials, counter-memorials and the methods of oral pleadings should be subjected to substantial modification.[63] This could save both time and cost. It has also been suggested that the Rules of Court be made to peg the length of the oral statements before the Court to say, one or two hours at the most.[64] This suggestion is certainly in consonance with the provision of Article 48 of the Statute which states that "The Court shall make orders for the conduct of the case, shall decide the form and time in which each party must conclude its arguments and make all arrangements connected with the taking of evidence."

It has also been suggested and we agree with the view, that the Registrar of the ICJ should be given wider powers than he has under existing rules to settle the records with agents and counsel on both

---

[63] Max Planck Inst. *op. cit.*, p. 29.
[64] *Ibid.*

sides in order to limit, as far as practicable, the bulk of the case record[65]

Elias wisely counsels that the Rules of Court regulating the examination of preliminary objections would require little if any changes because it is in consonance with the principles of natural justice that questions such as the refusal of one or more of the judges of the Court about to sit on a case, or the interpretation of its rules should be for the Court to determine.[66]

Another point which we find relevant is the suggestion that the giving of separate opinions in addition to the main opinion of the Court with which the majority of judges agree should be discontinued.[67] Dissenting opinions are, of course, in a different and necessary category. Thus our recommendation is that the technical aspect of rationalisation of procedure should be vigorously studied and furth er remedies to the existing situation made. However, we must not fail to mention that there may also be the possibility that States display contributory negligence in the slow prosecution of the cases in which they are involved. It is even within possibility that some States may seek a slow response by the Court to avert quick justice or to serve as a cooling down mechanism for domestic pressures.

Cost of litigation in the ICJ

Costs are doubtless a factor deterring States, especially younger ones, whose resources are limited, from making use of the Court.[68] Just as in the Nigerian society (or any other civil setting) the financially well to do find it easier to institute civil action to address their grievances, so also in the society of nations some States cannot litigate for financial reasons. As Castaneda rightly noted, it makes little difference whether the case is a contentious suit or one requiring an advisory opinion, the costs are comparable and

[65] *Ibid.*

[66] *Ibid.*, p. 30.

[67] George Elias, The International Court of Justice. (Leiden: A.W. Sijthoff, 1987) p. 160.

[68] Charles C. Okolie, *International Law Perspectives of Developing Countries: The Relationship of Law and Economic Development to Basic Human Rights*, (Lagos: NOK Publishers, 1978) pp. 50-51.

frequently too high.[69] As it is now, to take a case before the International Court, a State needs several millions of dollars. Maritime boundary litigation at the ICJ, for instance involves exceptionally high open and hidden costs. There would usually be the need for experts on geography, cartography, oceanography, geologists, and other specialists in addition to costs for exhibits, memorials and lawyers. Even for wealthy nations there is the problem of competing priorities and considerations of opportunity cost. For nearly all poorer and developing States, the risk of defeat might carry far greater financial weight especially since it is for sure that there is always a "winner and a loser"[70] in any such legal encounter. Thus the problem of costs needs urgent attention, especially as these costs are, as should be expected, on the increase.

One way of reducing costs is, of course, to limit the size of written pleadings to be kept within stated limits especially as regards bulk and complexity.[71] This, apart from saving costs, would save time, facilitating a somewhat more rapid assimilation of the essential data on the part of both the judges of the Court and counsel on the other side -

We are also in total alignment with Taslim Elias who submitted that:

> Agents, counsel and advocates of parties to disputes before the Court should be implored to enact a self-denying ordinance so that fees charged for service rendered to relatively impecunious clients or in respect of disputes not involving complicated commercial and industrial enterprises could be kept within reasonable bounds.[72]

Indeed, International lawyers should not only be concerned with personal monetary aggrandisement, but should be more concerned with their noble calling of aiding and abetting the administration of justice on the international plane. The Nigerian government is presently making use of the expensive service of Professor Ian Brownlie to defend its case at the ICJ. Needless to say, that is bound to be a further strain on the lean purse of the nation. We strongly

---

[69] Max Planck Institute., *op.cit.*p.30.
[70] *Ibid.*
[71] *Ibid.*, p. 301.
[72] Max Planck Institute, *op. cit.*, p. 30.

disagree with Taslim Elias that: "The idea of introducing a legal aid scheme for developing countries, which some have advocated in recent years, should be discountenanced as these countries would view with suspicion and even resentment any offer of financial assistance or charity in the prosecution of their claim for redress before an international tribunal.[73] Such reasoning is more typical of scholars and diplomats from the developed States[74] than of opinion in developing countries.

The basic fact, is that the Court is being under utilised by poor developing States. The situation is capable of getting worse and this cannot happen without more resort to armed conflict. A major reason for the poor turn out at the Court yearly is that some States cannot just afford the rising cost of justice. So it may not seem surprising and it is in fact very laudable that the Secretary-General of the UN in 1989 announced the creation of a legal aid scheme to financially assist developing states in litigating before the ICJ.[75]

The non-aligned States, a majority of which are indigent, sensibly pushed through the agenda for the creation of a trust fund in order to enhance the use of the Court by member States.[76] The trust fund idea might also have been inspired by Switzerland's commendable $400,000 assistance to Burkina Faso and Mali to help them implement the ICJ boundary decision in the Frontier Dispute Case.[77]

---

[73] Elias' comments in *ibid.*, pp. 30-31.

[74] See for instance, the views of Mary Ellen O' Connell "International Legal Aid: The Secretary-General's Trust Fund to Assist States in the Settlement of Disputes through the International Court of Justice" in International Courts for the Twenty-first Century, Mark W. Janis, ed. (The Hague: Kluwar Academic Publishers, 1992)

[75] Un Doc. A/44/PV. 43, at 7-11 (1989). This was based upon a directive of the UN General Assembly. See Provisional Verbatim Record of the Forty-Third Meeting, 44 UN GAOR (43rd Mtg.) at 7-11 UN Doc./44/PV.43 (1989).

[76] Ministerial Meeting of Non-Aligned Countries, UN Doc. A/44/PV.9, at 2 (1989); the Hague Declaration of the Meeting of the Ministers of Foreign Affairs of the Movement of Non-Aligned Countries to discuss the Issue of Peace and the Rule of Law in International Affairs, UN Doc. A/44/191 (!989); Bien-Aime, "Enhancing the Role of the World Court: An Examination of the Secretary-General's Trust Fund Proposal," New York University Journal of Internaitonal Law and Practice 22 (1991), p. 671.

[77] Burkina Faso v. Mali 1987 *ICJ Reports* 7 (Nomination of Experts, Order of 9 April 1987). The dispute was so contentious that an outbreak of military hostilities ensued during the case. Howeer, when the court ruled, the two States found they

Requests for Assistance from the fund are to be referred to a panel of experts who advise the Secretary-General.[78] The object of the fund is to provide "financial assistance to States for expenses incurred in connection with (i) a dispute submitted to the International Court of Justice by way of a special agreement, or (ii) the execution of a Judgement of the Court resulting from such special agreement.[79]

The Terms of Reference specify that the Fund will be financed out of voluntary contributions.[80] In addition to contributions from corporations, foundations, organisations with legal interests, etc.[81] To receive funds, a State must submit cost estimates for specified expenses involved in the suit. The Experts will then consider the expenses and issue funds along with a budget. In return, the requesting state must make an undertaking to submit receipts in a manner consistent with the UN audit system.[82]

There is no doubt that the Trust Fund can be one of the most important devices for facilitating access to the Court. Yet a lot still has to be done to achieve the dream of granting access to all poor States. In the first place, about ten years after the announcement of the Trust Fund not more than 35 States have contributed to it... Their total contributions have barely reached over half a million dollars. For the fund to become viable, more States, at least all those States which are Parties to the Court's Statute and which are by ascertainable economic indices available to the UN considered to be "developed nations" should donate to the Trust Fund. Transnational and Multinational Corporations many of which operate profitably

---

could not afford the cartograhers needed rto actually turn the Court's decision into a useable map. Switzerland's financial help supplied the needed experts. See O' Connell op.cit., p. 235.

[78] An annual report on the fund is made to the General assembly. and the Secretary-General may revise the Terms of Reference. Guidelines and Rules if circumstances so require. See Terms of Reference Guidelines and Rules of the Secretary-General's Trust Fund to Assist States int he Settlement of Disputes through the International Court of Justice, ILM 28 1590, Para. 17 1989, hereinafter, "Terms of Reference."

[79] *Ibid.*

[80] *Ibid.*, at para. 7.

[81] *Ibid.*

[82] See *ibid.*, para. 8(ii) and Financial Regulations and Rules of the UN., ST/SGB/Fin. Rules 1/Rev. 3 3. (1985).

from developing States should also be convinced to donate generously into the Trust Fund. While it must be stressed that donations to the Trust Fund should remain largely optional, developed States and Multinational Corporations should realise that there may be much more to lose in terms of lost investments, if developing States settle their disputes through armed conflict rather than through the ICJ. In any case, by 1993 not more than two States had as yet benefited from the Fund.[83] The process of receiving funds through the Trust Fund is still in practical terms shrouded in mystery. Chad which was the first recipient of an award under this scheme is undoubtedly an impoverished nation. It is landlocked and has far fewer resources than its adversary Libya (an oil rich African State). However, details of the award have for a long time not been made public. In this way, the potential of the legal aid scheme as an international public relations asset for the Court has been under-utilised since the aid scheme was set up. Furthermore, exactly how the "Experts" proceed in their consideration of applicants for funds is unclear. The Terms of Reference state that the Fund will finance only two categories of cases. That is, (i) those brought by special agreement and (ii) those brought by special agreement which have reached a final decision and require implementation as in the border demarcation in the "Frontier Dispute" between Burkina Faso and Mali , earlier referred to. Thus the fund may not be applied to cases submitted to the Court under its optional compulsory jurisdiction or pursuant to provisions of other treaties in force. There is no clear advantage to be derived from these limitation. If an ensueing legal dispute involves such important Treaties as the Genocide Convention or the Law of the Sea Convention 1983, States must not be discouraged from bringing them before the Court based on clauses recognising the Court's jurisdiction. This is exactly what the Terms of Reference achieves indirectly.

The aim of making these clauses exclusive of legal aid under the Terms of Reference would appear to be in effect to avoid funding cases where one party may refuse to cooperate. However, there is no concrete assurance that someday a State would not refuse to appear

---

[83] *ICJ Yearbook* 1992-1993, p. 249.

in a case even though it had agreed to submit the matter to the Court in a special agreement. Again, the refusal to supply funds in cases brought under the optional clause suggests the questioning of the Court's compulsory jurisdiction. Cases brought by consensus are thereby presented as more acceptable or at least the possibility of a successful litigation under them is suggested. This undermines the fact that the two modes of establishing jurisdiction are of equal legality and are in any case both based on "Consent." It may therefore be destructive of the painfully slow progress being made in advancing the acceptance of the compulsory jurisdiction of the Court under the Optional Clause as a form of consent *ante hoc*. In sum "the Fund's organisation gives the Experts most of whom are from the developed States ample opportunity to interfere with the way developing States may wish to handle their cases and forms an ominous cloud over the Court's compulsory jurisdiction.

The criticisms above do not diminish in any way the need and significance of the creation of the first ever global international legal aid scheme for Nation States. It is both a victory for developing States as well as an indication that sophisticated dispute resolution through international litigation will no longer be the preserve of Western States. There is no point in drawing analogies between the relevance and potential success of this scheme and that of legal aid schemes in domestic society. The differences are fundamental. One indigent person may quietly lose his entitlements in a legal relationship in the municipal setting and life simply goes on. The prospect of an entire population waking up to discover that their entire land and property now falls within the territorial sovereignty of another State as a result of poorly handled international litigation due to lack of funds is surely a fightening one. Life would surely go on, but it would not be the same for them. The seeds for future conflict would have been sown.

It can well be envisaged that frivolous suits may emanate from various quarters if the entire cost of litigation before the Court is to be borne by someone else. The Court, however, has a strong discretion to check any such occurrence. Legal aid for States is both a necessity and a progressive innovation. What remains to be done is to change and fine tune the operation of the Fund. Experts from developing States must be given priority position in the decision as to who gets what and how much out of the Fund.

Chapter 10

Alternative Futures

The ICJ is now over 50 years old. The system of having an international Court is even older with a history of nearly 80 years. The study so far points to the fact that there is a serious need for change. It is realised that "today's ICJ is in no small measure a creature of the nineteenth century put into the world of the twentieth."[1] There is peril in the likelihood that this largely unchanged and rigid system is about to be carried forward into the twenty-first century. This cannot happen without serious short comings both in the short, medium and long term.

However, change must not be pursued for its own sake. Change must be cautiously effected. As regards what exactly must be changed and how, it must be admitted that there is no small measure of variance, not even if all the judges of the Court, present and past, were gathered together to recommend changes to take the Court into the next 50 years would there be an exhaustive list nor would a foolproof system necessarily be developed. Their changes would be from the judges, point of view. Legalistic considerations would hold sway. Jurisdiction might be streamlined further and procedure would become even more unwieldy. The Court could slide away into obscurity and disuse.

If governments were to dictate the changes, political considerations would become supreme. Machiavellian expedients of diplomacy and international relations would have a free reign in such a newly designed Court. The value of the International Court could approach the level of ridicule and eventual neglect. Were jurists, academics and scholars of the Court appointed architects of the new order, this would still not guarantee success. They are further removed from the practical realities of the Court than they would

---

[1] Janis. *op. cit.*, p. 31

ever admit. The changes so designed would therefore be far removed from the realm of workability.

Hence, we can not pretend that the recommendations given so far in this work are ingenious or infallible. We prefer to speak in terms of Alternative Futures, for it is hoped that in the exercise of collating possible innovations, discovery of the correct mixture needed to reinvigorate the ICJ for the challenges ahead will be made easier. Indeed it may be admitted that some of the innovations recommended may be mutually exclusive.

However once it has been agreed upon that there are far reaching reasons to effect changes in the law and practice of the Court then it becomes imperative that the constitutive instruments upon which the Court operates must change. Thus, requisite amendments to the UN Charter, the Statute of the Court and the Rules of the Court must be made in view of the following considerations.

Opening the Floodgates

There is without doubt a recognisable trend in international law toward affording greater rights and duties to non-State actors. Therefore one of the crucial options facing the ICJ in the march towards the 21st century is whether or not to expand access to the Court in order to include the following non-State actors: (a) individuals; (b) Non-governmental Organisations (NGO's); (c) Nations and peoples struggling for independence; (d) Transnational Corporations, etc. Some of the suggestions for expansion are outright unbefitting of a World Court. Others raise the perennial issue of the expanding scope of subjects of international law. We will however focus our attention on the possibility of increasing the scope of participation of two of these-- individuals and NGOs. Whichever decision the Court may adopt on this matter will affect to a large extent the Court's work in the next 50 years.

Expanding access to the Court could be in two forms. The first is to allow non-State actors as Parties to proceedings. The second is to allow them greater participation so to speak as *amici curiae*. Furthermore it has to be decided if this expansion is necessary only for contentious proceedings or for advisory proceedings as well.

Increasing Access By Individuals

Throughout the existence of the ICJ there have been suggestions that it should accept individuals as Parties to proceedings.[2] There have also been numerous attempts by individuals to foist themselves as *amici curiae* on the Court. In the Namibia proceeding, Professor Michael Reisman asked about the possibility of submitting some form of *amicus curiae* brief to the Court.[3] Between August 1, 1990 and July 31, 1994 the Court received approximately 4,800 requests from private persons seeking a decision on matters at issue between them and the authorities of their own or of another country.[4]. On every occasion the writers were informed that in accordance with Article 34 of the Statute only States may be parties in cases before the Court. *Prima facie* the Court's decision on these applications are completely in consonance with the Statute as well as the Rules. As already noted, Article 34 of the Statute states clearly that only States are entitled to appear before the Court. Any injured individual must have his case espoused by his State of origin before obtaining redress in any way. In other words nothing prevents private interests from being the subject of proceedings before the Court if brought by their State of origin.

In practice, however, it has become clear that States do not often litigate the international rights of their citizens or the citizens of other States. There are many more requests from individuals for their States to expound their cases than we find States obliging these requests. One can find quite frequent advisory opinions by the PCIJ

---

[2] This view has been expressed by the Institute of International Law. Rosenne for instance believes that it is possible that the direct representation of the individuals concerned in the proceeding before the court would have the effect not only of stimulating public interest in the work of the court, but also and this may be more important, of enhancing its prestige and public confidence in the reality of the Court. Rosenne 1957 p 245.

[3] Dinah Shelton, "The participation, of Non-Governmental Organisations in International Judicial Proceedings" AJIL 1994. Vol. 88. Individuals may however under current procedures be invited as assessors to sit with the court for the consideration of particular cases. Unlike judges ad hoc, such assessors are not entitled to vote. They are chosen by the court itself and not by parties. Such persons may also be entrusted by the court with the task of carrying out an inquiry or may be asked to render an expert opinion

[4] See *ICJ Yearbooks* 1990, 1991, 1992, 1993 and 1994

concerning minority or trade union rights and as we have shown there are some ICJ cases which involve rights claimed by certain States for their corporate nationals. However, the two Courts have been more concerned with issues of sovereignty and jurisdiction, treaty law, land and maritime boundary delimitation and territorial acquisition.[5]

It must, however, be noted that it is not completely strange to international law for an individual to have rights, which are enforceable on the international plane without the intervention of his State. Thus, under Article 304(b) of the 1919 Treaty of Versailles, Nationals of the Allied and Associated Powers were allowed to present actions against Germany before the Mixed Arbitral Tribunal in their own names for compensation. Similarly, the Polish-German Convention of 1922 has been interpreted by the Upper Silesian Mixed Tribunal established by the Convention as recognising the independent procedural status of individuals as claimants before an international agency, even against their own State. The predecessor of the present court had reason to note in the case of Danzig Railway Officials (1928) that international law does not oppose the possibility of an individual enjoying directly rights conferred upon him by a treaty so long as this was intended by the Parties. The PCIJ in its advisory opinion sought by the Council of the League of Nations upon appeal by the Free City of Danzig, rejected the Polish contention and decided that the railway workers could actually claim directly whatever rights the treaty conferred on them.

Some prominent international courts also entertain legal action from individuals. For instance the European Court of Justice allows this. In addition, natural or legal persons establishing an interest in the result of any case submitted to the Court may intervene as *amicus curiae*. The question, however, is: Should the principal judicial organ of the UN open its gates for individuals as parties in contentious proceedings? The answer at least for now would appear to be in the negative. Acceptance of the Court's compulsory

---

[5] In most cases States will first of all seek an international or bilateral agreement governing the rights of the affected nationals before settlement is followed such as in the Ambatielos case where the Court was only called to decide the arbitration of the dispute under the Treaty of Commerce and Navigation 1926.

jurisdiction and recourse to its services is still too scanty to make such a bold attempt at expanding access to the Court. Such expansion will surely have a stultifying effect on acceptance of the optional clause, since in effect a national of another State might probably benefit from the Court's compulsory jurisdiction. The spectre of a national dragging his own State to the World Court will also not necessarily improve the acceptance of the Court among States. Besides, as already noted several international courts and tribunals already grant such access to individuals.

Nevertheless, granting the individual some rights before the ICJ should be allowed with greater frequency. While *Amicus* briefs add to the workload of courts they are nevertheless of much utility. They often provide detailed analysis of points of law, including discussion and citation of authorities which may not be contained in the Parties' arguments. They can provide detailed legislative or jurisprudential history and a scholarly exposition of the law on the subject under consideration. Invariably, the *Amici* present arguments the Parties are unable or unwilling to make due to political pressures or other tactical considerations. In the case of the ICJ the role of the *Amici* will undoubtedly be useful in charting new areas of novel concern in international litigation. This is particularly useful for an international court the judges of which are apparently of very similar basic legal training.

Unfortunately, the Court so far has taken an unduly limitative interpretation of its competence to receive offered assistance from individuals. In the Namibia case when Professor Michael Reisman asked the Court if he could submit some form of *amicus curiae* brief to the Court the reply of the Court's Registrar to him read in part, "With reference to your suggesting that there seems to be no explicit bar in the Statute or Rules to accepting a document from an interested group or individual… the court's view would seem to have been that the expression of its powers in Article 66, paragraph 2, is limitative and that *expressio unius est exclusio alterius*."[6]

This is an aspect of the Court's work that must change. Article 66 could therefore be amended to allow any person in addition to

[6] Dinah Shelton, *op. cit.*, p 624.

States and international organisations to submit written statements or oral statements relating to the question before the court. The right of the individual as *amicus curiae* in both advisory and contention cases should be recognised.[7] In any case the court like any court of law retains the discretion to use or not any such proffered assistance.

Non-governmental Organisations (NGOs) And The World Court

The Court does have a legitimate concern about opening the floodgates to participation by every non-governmental organisation that may wish to appear before it. In the first place NGOs are proliferating at an alarming rate the world over. Allowing all of them unrestricted access to the Court either as parties or *amicus curiae* in contentious and advisory proceedings could undoubtedly clog up the judicial machinery of the ICJ.

The court on its part clearly limits participation to "international organisations." Thus national NGOs are presently not under consideration.. The Civil Liberties Organisation (CLO) in Nigeria would, for instance, not be able under the present rules to appear as a party against the Nigerian Government. In like manner, even the Court cannot invite it to act as *amicus curiae* in proceedings before it.

However, grasp of issues and developments as well as the important work done in specialised fields of human endeavour by certain NGOs operating on an international scale makes them deserving of a special status before international courts. Based on quite subjective criteria NGOs like Amnesty International, The International Red Cross and Greenpeace can be considered worthy of such consideration. A simple way to delimit the number of such NGOs which may have access as *amicus curiae* to the Court is to interpret the term "international organisation" to include only NGOs with consultative status at the UN since Article 71 of the UN charter provides that: "The Economic and Social Council may make suitable arrangements for consultation with non-governmental organisations

[7]The court may indeed take a cue from the Inter-American Court of Human Rights which appears never to have rejected an amicus filing. See Shelton, *op. cit.*, p 638.

which are concerned with matters within its competence. Such arrangements may be made with international organisations and where appropriate, with national organisations, after consultation with the member of the United Nations concerned." This limitation could reduce the number of requests and also serve as a test of broad scope of interests, if not necessarily the overall competence of the NGO under consideration.[8]

Throughout the history of the Court, even when it seems that narrow issues are brought before it, broad human rights issues are usually lurking in the background. A boundary line litigated upon using historical title as root may inadvertently directly and seriously affect the right of self-determination of the population around the disputed region. More recently in the Gabcikovo-Nagymaros Dam project the need for active participation of some NGOs as *amici* of the Court became more glaring. In this case the interests at stake are much larger than those of the two claimants. Scholars believe that the full assessment of the potential environmental harm from the project can be best provided by NGOs which have been monitoring the river and flood plain for years.

It may indeed be recommended that NGOs which have been granted consultative status with the UN should on the authority of the General Assembly be allowed to request Advisory Opinions. This may necessitate the amendment of Article 96 paragraph 2, of the Charter in order to accept *amicus* submissions in the contentious cases, without changing the Statute, or alternatively to amend both Article 34(2) of the Statute and Rule 69(4). The first alternative would see the Court adopting a redefinition of the term "public international organisation" in Rule 69(4) to mean an international organisation composed of States or a non-governmental organisation holding consultative status with the UN. It is obvious that amending the Rules may be much easier than amending the Statute.[9]

Prior to these necessary changes the Court may indeed allow amicus participation before it by accepting requests from certain NGOs to prepare or submit expert opinions on appropriate issues, pursuant to Article 50 of the Statute.

---

[8] Shelton, *op. cit.*, p 625.
[9] *Ibid*

A Chamber Of International Criminal Justice

The call for an international criminal court has been a recurring decimal and a subject of continuous discussion since the end of the First World War. Pressure to institute such a court assumed a near hysterical level in the past few years. As a result the General Assembly is presently set to complete a draft convention for the establishment of an International Criminal Court. The competence to create such a structure is conferred on the General Assembly under Articles 7(2) and 22 of the Charter. The planned Court would have jurisdiction over four main crimes under general international Law: viz. genocide, war crimes, crimes against humanity , aggression and other exceptionally serious crimes of international concern. Thus, systematic violations of human rights, torture, hostage taking, apartheid, illicit trafficking in narcotic drugs, piracy and hijacking may fall under the preview of the Courts jurisdiction.[10]

But if the question is (as put by a scholar): Before what court and according to what law should an individual who has committed an international crime be tried?'[11] What better answer would there be than to reply:" Before the International Court of Justice." In essence, it is highly recommended that a standing and permanent chamber within the Court be established to administer criminal justice among States who are Parties to the ICJ. This can be done along the lines of the Chamber for Environmental Matters instituted by the Court in 1993. Thus judges of the Court who are known to posses special bias for criminal law, or who signify their interest in criminal law can be co-opted into this special chamber.

There is no inescapable consideration which bars the widening of the jurisdiction of the ICJ to include a criminal chamber. Though it is a fact that for the reasonable operation of such system the Charter would have to be amended, it must be realised that this would also be necessary if the proposed International Criminal Court were to have relevance within the UN system. Even those authors who are not exactly enamoured with the prospect of a

---

[10] See "Legal issues: work continues on Internationaal Criminal Court." *UN Chronicle*, December 1995, p. 76.

[11] John W. Bridge, "The case for an International court of Criminal Justice and The Formulation of International Criminal Law" in M.W. Janis (ed.) *op. cit.*, p. 213.

criminal chamber admit that it is important that any International Criminal Court to be created should to some extent be sponsored by the UN. One of the many benefits of this is the provision of the machinery to be used to execute sentences rendered. Already, binding Charter provisions and the pre-eminent role of the Security Council in ensuring compliance with UN decisions are natural advantages. At the very least the jurisdiction of the proposed Chamber of International Criminal Justice may be introduced under a Protocol which may be gradually acceded to the like Optional Protocol. The fear that because of the necessity of an amendment of the Charter "what is perhaps the ideal and most straight forward method of creating an international criminal court cannot be given practical consideration"[12] is not really justifiable. The increasing global concern with the adequate prosecution of war criminals for instance, means that if a charter amendment is what is required to cope with the problem once and for all, States would be favourably disposed towards achieving this aim.

It is important that there should be a clear definition of the crimes to be dealt with by this chamber of the Court. On the issue of State consent to the Chamber's Jurisdiction, it is likely that only the consent of the State in whose territory the crime was committed should be required. Thus in this particular instance the consensual basis of all jurisdiction may be comprised in the interest of mankind in general. For to require the consent of the State of nationality of the accused would in more cases than not lead to no jurisdiction. That a victorious side will not allow its heroes to stand trial for war crimes is clear from recent events in Bosnia and Rwanda. The general rules of criminal law and general international law should guide the Court's work in order to provide clear guidance to the Court and to Counsel. The completion of the draft Codes of Crimes Against the Peace and Security of Mankind would also be of much help. This would secure predictability and in fact protect accused persons

[12] Bridge, *op. cit*, p.229.

Developing Regional Chambers

The ICJ has actually been under -utilised by States. This is true both in terms of individual appearances and collective use. Sixty-nine cases in 50 years is not representative of the strife- filled and volatile situation of the international community in the past half century. This simply shows that other means, very frequently use of force, have been favoured by States in the settlement of disputes.

The older and more influential States of the world especially the Western actors, have demonstrated the most use and the most confidence in the Court. This raises the factual presumption of bias in the application of international law in their favour by the Court. Developing States and the newer generation of nations have displayed relatively less confidence in the Court's work. This however, does not mean that they have no confidence at all in the Court or that their attitude towards the Court will not change for the better in the near future.

Our analysis has shown that a judge's training in a specific legal system plays a large role in his contributions in the Court. This to a large extent accounts for the Euro-centric approach of the Court to legal interpretations. The requirement in Article 9 of the Statute that persons who sit as judges on the Bench of the ICJ should represent the main forms of civilisation as well as the principal legal systems of the world has not been properly adhered to throughout the existence of the Court. The obvious advantages and the enriching value of integrating and incorporating other legal systems and national traditions hardly needs to be restated. Thus we cannot but endorse the recommendations of Prott,[13] Luchman[14] Elias[15] and even Reigman[16] that judicial prejudices be technically annulled. In fact, it should be an affirmation rather than a repudiation of international law to strongly protest by any means whatsoever, any proven cases of prejudiced decisions by the ICJ.

The Court however, has for the past fifty years performed fairly well within the statutory parameters in which it operates and in

---

[13] Prott, *op. cit.*, p. 230 Passim

[14] N. Luchmann Legitimation Durch Verfahren (1969) p. 66.

[15] T. Elias (1983) *op. cit.*, p. 128

[16] Reigman, *op. cit.*, p. 128.

relation to the use to which it has been put. There is still ample opportunity for the Court to improve, correct past mistakes and prove itself to be a true arbiter of justice. Great care has to be taken in the handling of cases submitted by developing nations. The fragile confidence in which these States hold the Court must be reciprocated with very careful decisions as to what the ICJ considers tenable legal arguments, as opposed to historical, sentimental or even religious considerations that may be given weight by parties from the developing world as in the *Rights of Passage case* or *South-West Africa cases*. These might well be the significant part of the issue on which the disputants wish a decision to be based. The international law being developed by the Court on the basis of shifting stances of its judges from Europe and North America has been observed by the developing States. This obviously has not inspired confidence in the Court as a dynamic instrument of Justice to maintain the right balance between stability and change as well as between the rich and the poor.

Thus we recommend that a regional chapter or chambers of the court should be established at least for each continent. The possible objection that regional tribunals might result in fragmentation of the law and endanger its unity, is not particularly impressive. The great need in nearly all branches of international law is elaboration. If that can be bought on a regional basis only, so be it.[17] The hue and cry that arose from Latin American scholars and jurists over the Court's pronouncements in the Asylum cases could have been absent if a regional court for Latin America (composed of Latin American jurists knowledgeable in international law) had adjudicated upon the cases. A similar Court for the African continent would definitely have more speedily brought an end to Apartheid and racism on the continent through adequate legal pronouncements and decisions. Regional chambers of the Court can more readily and effectively recognise regional peculiarities, such as the Latin American view of what constitutes exhaustion of local remedies or Tanzania's doctrine regarding succession of States and government.[18] Not to take notice

[17] Max Planck Instutite., *op. cit.*, p. 26.

[18] See Edward Mc Whinney, *The World Court and the Contemporary International Law Making Process* (Leyden: Sijthoff, 1989) p. 176.

of such regional peculiarities where they exist would in our view be to detract from the true meaning of justice.

The power of the Court to form chambers to decide particular cases provided for in the Statute, Articles 26, 27, 29 and in the Rules of the Court 15-18 and 90-93 is of great utilitarian value. The use of that procedure has however been under-utilised though it is becoming increasingly popular. The procedural innovation and usefulness of the chambers procedure has been well proven in the Gulf of Maine case. This previously untested procedure proved appealing in this case where two nations from the common law tradition were involved.[19] The result was largely respected as equitable.[20] The fact that the Chamber consisted only of judges from North America and Western Europe was criticised by some, but in our view there is nothing wrong with such practise especially if the result as in this case is an equitable and well accepted decision.

The Parties should be free to select members of a Chamber. The make up of a Chamber should be premised upon the views of Parties to the dispute and not upon some abstract notion of geographical balance or blending of various legal systems when all that is needed is to determine a question of international law as existing between two countries of the same hemisphere or rank.[21]

Given the success of the Chambers system in its first decade rather than pulling back, it is more reasonable to consider an expansion of the notion. In the long run the establishment of regional courts will be necessary. The opening of regional courts in each of the continents will greatly reduce cost of litigation. A regional Court will be more at advantage in the taking and evaluation of evidence than a single court seated at the Hague. Our proposal does not mean that the present Court should be discarded. What is recommended is that the regional courts should adjudicate on intra-regional disputes in addition to acting as an appellate body to the regional

---

[19] Davis R. Robinson *et al.* "Some Perpective on Adjuiciating before The World Court: The Gulf of Maine Case" American Journal of International Law, 79 (1985) p. 581.

[20] G.O.M. Gross Disent. para 3 *et. seq.* See also Jan Schneider, " The Gulf of Maine Case: The Nature of an Equitable Result" AJIL 1985, p. 541.

[21] Robinson, *et al*, *op. cit.* 582.

international courts. Thus we subscribe wholeheartedly to the submissions of the legal scholars who wrote:

> Some change and modifications in the present international system are essential. In the first place, a single permanent World Court situated at the Hague, however impartial, was not sufficient for the whole globe. Both the Courts and justice should move closer to the customer... There was a strong feeling that the Hague Court was neither suitable nor economic for trade disputes in the remote areas, especially of Asia, Africa and Latin-America.[22]

Yet another possibility would be to convert the long dormant Permanent Court of Arbitration into a chamber. For two decades through the 1970s and 1980s no new cases were submitted to the PCA; its staff and facilities would serve a better function if they were converted into use as an arbitral chamber of the Court after necessary refinement.[23]

An ICJ Bar Association

As is characteristic of many legal bars, in their earlier years there is an era of nearly uncontrolled or at least poorly co-ordinated existence.[24] The case of the ICJ has not been very different. There is up till now no tightly regulated international bar organisation regulating the practice of international lawyers before the Court[25]. In

---

[22] Nascimento Da Silva, *op. cit.*, p. 181. See also the submissions of Vratislav Pechota, "Complimentary Structure of Third Party Settlement of Disputes," *Dispute Settlement Through the United Nations* (New York: UN Institute of Training and Research (UNITAR), (1977) p. 156.

[23] Cf Janis, *op cit* p. 35.

[24] As in Nigeria at one time so it was with bar groups of many countries during and after the nineteenth century. The American Bar Association's original canons of Ethics date back only to 1908 while the British Solicitors Practice Rules date back to 1936 , France accorded out-of-Court lawyers unregulated existence up till 1971. The Swedish Bar Association did not exist till as recent as 1987; there are even now still many jurisdictions where rules of professional conduct are merely handed down from generation to generation as some kind of "oral law," uncodified and restricted to prohibitions of the most obvious conflicts of interest. See Detlev F. Vogts, "The International Legal Profession : A need for more Governance?" AJIL, v. 90 1996, p.250; See also Ivo Gaytas, *Transnational Legal Practice :Conflicts in Professional Responsibility* (1992) p. 19.

[25] The ultimate persisting nightmare is that it is not even necessary to be a member of the bar of any country in order to appear at the Hague. Thus, "Herbert Briggs, who

fact it appears not to be necessary to be an international lawyer at all to appear before the Court. It does not take much ingenuity to realise that such a situation is far from perfect. Though in practice many of the advocates who have appeared before the Court are indeed international lawyers, the *de facto* bar operating at Hague can be best described as:

> Those international lawyers who have practised and continue to practise as Oral advocates before the Court, who represent a variety of foreign states other than their own governments, who are well known to the Judges and Registrar of the Court, who know how things work out in practise, and who understand by experience the difficulties, pitfalls and tricks of the trade.[26]

The absence of a regulated ICJ bar means also there is a lacunae of sorts regarding various aspects of professional behaviour in litigating before the Court. Other deleterious effects include possible overcharging of professional fees, economic exploitation of poor States or of the ICJ Trust Fund, protectionist tendencies and other sharp practices by lawyers from the same or similar legal systems, bias of the bench, etc. Some of these problems already exist, but the low level of patronage the Court receives from States now hides the urgent need for regulation via the creation of an ICJ Bar. Sure, slowly and inexorably traffic before the Court will increase dramatically within the first quarter of the next century. The day will soon arrive when the Courts docket will be so full as to be overwhelming. At such a time, if not now, it will be intolerable for non-experts in the Courts practice and procedures to continue to waste valuable time and resources while acting as advocates, agents, assessors, etc. in cases before the Court.

The existing situation where most of the lawyers litigating before the Court are of western extraction is a matter for obvious criticism. Even if the situation was not obviously engineered, it cannot but have an effect on the chances of third world litigants. Acrimony in the early years of the Iran-U.S Claims Tribunal showed that difficulties could surface when newcomers to the international

---

as not a lawyer, appeared in four cases before the Court. See M. Schwebel," Herbert W.Briggs (1900-1990)" *AJIL*, 84 (1990) pp. 531, 531-52.

[26]Keith Highet, "A personal memoir of Eduardo Jiménez de Archaga," *American Society of International Law Proceedings*, 88 (1994) pp. 577, 579.

law community represented a non-European client distrustful of the establishment. As the activities of international law agencies , both public and private, involve more countries and more cultures, disputes about standards of behaviour will expectedly multiply. Apart from the possibilities of bias the question of regulation of professional ethics is not one that can be easily avoided. The silence of the Statute of the Court on this matter is unacceptable, and practical problems are begging for solutions. The Statute spells out clearly the do's and dont's of a judge, the judge's position in case of conflicts of interest, requirements of independence and the enforcement powers to effect punishment on erring judges. Very soon leaving untouched matters relating to lawyers will lead to unpalatable consequences. Recently an American lawyer who participated in various government decisions in the wake of the destruction of the Pan American airliner proposed to represent the Libyan government in a suit brought by survivors of the aerial disaster.[27]

The question that comes to mind is: If he had actually represented the Libyan government in the US case would that fact have disqualified him from representing the US ever again before the ICJ? There are no clear rules on such matters. It cannot be hoped that Agents of governments before the Court will continue to be of exceptional behaviour. Though the mere fact that one stands before a World Court in the daunting presence of over a dozen imposing judges gathered from the world over is surely capable of aweing the most errant mind, it cannot be simply assumed that this will always hold true. Once in a while interesting cases of misbehaviour may emanate even from no less a place than an international Courts bench. In a spectacular occurrence two Iranian Judges at the Hague physically assaulted Judge Nils Mangard, a neutral Judge.[28]

In at least two cases the ICJ rebuked counsel for unduly delaying proceedings or producing evidence in negligent and disorderly

---

[27] In Re Sofaer No. 280 93 (D.C. Ct App. 1995).

[28] Vagts, *op. cit.*, P. 257.

manner.[29] In another case criticisms were generously levelled at the performance of counsel in presenting evidence, an overstraining of the facts which may have arisen due to the awkward relationship between the agents of the US and the counsel for company whose claim was being espoused.[30]

As to qualification of membership in the recommended international Bar of the ICJ it need not be radically different from what obtains now as regards who can appear before the Court to argue cases. It is important though that there must be the basic qualification of a law degree from a recognised institution from any of the States Parties to the Statute: in addition such persons as aspire to be members must have been called to the Bar in their respective countries and must be eligible to appear in Court there. It is now, however, not considered important that he or she must have actual litigating experience in municipal Court. What is important is that such persons must posses demonstrable knowledge of Public International Law. It is important that the ICJ bar itself embarks on varied but regular training courses, symposia and seminars to help in the continuous development and skills necessary for practice before the Court. The conduct of an ICJ bar exam may well be within contemplation.

The chief utility of the recommended changes may well be found in the maintenance of discipline, ethics and standards. Thus remuneration schedules need to be standardised. A concise set of rules to guide the behaviour of lawyers before the ICJ would be useful. Rules such as how to appear before the Court (dressing) should be revised. Appropriate gowns, apparels or wigs may be fashioned out for uniformity. Delicatesse, courtesy and tact have to remain the watchword of the lawyers at all times.

---

[29] *Ibid.*; Application of the Convention on the prevention and punishment of the Crime of Genocide (Bosnia and Herzegovina v. Yugoslavia (Serbia and Montenegro), Provisional Measures, 1993 *ICJ Reports* 325, 336 37 (Order of Sept. 13)

[30] See Keith Highet, Evidence, the Chamber and the ELSI Case, in *Fact Finding Before International Tribunals.* Ricardo Lillich ed,. (1992, pp. 33, 65 68)

It will probably be advantageous to ICJ Court if the Registrars of the Court are drawn from the pool of lawyers at the ICJ bar. To ensure that the bar is not monopolised or dominated by certain States it may make much sense to insist that each State Party to the Statute be allowed to present at least five eminent lawyers into the ICJ bar.

On the whole, the limitations of judicial settlement in international relations must be accepted; a judgement might not always constitute a settlement. This is a fact each international lawyer must impress on the State he represents. Indeed, authoritative statements of legal rights could even impede settlement by encouraging rigidity by one side in a controversy which might have been settled through political compromise. Despite all these, States must be brought to see the need to accept judicial settlement in their international relations. The obligatory jurisdiction of the ICJ under the Optional Clause for instance should be accepted by all States. The reward for this in the world will be justice and peace under law. However, each State must realise that the day will come when the Court will give some decision which will be very unpopular to its own population and the Court will not necessarily be wrong because it decided against any particular State.

Bibliography

BOOKS

Ajomo, M.A.: *Proceedings of the Seventh, Eight and Ninth Annual Conference of the Nigerian Society of International Law 1975-1978*, Ibadan: University Press, 1979.

Anand, R.P.: *Compulsory Jurisdiction of the International Court of Justice*, Bombay: Asia Publishing House, 1961.

Anand, R.P.: *The Fúture of the International Court of Justice*, Vol. 1 Dobbs Ferry, New York: Oceana Publications, 1986.

Brownlie, *Ian: Principles of Public International Law*, 3rd ed. Oxford:Clarendon Press, 1979.

Bruno Simma (ed) *The Charter Of The United Nations: A Commentary. 1994.*

Cassese, A.:*International Law in a Divided World.* Oxford: Clarendon Press, 1990.

Da Silva, Nascimento E.:*Diplomacy in International Law*. Leyden: A.W. Sijthoff, 1977.

Ehrlich, L. *Prawo Mic Dzynour Odowe.* Warsaw: 1958

Elian, G.: *The International Court of Justice*, Hague: A. W. Sijthoff, Leiden, 1987.

Elias, Taslim Olawale: *The International Court of Justice and Some Contemporary Problems: Essays on International Law.* Dordrecht: Martinus Nijhoff, 1983.

Elias, Taslim Olawale: *United Nations Charter and the World Court Law Series No. 1.* Ibadan: Nigerian Institute of Advanced Legal Studies, 1989.

Elias, Taslim Olawale: *Africa and the Development of International Law.* Dordrecht: Martinus Nijhoff, 1974.

Ferencz, Benjamin B. *Enforcing International Law -- a Way to World Peace.* V. 2. Dobbs Ferry, NY: Oceana, 1983

Good News Bible: Deuterocanomical Books/Apocrypha, "Today's English" Version, Britain: The Bible Societies, Collins, 1979.

Gowland-Debas Vera. "The Relationship Between The International Court of Justice And The Security Council In The light of the Lockerbie Case," *American Journal of International Law, AJIL* Vol. 88 1997.

Gross, Leo (ed): *The Future of the International Court of Justice*. Dobbs Ferry, N.Y: Oceana Publications, 1979.

Harris D.J. *Cases and Materials on International Law.* Third edition London, 1983.

Janis, Mark W. "The International Court," in Mark W. Janis, ed, International Courts for the Twenty-First Century. The Hague: Kluwer Academic Publishers, 1992.

Jenks, C. Wilfred,:*The Prospects of International Adjudication.* London: Stevens, 1964.

Jessup. *The Price Of International Justice.* 1971.

Lauterpacht, *Sir* Hersch: *The Development of International Law by the International Court.* New York: Praeger; Dobbs Ferry, N.Y. Oceana Publications 1958.

Lauterpacht, *Sir* Hersch:*The Function of Law in the International Community*, London: 1933.

Levi, Werner: *Contemporary International Law: A Concise Introduction.* Boulder, Colorado: West View Press, 1979.

Lissitzyn, Oliver J.: *The International Court of Justice: Its Role in the Maintenance of International Peace and Security.* Westport, Connecticut: Greenwood Press, 1970.

Luchmann, N.: *Legitimation durch Verfahren* Bonn, 1989.

Lund. Michael S. *Preventing Violent Conflicts : A Strategy For Preventing Diplomacy. Washington D.C* : United States Institute Of Peace Press, 1997.

Marak, Krystyna. *A Digest of the Decision of the International Court of Permanent Courts of International Justice.*. The Hague: Martinus Nijhaff, 1974.

Max Planck Institute for Comparative Public Law and International Law: *Judicial Settlement of International Disputes: An International Symposium*. New York: Max Planck Institute, 1974.

McWhinney, Edward,:*The World Court and the Contemporary International Law Making Process.* Dordrecht: Sijthoff and Nordhoff, 1989.

International Court of Justice. *Background Note VI Collected Unofficial Summaries of Decisions Concerning the Law of the Sea 1976 - 1986.* 1987

Iwanejko, M. *Miedzynardowy Trybunal Sprawied- Liwosic Krakow.* 1969.

Northrop. *The Training Of the Nations. 1952*

Okeke, Nwachukwu,:*The Theory and Practice of International Law in Nigeria.* Enugu: Fourth Dimension Publishers, 1986.

Okolie, Charles C.:*International Law Perspectives of the Developing Countries: The Relationship of Law and Economic Development to Basic Human Rights*. Lagos: NOK Publishers, 1978.

Oppenheim, L.: *International Law: A Treatise* Vol. II *Disputes, War and Neutrality*, Lauterpacht, H. (ed.); 7th ed. London, Longmans Green and Co., 1952.

Prataap, Dharma,: *The Advisory Jurisdiction of the International Court*, Oxford: Clarendon Press, 1972.

Prott, Lyndell V.: *The Latent Power of Culture and the International Judge*, London: Billing and Sons, 1979.

Rosenne, Shabtai: *Law and Practice of the International Court of Justice*, Vol. 1. 2nd ed. Leyden: Sijthoff, 1965.

Rosenne, Shabtai:*The International Court of Justice*. Leyden: Sijthoff, 1957.

Rosenne, Shabtai: *The World Court: What It is and How it Works*. Leiden: A.W. Sijthoff; Dobbs Ferry, N.Y., Oceana Publications., 1973.

Satow, *Sir* Ernest:: *Satow's Guide to Diplomatic Practice*, Fifth ed. ed. by Gore-Booth. London: Longman Group, 1959.

Schwarzenberger, Georg: *International Law as Applied by International Courts and Tribunals*, Vol. 3, London: Stevens and Sons, 1976.

Shaw, M.N.:*International Law*, 3rd ed. Cambridge: Grotius Publications Ltd, 1991.

Simpson, J.L. and Fox, H.:International Arbitration Law and Practice, London: Stevens, 1959.

Syatauw, J.J.G.: *Decisions of the International Court of Justice: A Digest*, Dobbs Ferry, N.Y., Oceana; Leyden: A.W. Sijthoff, 1962.

Syatauw, J.J.G.: *Some Newly Established Asian States and the Development of International Law*. New York: Leyden: Sijthoff, 1981.

Szafaria Renata. *The Compulsory Jurisdiction of The Internal Court of Justice*. Netherlands: Martinus Nijhoff Publishers, 1993.

Taraconzio, T.A.: *The Soviet Union and International Law*, New York: Macmillan Co., 1985.

UN Office of Public Information. *Basic Facts About the United Nations*, New York: United Nations Publications, 1987.

U.N. Office of Public Information. *The International Court of Justice*, 6th ed., New York: United Nations Publications, 1967.

Venkata, Raman K. (ed.):*Dispute Settlement Through the United Nations*. New York: U.N.' Institute of Training and Research (UNITAR), 1977.

Wheeler, Bennett, Fanshawe,:*Information on the World Court 1918-1928* London: George Allen and Unwin Ltd., 1929.

YEARBOOKS

International Court of Justice Yearbook, 1946-7. The Hague: *ICJ*, 1948.
International Court of Justice Yearbook, 1971-72, The Hague: *ICJ*, 1973.
International Court of Justice Yearbook, 1992-93. The Hague: 1994.
International Court of Justice Yearbook, 1993-94, The Hague: 1995.
International Court of Justice Yearbook, 1995-96, The Hague: 1997.
Nigerian Annual of International Law. Vol. 1, Ibadan: Oxford University Press. For the Nigerian Society of International Law, *N.I.A.*
United Nations Yearbook, 1946-7.
World Court Reports, Vol. IV, 1938. ed. by Hudson.

ARTICLES

Becker, Elizabeth. "On Its Last Legs, the Saddest Cambodian Army," *New York Times*. October 20, 1997.
Bekker, Peter H.F. "International Decisions: April 1996 New Zealand Challenge to Underground Nuclear Testing by France in Sahara Pacific - ICJ Judgment in 1974 nuclear testing case (New Zealand. France)," *AJIL*, 1996.
Bien-Aime, "Enhancing The Role of the World Court: An Examination of the Secretary - General's Trust Fund Proposal," *New York University Journal of International Law and Practice* 22, 1991.
Brownlie, Ian. "The Justiciability of Disputes and Issues in International Relations," *BYIL* 42. 1967.
Brierly, J.L. "British Reservations to the General Act." *BYIL*., 1931.
Crawford, J. "The Legal Effect of Automatic Reservation to the Jurisdiction of the International Court," *BYIL*, 1979.
Castenada, Jorge. "The Underdeveloped Nations and the Development of International Law," *International Organisation*,15, 1961.
Cheng, Bin. "The 1966 South-West Africa Judgment of the World Court" *Current Legal Problems*, 20, 1967.
Donner, A.M. "National Law and the Case Law of the Court of Justice of the European Communities,." *Common Market Law Review*, 1983.
Epstein, William. "Nuclear Powers Take a Hard Line," *Bulletin of Atomic Scientists*, Vol. 53, Issue 2 March - April 1997.
Fitzmaurice, G. "The Law and Procedure of the International Court of Justice, 1951-4: Questions of Jurisdiction, Competence and Procedure," *BYIL*, 34, 1958.

Fitzmaurice, G. "Hersch Lauterpacht- The Scholar as a Judge," *BYIL* 137 *1961*.

Hambro, Edward. "On compulsory Jurisdiction and Advisory Opinio~s," *BYIL*, 1972.

Higgins, R. "The International Court and South West Africa: Implications of the Judgment," *International Affairs*, 5,42, 1966.

Higgins, R. "Diverging Anglo American Attitudes to International Law Introductory Statement " *JICL*, 2,Ga 1992.

Higgins, R. "Policy Considerations and the International Judicial Process," *ICLQ,* 17, 1968.

Highet, Keith. "Evidence, the Chamber and the ELSI Case," *Fact Finding Before International Tribunals.* Ricordo Lillich ed. 1992.

Highet, Keith. "A Personal Memoir of Eduardo Jiminez de Archaga," *American Society of International Law Proceedings* 88, 1994.

Hudson, M.O. "The Effect of Advisory Opinions of the World Court," *BYIL*, 1958.

Hudson, M.O. "The Twenty-Ninth Year of the World Court" *AJIL*, 4, 1951.

Jennings, R. "The Role and Functioning of the Court," *Year Book of the International Court of Justice.* YBICJ 1993.

Jennings R.Y. "The United Nations At Fifty: The International Court of Justice After Fifty Years" *American Journal of International Law, AJIL* 1995.

Kelly, G.M. "The Temple Case in Historical Perspective," *BYIL,* 39, 1993.

Lissitzyn, Oliver J. "International Law in a Divided World." *International Conciliation,* No. 542, 1963.

"Mandela Presses for Neutral: Nation Trial of Lockerbie Suspects." *New York Times*, October 26,

Markensinis, Basil.S. "Litigation-Mania in England and Germany." *Cambridge Law Journal*, July 1990.

Mendelson, "Interim Measures of Protection." *BYIL*, 1922-23.

Ogan, C.A. "Potency and Weakness of a Jurisdictional Weapon: The Odyssey of the Connally Reservation," *Justice.* 21, 1991.

Perlez, James. "World Court Leaves Fight over Danube Unresolved." *New York Times.* Sept. 26, 1997.

Reigmann, M. "Has the International Court Exceeded Its Jurisdiction?" *BYIL,* 80, 1986.

Renouff, T. "Reception of Advisory Opinions by the General Assembly of the United Nations." *Canadian Bar Review*, 28, 1950.

Robinson, D.A. *et al* "Some Perspectives on Adjudicating Before the World Court: The Gulf of Maine case." *AJIL*, 79, 1985.

Roggers, "The Rule of Law and the Settlement of International Disputes." *AJIL*, 64, 1970.

Schacter " The Enforcement of International Judicial and Arbitral decision," *AJIL*, 54 *American Journal of International Law.* 1960.

Schachter, Oscar. "The Generation Gap in International Law." in *Proceedings of the American Society of International Law.* Boulder, Colorado: West View Press, 1969.

Schneider, J. "The Gulf of Maine Case: The Nature of an Equitable Result." *AJIL* 1985.

Sloan, F. B. "Advisory Jurisdiction of the International Court of Justice." *California Law Review*, 38, 1950.

Szasz, Paul C. "Enhancing The Advisory Competence Of The International Court of Justice," Leo Gross Ed., The *Future Of The International Court of Justice.* 1976.

Szasz, Paul. "Addendum: the Vote In The General Assembly," *AJIL*, Vol. 91, 1997.

Tenekides, I.G. "International Law and Federal Communities in the Cities of Greece." R.A.D.K. 90, California, 1956.

Vogts, Detler F. "The International Legal Profession: A Need for more Government?" *American Journal of International Law, AJIL* 90 1996.

Waldock, C.H.M. "Decline of the Optional Clause." *BYIL*, 1955-6.

Weight, "The Mosul Dispute," *AJIL*, 20, 1926.

DOCUMENTS

I.L.O Official Bulletin No. 2 (Dec. 1st 1944)

"Report on the Peaceful Settlement of Disputes" U.N. Document, 1973.

Report on the UN Conference on International Organisations (UNCIO) 13 UNICIO 395 (1945) (Dec. 913 IV /1/ 74 (1), June 12 1995U.N.C:I.O., Document Vol. XIV.

UN DOC.A/ PV. 52 (1/2) (1946)

UN DOC . A/PV 269 (IV) (1949

UN DOC. A/ 49 / PV. 90 (1994)

U.S. Department of State *Bulletin* XV, 1946. U.S. Congress, Senate Committee on Foreign Relations, "Compulsory Jurisdiction, International Court of Justice." Hearings on Senate Resolutions, 126, 11, 12 and 15 July, 1946.

Index

A

Arbitration, 4, 10, 12-15, 17, 25-27, 48, 72, 78, 135, 177, 181
Adjudication, 1, 4, 5, 7, 8, 12, 13, 25, 34, 38, 39, 57, 73, 78, 157, 178, 208
Administrative Tribunals, 31
Advisory Jurisdiction, 5, 103-105, 107, 169, 183, 225
Advisory Opinion, 4, 43, 46, 103, 142, 183, 204
Advisory Cases, 5, 103, 107, 115, 121, 142, 166-168, 170
Africa/African, 2, 5, 28, 40, 44, 72, 137, 140, 144, 148, 150, 152, 156, 157, 159, 160, 166, 170, 173, 177, 183, 185, 193, 203, 205, 207, 218, 220, 222, 224, 233, 245, 247
Asylum, 6, 37, 50, 143, 176, 177
Arab, 41, 139, 145, 160, 162, 174
Albania, 136, 142, 146, 174
Ajibola, 171, 193, 196, 200, 222
Anand, 59, 61, 62, 72, 202, 204, 207, 225
Agents, 85, 92, 94, 97, 124, 126, 197, 202, 227, 230
Antarctica, 171

B

Bakassi, 36, 137, 159, 194, 195
Brierly, 72, 73
Boundary, 68, 144, 155, 158, 160, 162, 172, 174, 196, 198, 230
British, 63, 72, 99, 125, 171, 175, 177, 181, 209
Brazil, 137, 185
Bosnia, 66, 91, 93, 145, 153, 155, 212
Benin, 137, 219, 223
Brownlie, 7, 33, 49, 55, 71, 103, 116, 230
Bench, 44, 66, 68, 193, 216, 218, 219, 220, 221, 223, 224, 244, 248, 249
Bar, 8, 92, 179, 221
Barcelona Traction, 21, 43, 154, 160, 179, 180, 202

C

Conciliation, 13, 20, 27, 29, 60, 215
Contentious Jurisdiction, 41, 45, 64, 103, 149, 152, 159, 183, 185, 225
Consent, 17, 47, 49, 50, 52, 55, 69, 73, 111, 125, 177, 214, 225, 234
Chambers, 66, 67, 68, 98
Cameroon, 2, 6, 34, 36
Charter, 3, 11, 12, 18, 20, 31, 38, 44, 46, 56, 60, 73, 81, 84, 99, 102, 105, 108, 113, 115, 118, 129, 134, 137, 167, 170, 187, 215, 221
Continental Shelf Case, 22, 50, 90, 103
Civil War, 11
China, 23, 29, 65, 131, 132, 151, 223
Compromise, 7, 22, 66, 207, 215
Competence De la Competence, 31, 46
Cheng, 79, 185, 223
Communism/Communist, 26, 39, 151, 152, 162, 165, 170, 190, 202, 208, 224
Corfu Channel, 47, 50, 52, 57, 63, 87, 89, 100, 142, 159, 165
Committee of Experts, 59
Christian, 204
Connally, 193, 202
Composition, 136, 216
Cold War,165, 166
Canada, 68, 72, 82, 137, 144, 146, 148, 152, 153, 155, 161, 162, 175
Compulsory Jurisdiction, 4, 8, 15, 16, 53-55, 60, 70, 71, 74, 75, 77, 79, 82-84, 112, 113, 163, 164-165, 178, 179, 193, 194, 198, 203, 208, 209, 215, 233, 234, 239
Colony/Colonial, 144, 154, 150
Continental Shelf, 7, 21, 49, 90, 158, 161, 162, 175,
Criminal Law, 171, 185, 242, 243
Costs, 66, 97, 227, 229, 230

D

Diplomacy/Diplomatic, 9, 20, 21, 22, 27, 34, 37, 38, 40, 57, 87, 92, 100, 144, 156, 161, 176, 178, 181, 182, 185 191, 211, 212, 217, 235,
Declaration, 51, 53-55, 60, 69, 70-78, 80-82, 84, 164, 178, 184, 192-194, 198, 211
Developed States, 26, 75, 153, 156-158, 205, 222, 231, 233, 234
Developing States, 2, 4, 6, 75, 130, 150, 151, 154, 156-158, 169, 172, 177, 183, 202, 203, 206, 220, 225, 227, 230, 231, 234, 244, 245
Declarations, 4, 53-55, 60, 69, 72, 75, 78, 80-82, 84, 164, 184, 193, 194, 198, 211
Dissenting Opinions, 43, 96, 190, 229

E

Enquiry, 4, 11, 20, 23, 27, 220
Ex Aequo et bono, 42, 61, 62, 226
Environment, 67, 112, 171, 188, 189, 190-192, 241, 242
Europe, 2, 12, 13, 27, 151, 152, 153, 173, 176, 202, 212, 218-224, 238, , 245, 246, 249
Elias, 55, 117, 189, 193, 218, 221, 224, 229, 230, 231, 244
Eastern Carelia, 134
Extra Territorial, 171, 185

Experts, 23, 40, 59, 62, 85, 125, 230, 232-234, 248
East Timor, 145, 155, 161, 164
Electricite de Beyrouth, 156
Electronica Sicula, 155

F

France, 28, 34, 72, 76, 130, -132, 138, 142-144, 151, 152, 154, 155, 156, 159, 160-163, 171, 172, 173, 174, 178, 180, 187-190, 219, 220, 223
Fitzmaurice, 6, 34, 42, 43, 45, 127, 219, 222, 223
Forum Prorogatum, 46, 50-52
Fisheries, 99, 100, 142, 144, 146, 154, 155, 160, 161, 163, 175
Ferencz, 214, 215

G

Good Offices, 26, 28, 29, 177
Germany/German, 15, 50, 100, 138, 144, 148, 151, 152, 154, 155, 160, 162, 175, 181, 219, 220, 238
General Assembly, 6, 17, 18, 23, 25, 29, 31, 32, 43, 99, 105, 108, 109, 118, 120, 126, 127, 129, 131, 133, 166, 168, 169, 170, 183, 185, 187, 211, 216, 217, 241, 242
Genocide, 65, 66, 91, 93, 143, 153, 155, 160, 66, 68, 211, 233, 242
Gorbachev, 208
Gross, 204, 255
Geographical Balance, 246
Gabcikovo Nagymoros, 155

H

Hague Conference, 14-16
Haya de la Torre, 37, 143, 157, 177
Hudson, 55, 133, 155
Harris, 98
Humanitarian, 187, 188, 222

I

International Disputes, 1, 2, 5, 8, 10-12, 14, 16, 20-23, 26, 28, 29, 34, 55, 78, 98, 142, 157, 203, 206, 208, 213-215
International Court of Justice/ICJ, 1, 2, 17, 18, 33, 41, 45, 54, 58, 74, 99, 105, 108, 113, 132, 152, 175, 187, 193, 194, 205, 206, 232, 242
Interim Measures, 63-66, 102, 179, 186, 199, 200, 216
ICJ Bar Association, 247
I.B.R.D, 26
I.C.S.I.D, 26
Iranian Oil Co., 47, 52, 56, 64, 99, 100, 143, 155, 159, 163, 177, 205, 249
I.L.O, 30, 57, 106, 107, 124, 126, 166, 169
Interhandel, 64, 143, 154, 160, 163, 178, 179
International Law, 3, 6, 7, 9, 11, 19, 20, 25, 42-44, 47, 48, 50, 53, 61, 74, 75, 78, 98, 99, 101, 108, 127, 128, 135, 165, 174, 175, 178, 185, 186, 188, 189, 191, 194, 195, 202-206, 214, 218, 223-227, 230, 236, 238, 242-251
I.M.O, 119
International Organisation, 3, 15, 28, 43, 46, 99, 103, 115, 118, 120-123, 135, 140, 147
Immunities, 113, 135, 167, 169, 170, 217
International Relations, 4, 9, 38, 60, 132, 165, 169, 185, 207, 210, 225
Iron Curtain, 166
Interim Measures, 63-66, 102, 179, 186, 199, 200, 216
Islam/Islamic, 12, 138, 145, 160, 221
International Lawyer, 6, 61, 78, 208, 224, 227, 230, 247, 248, 251
Individual, 14, 29, 75, 76, 95, 103, 122, 123, 126, 127, 133, 135, 169, 182, 201, 206, 217, 223, 227, 228, 236240, 242, 244
International Criminal Court, 242, 243

J

Jurisdiction, 3-8, 11, 15-19, 25, 32, 41, 45, 56-67, 69-84, 90, 99, 101, 103-108, 111, 112-119, 127, 142, 144, 146, 149, 152, 154, 155, 158, 163-165, 169, 177, 180, 183-186, 189, 193, 194, 195, 197-199, 203, 205, 206, 208-210, 215, 223, 225, 226, 233-235, 238, 239, 242, 243, 251
Judges, 24, 35, 41-43, 66-68, 75-77, 92, 93, 95, 96, 124, 172, 182, 193, 196, 201, 207, 216, 217, 220, 221-224, 228-231, 235, 239, 242, 244, 246, 248, 249
Jay Treaty, 13
Jennings, 44, 55, 68, 84, 220
Judgment, 30, 97, 98, 102, 103, 107, 115, 119, 123, 129, 132-135, 149, 150, 167
Jurisprudence, 3, 40, 41, 43, 44, 58, 75, 76, 78, 85, 108, 165, 171, 192, 204, 221
Jessup, 209, 223

K

Khmer Rouge, 41, 172
Kasikili/Sadudu Island, 50, 146, 158, 162
Klarestad, 77

L

Law of the Sea, 101, 171, 174, 175, 233
League of Nations, 1, 16, 17, 23, 27, 58, 69, 104, 114, 120, 135, 177, 183, 184
Legal Disputes, 8, 47, 53, 69, 72, 74, 80, 84, 97, 98, 193, 213
Liberation Movements, 10, 30

Liberia, 10, 75, 82, 139, 144, 148, 152, 156, 160, 184, 185, 205, 212, 222
Levi, 5, 11, 21, 26, 42, 69
Lockerbic, 2, 37, 40, 145, 156, 157, 160
Libya, 2, 37, 38, 40, 41, 90, 139, 144, 145, 148, 151, 152, 156-160, 162, 173-175, 233, 249
Lauterpacht, 41, 42, 43, 61, 62, 76, 219, 225
Languages, 97, 119
Latin American, 153, 176, 245
Locus Standi, 179, 180, 184, 226
Legal Aid, 231, 233, 234
Luchman, 244

M

Mediation, 11, 20, 26, 29, 30, 198
Mozambique, 10, 139
Montreal Convention, 37, 38, 145, 156, 157, 160, 180
Monetary Gold, 48, 143, 154, 159, 180
Minority Schools, 50
Minquer and Ecrehos, 9, 57, 143, 154, 162
Maritime, 2, 64, 68, 90, 91, 93, 100, 119, 144-146, 155, 158, 160-164, 166, 169, 175, 194, 195, 230, 238
Memorial, 51, 77, 85, 87, 88
Malaysia/Malaysian, 130-132,139, 209, 210
Mandate Territories, 183
Machiavellian, 235

N

Negotiation, 9, 11, 20-22, 24, 28, 29, 39, 40, 47, 130, 131, 180, 182, 185, 188, 213, 215
Non Ultra Petition Rule, 160, 164, 193-201, 218, 219, 221, 223, 229, 230, 240, 247,
Nigeria, 2, 23, 26, 31, 36, 54, 64, 81, 83, 139, 146, 149, 152, 158
Nuclear, 34, 35, 63, 100, 108, 110-112, 129-132, 129-132, 144, 146, 155, 160, 163, 166,-170,187, 188, 189, 191, 192, 211
Nottebohm Case, 45,143, 145, 159 163, 181, 182
Nicaragua, 44, 48, 68, 77-79, 81-83, 139, 143-145, 147, 151, 152, 156-159, 161, 163, 165, 186
Norwegian 171, 175, 100, 101, 143, 154, 160, 163
Nemo Judex, 79
Non Aligned Movement, 170
Nascimento, 176

O

Optional Clause, 4, 47, 49, 53-55, 60, 69-71, 73, 74, 76, 79-83, 163, 164, 193, 215, 234, 239, 251,
Oil Platforms, 56, 145, 157, 160
Oppenheim, 47, 48
Ogan, 79
Oda, 68, 109
Objections, 4, 51, 60, 65, 71, 107, 159, 164, 178, 180, 183, 184, 189, 197, 198, 205, 229
Oral, 37, 39-41, 66, 85, 86, 90-95, 98, 99, 101, 119-121, 123-125, 134, 228, 240, 248

P

Permanent Court of Arbitration, 4, 14-16, 26, 216, 247
Proceedings / Procedures, 20, 21, 23-27, 29, 30, 37- 41, 45, 48, 50, 57, 58, 63, 65-67, 72, 77, 78, 85-87, 89-95, 97, 99, 102, 104, 106, 109-113, 116, 119-126, 134, 135, 152, 157, 169, 166, 168, 170, 173, 177-184, 186, 189, 194, 199, 227, 228, 236-238, 240, 248,
Permanent Court of International Justice (P.C.I.J.), 1, 16, 17, 58, 226
Politics, 4, 8, 165, 169, 224
Political Question, 6, 7
Palestine, 5, 27, 29, 108
Prott, 33-35, 43, 172, 221, 223, 224, 244
Peace Treaties, 6, 34, 47, 127, 132, 133, 166, 168,
Preliminary Objections, 6, 47, 50-52, 56, 64, 65, 71, 94, 132, 142, 159, 164, 180, 183, 184, 189, 197, 198, 229
Prataap, 104, 114, 115, 121, 128, 129, 134
Privileges, 113, 135, 167, 169, 170, 217
Perestroika, 90, 92-96, 121, 125, 150, 177
President, 33, 34, 40, 53, 67, 68, 77, 86, 87, 187, 193, 196-199, 208, 214, 218, 221, 228
Peace Keeping, 27, 212

Q

Qadaffi, 40, 49, 53, 54, 55

R

Reservations, 4, 69, 70-84, 122, 116, 168, 178. 193, 198, 228
Rosenne, 9, 12, 13, 30, 33, 36, 37, 45, 46, 48-50, 52-55, 58, 71, 85, 87, 89, 90, 92, 95, 103, 106, 109, 113, 115, 132, 134, 179, 200, 217, 235, 237
Russia, 28, 73, 98, 130, 131, 132, 140, 141, 151, 220
Reparations, 35, 43, 47, 99, 126, 128, 129, 166, 168, 169, 179, 186, 188, 189, 195, 196
Reigmann, 78
Ratione Personae, 52, 80, 82
Ratione Tempories. 81
Rapporteur, 177
Roman Law, 206
Regional Chambers, 244, 245

Registrar, 92, 96, 97, 199, 121, 123, 124, 227, 228, 239, 248, 251

S

Super Powers, 10, 151, 165, 209
Sam Francisco, 106
Security Council, 10, 18-20, 27, 37, 38, 59, 64, 99, 102, 105, 111, 117, 118, 120, 126, 128, 129, 151, 167, 168, 170, 183, 187, 199, 208, 216, 217, 243
Secretary-General, 22, 23, 29, 30, 40, 53, 78, 81, 99, 118-120, 123, 126, 129, 199, 200, 231, 232
Scheuner, 7
Szafara, 8
Singh, 34, 68
South West Africa, 5, 44, 92, 110, 117, 131-133, 144, 150, 156, 160, 166-168, 170, 183-185, 207, 222, 224
Seizing, 45
Shaw, 48, 55, 66, 209, 215, 217, 222, 223
Sudan, 75, 83, 140
Stare Decisis, 42, 98, 133
Statistics/ Statistical, 136, 164, 203
Sovereignty, 15, 36, 37, 54, 101, 143, 162, 171, 175, 186, 194, 195, 206, 209, 210, 234, 238
Sanctions, 37, 38, 212

T

Treaties, 5, 6, 11, 13, 17, 19, 24, 27, 28, 34, 46, 47, 54-59, 127, 132, 133, 166, 168, 182, 188, 193, 204, 233
Test Ban Treaty, 130
Trust Fund, 98, 231, 232, 233, 248

U

U.N. /United Nations, 1, 3, 10, 14, 16-19, 23, 26, 27, 30, 31, 43, 56, 59, 81, 97, 103, 108, 113, 114, 118, 119, 126, 127, 129, 132, 135, 142, 164, -170, 177, 179, 184, 187, 192, 193, 199, 200, 206, 214, 221, 241, 247
U.N. Decade of International Law, 3
U.S./United State, 2, 13, 16, 21, 24, 56, 68, 70, 72-74, 87, 100, 130, 132, 141, 143-146, 156, 159, 160-165, 175, 179, 181, 186, 187, 211, 228
U.K / United Kingdom, 2, 25, 52, 57, 64, 72, 127, 141-146, 156, 159, 160-163, 171, 174, 175
U.S.S.R; 10, 73, 143, 144, 147, 151, 153, 161, 162, 166, 219, 223
Umezurike, 100
UNESCO, 107, 119, 120, 126, 166, 169
U.N Administrative Tribunal Case, 87, 122-124, 126

V

Vandenberg, 78
Voting/Votes, 96, 102, 109, 166, 168, 170, 187, 191, 216, 223

W

World War, 1, 2, 16, 127, 164, 165, 178, 181, 202, 203, 242,
WHO, 111, 112, 119, 167, 169, 191, 192
Western, 2, 131, 151, 152, 167, 168, 170, 171, 177, 202, 204, 220, 221, 223-226, 234, 244, 246, 248
Western Sahara, 167, 168, 170, 171
Weisberg, 206, 208, 210, 213
World Court, 5, 12, 14, 31, 33, 42, 55, 60, 73, 97, 98, 103, 110, 115, 126, 130, 132, 185, 188, 190, 202, 209, 215, 231, 236, 239, 240, 247, 249

Y

Yemen, 10, 141
Yugoslavia, 10, 65, 91, 93, 141, 145, 149, 153, 155, 160, 212